Let's Get
Real
About
Money!

Let's Get Real About Money!

Profit from the Habits of the Best Personal Finance Managers

Eric Tyson

Vice President, Publisher: Tim Moore
Associate Publisher and Director of Marketing: Amy Neidlinger
Executive Editor: Jim Boyd
Editorial Assistant: Pamela Boland
Development Editor: Russ Hall
Digital Marketing Manager: Julie Phifer
Marketing Coordinator: Megan Colvin
Cover Designer: 4 Eyes Design
Managing Editor: Gina Kanouse
Project Editor: Betsy Harris
Copy Editor: Water Crest Publishing
Proofreader: Karen A. Gill
Indexer: Lisa Stumpf
Compositor: TnT Design, Inc.
Manufacturing Buyer: Dan Uhrig

© 2008 by Eric Tyson
Published by Pearson Education, Inc.
Publishing as FT Press
Upper Saddle River, New Jersey 07458

FT Press offers excellent discounts on this book when ordered in quantity for bulk purchases or special sales. For more information, please contact U.S. Corporate and Government Sales, 1-800-382-3419, corpsales@pearsontechgroup.com. For sales outside the U.S., please contact International Sales at international@pearsoned.com.

Company and product names mentioned herein are the trademarks or registered trademarks of their respective owners.

Printed in the United States of America

First Printing November 2007

ISBN-13: 978-0-13-234161-5
ISBN-10: 0-13-234161-1

Pearson Education LTD.
Pearson Education Australia PTY, Limited.
Pearson Education Singapore, Pte. Ltd.
Pearson Education North Asia, Ltd.
Pearson Education Canada, Ltd.
Pearson Educatión de Mexico, S.A. de C.V.
Pearson Education—Japan
Pearson Education Malaysia, Pte. Ltd.

Library of Congress Cataloging-in-Publication Data
Tyson, Eric (Eric Kevin)
  Let's get real about money : profit from the habits of the best personal finance managers / Eric Tyson.
    p. cm.
  ISBN 0-13-234161-1 (pbk. : alk. paper) 1. Finance, Personal. 2. Investments. I. Title.
  HG179.T966 2008
  332.024—dc22
                            2007014118

This book is dedicated to all people who aspire to improve their financial health to better accomplish their personal goals and who have the courage and confidence to admit what they don't know and to learn from others.

Contents

About the Author

With more than 5 million books sold, **Eric Tyson** is one of the top best-selling personal finance authors in the country and has penned five national best-sellers. (He is also the only author to have four of his books simultaneously on *Business Week*'s business book best-seller list.) His syndicated newspaper column, "Investor's Guide," is read by more than 4 million people nationwide.

His *Personal Finance for Dummies*, which was a *Wall Street Journal* best-seller, won the Benjamin Franklin Award for Best Business Book of the Year. Eric's work has been featured and quoted in hundreds of publications and media outlets, including *Newsweek*, *The Wall Street Journal*, *Los Angeles Times*, *Chicago Tribune*, *Forbes*, *Kiplinger's Personal Finance Magazine*, *Money*, *Worth*, *Parenting*, *USA Today*, and on ABC, Fox, PBS Nightly Business Report, CNN, CNBC, and on CBS national radio, NPR's Marketplace, and Bloomberg Business Radio. He's also been a featured speaker at a White House conference on retirement planning.

Eric is a former management consultant to Fortune 500 financial service firms. In 1990, Eric founded a financial counseling firm that worked exclusively on an hourly basis. In addition to his counseling work, Eric also hoped to make an impact in the writing and media fields. Much of the personal finance writing and reporting he saw and heard was biased, jargon-laden and, in some cases, provided bad advice.

In addition to his writing and counseling, Eric also taught the nation's most highly attended personal financial management course at the University of California. He has spoken at many corporations and non-profits. His educational background includes having earned his bachelor's degree in economics at Yale and an MBA at the Stanford Graduate School of Business.

From the Author

Nearly two decades ago when I first began my work in financial counseling, I believed that people made financial mistakes because of a lack of personal financial education and because of sales pitches and misleading advertising that led them astray. Although I still believe these factors contribute to a lot of money misery, I've learned over the years that counterproductive habits and beliefs sabotage the best laid plans, too.

This book represents a compilation of what I have learned in my one-on-one work with individuals in addition to current research into how to best develop productive financial habits and extinguish problematic ones.

Whether you play sports, card games, or enjoy solving crossword puzzles, there's always room for improvement. This book contains the information, strategies, and tools that can truly help you and yours make the most of your money and dreams.

1

Getting Real, Not Real Obsessed, About Your Money

"Being rich is having money; being wealthy is having time."
—Margaret Bonnano

"Some folks seem to get the idea that they're worth a lot of money just because they have it."
—Seth Parker

"The trouble with the rat race is that even if you win you're still a rat."
—Lily Tomlin

The implicit message from most money books is that more is better. Quite simply, it's not. I know this from direct experience with many clients and readers over the years, and this is supported by a wealth of cross-cultural research. It's all about *balance* and making the most of what money does pass through our hands. Harmony comes from striking balances and avoiding extreme behaviors.

I don't know if there's life in outer space, but I've tried to imagine what an alien who landed here would think of our most "advanced" civilizations. If such a being could understand our society and publications, it might deduce that money has a high level of importance given how much time and effort so many of us put into acquiring, spending, and managing it. And, for goodness sakes, we have standings that rank who has amassed the most. More amazing is that some people actually care if Gates, Buffett, or someone new is in the lead!

Our culture not only worships those with a large net worth but also those who adhere to workaholic schedules to earn their wealth. America prides itself on its strong work ethic. Our popular history is rooted in ideas of economic self-reliance and the ability of every person to pull up himself or herself by the bootstraps to carve out a better life.

Burning the midnight oil is revered in our culture, and the path to success is paved with 50-, 60-, and 70-hour work weeks. And we still love the rags to riches stories that give us hope for having a better life. Magazine covers, from *Fortune* to *People*, along with television shows of all stripes, are filled with the beaming faces of those who came from humble backgrounds to achieve great "success" and wealth—that is, of the financial variety.

Famous and wealthy execs then may write a book that publishers flog as supposedly being able to teach the masses how they too can amass their own billion-dollar nest eggs in the business world. Donald Trump has numerous books out, as well as a television series purporting to teach you his secrets of amassing wealth. Michael Bloomberg, self-made billionaire media mogul, offered these career management insights in his biography, *Bloomberg on Bloomberg*: "The rewards almost always go to those who outwork the others. You've got to come in early, stay late, lunch at your desk, and take projects home nights and weekends." Personally, I have a hard time identifying with a man who describes his "perfect day" as "…one where I'm hopelessly overscheduled…to work by 7:00 A.M.; a series of rushed meetings; phone call after phone call; 50 or more voice messages and the same number of e-mails demanding a reply; a hurried business lunch between myriad stand-up conferences to solve firm personnel, financial, and policy problems…" that culminates when he "…falls into bed, exhausted but satisfied with the day's accomplishments. That's the best weekday one could ever have!"

One magazine appropriately called Bloomberg's biography "Confessions of a Workaholic." Behind nearly every super successful workaholic man (or woman) like Bloomberg lies a personal and family life in tatters—or no family life at all. (For insight into "successful" CEOs' lives outside of the office, read Christopher Byron's *Testosterone Inc.: Tales of CEOs Gone Wild* and *Martha Inc.: The Incredible Story of Martha Stewart Living Omnimedia*.)

For sure, some people have to work long hours to put food on the table and keep a decent roof over their family. However, in my work as a financial counselor, I have observed far too many people—the vast majority of whom have not and will not achieve overwhelming success in their careers—who sacrifice their personal lives, family relationships, and friendships for the sake of working more than is necessary or healthy.

With competitive workplace pressures and the high cost of housing in desired areas, increasing numbers of people are working longer hours than they'd like. Many employers exacerbate this problem with the culture they foster, encouraging and rewarding workaholics.

Like bartenders and bar owners who profit from big drinkers, corporate (and even non-profit) managers often implicitly and explicitly support and encourage overworking. Unfortunately, many corporations view squeezing more hours from employees as cost effective—employees on salary are a fixed cost, so the more hours you can wring out of your people, theoretically, the more work gets accomplished. Joe Robinson, director of the Work to Live campaign, comments, "We're the most vacation-starved country in the world. … In total hours, we now work two months longer every year than Germans; two weeks longer than the Japanese."

The Surprising Wealth-Happiness Connection

Many of us feel fortunate to live in a country where we have the freedom and ability to work hard at something of our own choosing to accomplish our goals and dreams. I know that I do.

That said, too many people are working too many hours due to explicit and implicit pressure from their bosses and the desire to move ahead and make more money. Given the choice, most people prefer having more money to less money. Of course, if you don't have enough money to put food on the table, keep a roof over your head, or pay for needed transportation, lack of sufficient funds for basic (subsistence) necessities certainly can contribute to unhappiness even among the most optimistic of people.

Quite a lot of research has been conducted not only in the U.S., but worldwide, examining the link, or lack thereof, between affluence and happiness. Psychology professors Richard Ryan and Timothy Kasser interviewed and studied people in 13 countries. Through questionnaires, researchers are able to measure how important (extrinsic) materialistic values such as image, status, and financial success are to various people and then measure these folks' psychological happiness. Ryan and Kasser found that having more money, in and of itself, did *not* increase people's happiness or cause problems.

> *"Money brings some happiness. But, after a certain point, it just brings more money."*
> —*Neil Simon*

The pursuit of wealth and adoption of money as one's primary motivator, however, led to psychological unhappiness, severe depression, anxiety, and other problems, including a far higher incidence of alcohol, drug, and tobacco abuse. Kasser, the author of *The High Price of Materialism* (MIT Press), has himself conducted extensive research into this topic and compiled others' studies. Kasser states, "The results consistently pointed towards the conclusion that materialistic people were less happy and satisfied with life, and that they also reported more distress. Thus, the more people buy into the messages of consumer society, the lower their levels of personal well-being and the higher their levels of distress."

You've probably heard the expression, "Money is the root of all evil." Actually, this is misquoted—the real phrase, which comes from the Bible, is "The love of money is the root of all evil."

Robert Lane, author of *The Loss of Happiness in Market Democracies* and Yale University professor, has deeply researched money and life satisfaction and has found that the primary sources of long-term happiness are friends and family. "Amidst the satisfaction people feel with material progress, there is a spirit of unhappiness and depression haunting advanced market democracies throughout the world...Once you get past the poverty level, there's no correlation between increased wealth and greater happiness. If anything, it's quite the reverse."

Social psychologist Dr. David Myers has studied happiness for decades. He has found that wealth, gender, age, education, and occupation do *not* determine happiness. What he has found leads people to be happy are optimism, self-esteem, a sense of personal control, and extroversion. People also derive happiness from investing in friendships and family ties, being with people with whom they can openly share.

"Having food, shelter, and safety is basic to our well being. But once able to afford life's necessities, increasing levels of affluence matter surprisingly little. Wealth is like health: Although its absence can breed misery, having it is no guarantee of happiness," writes Myers, who is the author of *The Pursuit of Happiness*.

> *"Money buys everything except love, personality, freedom, immortality, silence and peace."*
> —*Carl Sandburg, Poet and Author*

In my experience working with and observing people, it's clear to me that many Americans have lost sight of the differences between "necessities" and luxuries, especially in affluent and upper-middle class communities and circles. We can always find people with bigger homes and more expensive cars and who have taken more exotic vacations. The bar continually is set higher and higher in terms of how much money we "need."

A business professional I know, who I'll refer to as Mark, presents what I think is an absurd extreme in this regard. He puts in long work hours and is a multi-millionaire. Based on conversations that I've had with him, his net worth is at least $5 million and probably as much as $10+ million. Mark grew up in a middle class family that often struggled to make ends meet. Mark is an extremely competent businessman but a workaholic who doesn't feel the least bit financially secure. For years, he even balked at buying a modest home, which his wife really wanted to do so their family with young children could settle down.

If he wanted to, Mark could retire and shift careers to spend more time with his wife and kids and on his hobbies. But he doesn't and didn't. Mark doesn't feel the least bit financially secure. He truly believes that he needs at least $20 million to be financially comfortable. $20 million! Mark was surprised, but I was not, when his wife filed for divorce. What surprised me was that it didn't happen sooner.

Which bring me back to my favorite quote from Dr. David Myers, which is apropos to Mark and his pursuit of grand levels of financial health while he neglected the emotional health of his family:

"Satisfaction isn't so much getting what you want but wanting what you have. There are two ways to be rich: one is to have great wealth, the other is to have few wants."

> *"It is not the man who has little, but he who desires more, that is poor."*
> —*Seneca, A.D. 40*

Buying the Good Life

Consumption expectations play a significant role in why some people work the hours that they do and why career is the focus of their lives. I've seen this problem with single people, couples, and families with children. Some childless couples and single people have even greater temptations to get caught up in working harder to finance a higher lifestyle.

Over the years, I've seen surprising numbers of people with modest incomes make the decision to fit work into their lives rather than continuing to try to fit their lives into their work. So often, though, people twist and contort their lives and priorities to meet the perceived expectations and demands of their bosses and employers. Fitting work into the rest of your life often involves choosing employers and even careers that enable you the flexibility and ability to accomplish your personal and family goals.

Early in my career, I was working at a leading management consulting firm where the managers and partners logged many hours and were constantly on the road, away from their families. At the firm's holiday party one year, I was standing around the shrimp bowl, always a popular spot, and overheard a large group of spouses complaining about how their mates were rarely around. I heard a lot of anger, disappointment, and resentment. These comments provided me with a new perspective on everyday events around the office. And my observations of the senior people at this consulting firm convinced me that I had no interest in staying there long-term, especially since I hoped to raise children and be an active, involved dad.

Our culture, though, too often focuses on getting ahead, promotions, and pay raises. But if you're going to make time for the important things in life, you must resist the temptation to be envious of those with loftier titles and bigger salaries at your place of business and in your field. You can begin that process by realizing that there are no free lunches. Although some people are blessed with extraordinary talent and luck, you'll often find that the super-successful people in this world, with their mugs on the cover of every magazine, are workaholics. Don't emulate these workaholics to get "ahead." Perhaps the news media should cover the realities of the personal lives and emotional well being of these career superstars as thoroughly as they tally their business and financial success. Then, we'd have a realistic perspective of the rewards and consequences of chasing after capitalism's spoils.

Choosing Your Role Models

I met Dr. Laird Stuart during my years living in California. He does an outstanding job of combining religious instruction with practical, real-world issues that people struggle with. One morning, he was especially on his game when he said, "We all lose our bearings sometimes." He continued with the story of baseball player Matt Williams, who at the time, was playing for the San Francisco Giants. Matt Williams worked to get traded, and agreed to less money, to be in Phoenix where his family and kids are. "Anyone who will take less money to be with his children has got his bearings," said Dr. Stuart.

Unlike Matt Williams, basketball legend Michael Jordan didn't put his family first, even though he clearly could afford to do so. Comments and quotes from Jordan when he "retired" from basketball cited his supposed desire to spend more time with his family. But, after retiring from his playing career and despite being worth hundreds of millions of dollars, Jordan signed on with the Washington Wizards basketball team in Washington, D.C., far away from his family and home in the Chicago area. Not only did he take on a demanding management role and an ownership interest in the team, but he also eventually returned to playing full-time. With children who were 9, 11, and 13 years old at the time, Jordan and his wife filed for divorce. When interviewed by Reuters, Jordan said, "I come out, do my job, and focus on what's enjoyable for me, which is playing the game of basketball." A young man on a Yahoo message board said in response to this comment, "Which is his game, not his kids or marriage. Nice priorities Michael. I once actually admired you."

While there's far, far less excuse for wealthy people not to cut back on workaholic schedules, few do it. In fact, it's so unusual that, when it happens, it actually makes news. Tom Bloch resigned as CEO of H&R Block to become a teacher in a Missouri middle school. He had recognized that his hectic CEO schedule interfered with his top priority, which he said was his wife and two sons. He added that he didn't want to look back on his life and say, "Gee, you had an opportunity to play a bigger role in your children's lives and didn't take it."

Well said, Tom Bloch!

> *"That man is admired above all men who is not influenced by money."*
> —*Cicero, 60 B.C.*
>
> *"Money never made a man happy yet, nor will it. There is nothing in its nature to produce happiness."*
> —*Benjamin Franklin*

The Power of Money Knowledge

The knowledge of how to manage the money that comes into our hands and that we spend and that we save is vital. This knowledge will enable you to work smarter with your money, not harder for it. Unfortunately, too many adults graduate from their childhoods without a mastery of personal finance, investing, and so on.

Imagine for a moment that you were blindfolded and helicoptered into a remote location for a fabulous hiking adventure up a reasonably safe mountain, but where accidents sometimes have been known to happen. If you had never been mountain climbing before, trepidation if not outright fear might be your emotions du jour. Even with prior mountain climbing experience, this new challenge could strike both excitement and concern in you. You would likely wonder how high the mountain is and what tools and resources you would need and actually have at your disposal for the adventure.

Understanding and managing your personal finances has much in common with this mysterious mountain climbing expedition. Your IQ, formal education, and work experience do not matter—*no one* is born knowing how to competently direct their money matters. Even the nation's best high schools, colleges, and graduate programs don't teach a course called "Personal Finance 101."

Personal Finance Quiz I—The Basics

I've excerpted and adapted the following personal finance quiz from the non-profit JumpStart Coalition for Personal Financial Literacy. Please take this quiz, which has been administered to our nation's high school seniors, without using any resources or references and without doing any further preparation:

1. If you have caused an accident, which type of automobile insurance would cover damage to your own car?

   a) Term

   b) Collision

   c) Comprehensive

   d) Liability

2. Matt and Eric are young men. Each has a good credit history. They work at the same company and make approximately the same salary. Matt has borrowed $6,000 to take a foreign vacation. Eric has borrowed $6,000 to buy a car. Who is likely to pay the lowest finance charge?

   a) Matt will pay less because people who travel overseas are better risks.

   b) They will both pay the same because they have almost identical financial backgrounds.

   c) Eric will pay less because the car is collateral for the loan.

   d) They will both pay the same because the rate is set by law.

3. Many savings programs are protected by the federal government against loss. Which of the following is not?

   a) A bond issued by one of the 50 states

   b) A U.S. Treasury Bond

   c) A U.S. Savings Bond

   d) A certificate of deposit at the bank

4. If each of the following persons had the same amount of take-home pay, who would need the greatest amount of life insurance?

   a) A young single woman with two young children

   b) A young single woman without children

   c) An elderly retired man, with a wife who is also retired

   d) A young married man without children

5. Which of the following credit card users is likely to pay the GREATEST dollar amount in finance charges per year, if they all charge the same amount per year on their cards?

   a) Vera, who always pays off her credit card bill in full shortly after she receives it.

   b) Jessica, who only pays the minimum amount each month.

   c) Megan, who pays at least the minimum amount each month, and more when she has the money.

   d) Erin, who generally pays off her credit card in full but, occasionally, will pay the minimum when she is short of cash.

6. If you had a savings account at a bank, which of the following would be correct concerning the interest that you would earn on this account?

a) Sales tax may be charged on the interest that you earn.

b) You cannot earn interest until you pass your 18th birthday.

c) Earnings from savings account interest may not be taxed.

d) Income tax may be charged on the interest if your income is high enough.

7. Inflation can cause difficulty in many ways. Which group would have the greatest problem during periods of high inflation that last several years?

a) Young couples with no children who both work

b) Young working couples with children

c) Older, working couples saving for retirement

d) Older people living on fixed retirement income

8. Lindsay has saved $12,000 for her college expenses by working part-time. Her plan is to start college next year, and she needs all of the money she saved. Which of the following is the best place for her college money?

a) Corporate bonds

b) A bank savings account

c) A money market fund

d) Stocks

9. Which of the following types of investment would best protect the purchasing power of a family's savings in the event of a sudden increase in inflation?

a) A 25-year corporate bond

b) A house financed with a fixed-rate mortgage

c) A 10-year bond issued by a corporation

d) A certificate of deposit at a bank

10. Which of the following statements best describes your right to check your credit history for accuracy?

a) All credit records are the property of the U.S. Government, and access is only available to the FBI and lenders.

b) You can only check your record for free if you are turned down for credit based on a credit report.

c) Your credit record can be checked once a year for free.

d) You cannot see your credit record.

11. Your take-home pay from your job is less than the total amount you earn. Which of the following best describes what is taken out of your total pay?

    a) Federal income tax, Social Security, and Medicare contributions

    b) Federal income tax, state sales tax, and Social Security contribution

    c) Social Security and Medicare contributions

    d) Federal income tax, property tax, and Social Security contributions

12. Retirement income paid by a company is called:

    a) Rents and profits

    b) Social Security

    c) 401(k)

    d) Pension

13. Many people put aside money to take care of unexpected expenses. If John and Jenny have money put aside for emergencies, in which of the following forms would it be of LEAST benefit to them if they needed it right away?

    a) Stocks

    b) Savings account

    c) Invested in a down payment on the house

    d) Checking account

14. Kelly and Pete just had a baby. They received money as baby gifts and want to put it away for the baby's education. Which of the following tends to have the highest growth over periods of time as long as 18 years?

    a) A U.S. Government savings bond

    b) A savings account

    c) Corporate bonds

    d) Stocks

15. Karen has just applied for a credit card. She is an 18-year-old high school graduate with few valuable possessions and no credit history. If Karen is granted a credit card, which of the following is the most likely way that the credit card company will reduce its risk?

a) It will charge Karen twice the finance charge rate it charges older cardholders.

b) It will start Karen out with a small line of credit to see how she handles the account.

c) It will make Karen's parents pledge their home to repay Karen's credit card debt.

d) It will require Karen to have both parents co-sign for the card.

Source: Excerpted and adapted from JumpStart Coalition for Personal Financial Literacy.

Answers to Personal Finance Quiz I

1. **b)** Collision is the portion of your policy that pays for damage to your car.

2. **c)** Eric will pay less because his lender can go after his car as collateral for the loan, whereas Matt's lender has nothing to recover once Matt spends the borrowed money on the vacation.

3. **a)** A bond issued by one of the 50 states. That's not to say that state bonds are unsafe, but they do lack federal government backing. CDs from a bank (choice "d") are backed by the federal government through the FDIC insurance program.

4. **a)** The young single parent with two young children would need the most life insurance. (It's possible that the young married man without children would need some life insurance if his spouse is dependent upon his income and would want his income replaced in the event of his passing.)

5. **b)** The person who is only paying the minimum amount on her credit card bill each month will be carrying the most debt month-to-month and therefore incurring the greatest interest charges.

6. **d)** Interest on a bank savings account is taxable (for income tax purposes).

7. **d)** If your income is fixed, continued large increases in the cost of living erode the purchasing power of your money.

8. **c)** Money market funds, which are offered by mutual fund companies, and not banks, typically offer higher rates than bank savings accounts and a high level of safety. Bonds and stocks, while offering higher potential, are too risky for such a short period as they can fall in value.

9. **b)** Housing values generally keep up with increases in the cost of living. Bonds and CDs have fixed interest rates and would not protect purchasing power due to sudden inflation.

10. **c)** You are entitled to receive a free copy of your credit record once annually from each of the credit reporting agencies.

11. **a)** Federal income taxes and Social Security and Medicare contributions are deducted from paychecks. (If your state has an income tax, that may be deducted too.)

12. **d)** Pension income is paid by a company to its employees who are retired and have worked enough years to earn a pension benefit.

13. **c)** Down payment money would be the slowest to access (unless you had a home equity line of credit already established and could simply tap into it when needed). Although stocks can be sold any day the financial markets are open, they would not be a good place to keep emergency money because the price might be down when you needed to sell.

14. **d)** Stocks have the best long-term returns, by far, easily beating bonds and savings accounts (by about double[d]10 percent versus about 5 percent or less).

15. **b)** It's easy to get a credit card. Karen will be granted a relatively small line of credit until the credit card company can see that she won't default on repaying any borrowings on the card.

Scoring and Evaluating Your Quiz Results

The average score for high school seniors on the preceding quiz was just 52 percent, which isn't too hot when you consider this is a multiple choice quiz and simply through random selection of answers, you should get at least 25 percent correct! These questions are testing pretty basic personal finance concepts and you should, as an adult, be getting 100 percent correct. If not, don't despair—this book (and other recommended resources) can help you close the gaps in your knowledge. The lower your score, the more room you've got for improvement.

Personal Finance Quiz II—Key Concepts

I developed the following quiz to test some personal finance concepts that are key to successfully managing your money. As with the prior quiz, choose the best answer from among those offered:

16. Marie and John have suffered through some tough times in recent years due to John's being out of work for an extended period of time. Prior to his job loss, they were planning on buying new living room furniture to replace the horrible-looking pieces they've owned for too long. Now that John is back at work, albeit at a lower-paying job than before, they feel that the time has finally come for them to buy that long-put-off furniture. Should they:

    a) Borrow on Marie's credit card since she has had a more stable job.

    b) Put off the purchase until they have enough cash saved to buy what they want.

    c) Take out a line of credit from Ethan Allen since that is large national chain of furniture stores and their interest rate should be pretty good.

    d) Finance the purchase through taking out a second mortgage on their home (the interest on which will be tax deductible).

17. Karl is in his 20s, working at his first job, and readily admits he doesn't know much about dealing with money. He has some student loan debt from college and is currently renting an apartment. He feels that he has no free time between his job, commuting, preparing most meals, keeping up with laundry and cleaning, and some recreation with friends and dating. Regarding his personal finances, Karl should:

    a) Not stress out. He is young, has many years ahead, and should enjoy life as a young single adult.

    b) Ask his parents for advice since they have handled all of his money issues through college and getting his first apartment set up. He should wait a few years so that he won't feel so stupid and dependent as he does now.

    c) Make learning how to manage his money a top priority now. He should begin saving and developing a plan for his financial priorities and tasks.

    d) In a year when he's eligible for all of his employer's benefits, hire the financial planner who recently came to his company's offices and is with a large insurer whose ads he sees all the time on television.

18. The Longstreets' family has grown in recent years, and now they have four children, so their home suddenly seems way too small. After hiring an architect, plans were drawn up for a major addition to the house. They've also finally hired a decorator since neither mom nor dad seems to have the aptitude or time. Thanks to the strong real estate market since they originally bought their home, they have quite a bit of equity and can just barely totally finance their projects by refinancing their mortgage and taking cash out. Should they:

    a) Take out an adjustable rate mortgage to keep their rate (and payment) as low as possible.

    b) Lock in a fixed rate so they know exactly how much they'll owe every month.

    c) Consider an interest-only loan so that their payments will stay very low in the early years.

    d) Reevaluate and scale back on their projects.

19. Proud parents of a one- and two-year-old child, Amy and Walter have been looking at housing for a long time. This past weekend, some people they know who live near a preschool that they really like and anticipate sending their children to are planning to put their two-bedroom home up for sale and are willing to sell it to Amy and Walter at a 5-percent discount—the savings realized from not having to pay real estate agents. They love the home and the neighborhood (although the lot is small) and will be able to walk to the preschool! This will be a huge benefit to them as they anticipate having at least two more children once Walter's income increases with an expected promotion in the next few years. Should they:

    a) Find a good real estate attorney to help with a real estate contract.

    b) Tour area homes to be sure they are paying a fair price for the home.

    c) Not buy the home, continue renting, and stay on the sidelines.

    d) Check with the preschool to be sure it plans on not moving for the foreseeable future.

20. Jason got his first full-time job at the age of 21, fresh out of college. He saved money from every paycheck in a 401(k) plan into a money fund. Seven years have passed quickly, and now he is changing jobs because a terrific opportunity came up that is more in his true field of interest. The only downside is that he can expect long hours, especially in his first year or two. His new employer does not offer a retirement savings plan, so he's deciding what to do with his money in his previous employer's plan, which he has had invested in a money market fund. He had started with that and never changed because he felt that he lacked the expertise and time to evaluate his investment options. Should he:

a) Use some of his vacation time to figure out how and where to invest his money on his own.

b) Given his lack of time, keep his money in the money market fund in his previous employer's plan, if they allow that.

c) Withdraw his money and use it to buy a house rather than continuing to rent.

d) Wait until his new employer opens a retirement plan and then transfer the money into that plan.

21. A year into his new job, Jason gets a phone call from a very smart college classmate of his, Ken, who went on to get his MBA at Harvard Business School. Ken has been working for several years at a new medical device company whose main product is one that promises to revolutionize the way that diabetic patients are treated. Ken tells Jason that his company is about to go public and that Jason should use some of his spare cash in his retirement account to buy shares in the initial public offering (IPO), which is happening in one week. According to Ken, the stock price will skyrocket once the shares are issued, so he should not wait. Jason should:

a) Buy shares in the IPO since he has spare cash and Ken is a smart, successful professional and investor.

b) Withdraw the retirement money and use it instead to buy a home since he is still renting.

c) Conduct some research on the company and the stock valuation and then make a decision.

d) Buy the stock and then do research as time allows.

22. Richard is unhappy with the amount of money he is spending on all of his insurance policies. He needs life insurance because he has a mortgage, is the sole breadwinner (he makes $50,000 annually) in his family, and has a wife and three dependent children (ages 6, 4, and 1). He is quite happy with his universal life policy, which provides $200,000 of coverage and is growing an investment balance that he could draw from to pay for his kid's future expenses, such as college. In taking an inventory of all of their other insurance policies, they have health insurance, auto insurance, and homeowners' insurance for their home in Chicago. He should:

   a) Speak with the insurance agent who sold him the life insurance policy about what he should do with his other policies to keep his insurance expenditures under control.

   b) Shop around for his auto insurance policies since that coverage can be quite expensive in urban areas.

   c) Suck it up and realize that with a family, a house, and cars, insurance costs add up fast.

   d) Buy more insurance: a different, less costly life insurance policy for himself that provides more coverage and disability insurance.

23. Two years ago, Marva, age 35, invested about 10 percent of her money earmarked for the stock market overseas—specifically into two foreign stock mutual funds. She had heard that she should be diversified and lacked any foreign stocks. Since that time, while her U.S. stocks have appreciated 50 percent, her international stocks have badly lagged—rising just 15 percent. On CNBC, a commentator who hosts his own television show on investments said that investors should dump all foreign stocks for at least the next year due to a strengthening dollar. Marva should:

   a) Sell her foreign stocks and find a better investment in the U.S.

   b) Invest more overseas.

   c) Dump her foreign funds and buy individual foreign company stocks.

   d) Keep things the way they are.

Answers to Personal Finance Quiz II

When I worked as an hourly-based, personal financial counselor, I had new clients complete a detailed questionnaire, which I then discussed with them in our first meeting. Completing the form required accessing many financial documents as well as reflecting on short- and long-term financial goals and concerns as well as financial decisions and issues that caused discomfort and displeasure. The point of going through all of this was so that I could develop a specific action plan for them to improve their overall financial situation. (I will walk you through a similar exercise in later chapters.)

Every client that I ever worked with had made mistakes. Whether it's training airline pilots or paramedics, learning from and avoiding the mistakes of those who have come before you goes a long, long way toward doing your best at the endeavor at hand. Managing your money is no different. The preceding quiz, which I developed, unearths the more common mistakes, so don't feel surprised or bad if a number of the questions tripped you up:

16. **b)** They should put off the purchase until they can afford to pay cash. (Ideally, they should have some emergency reserve money put aside as well.) Buying consumer goods (which would include furniture, vacations, cars, dinners out, etc.) with credit cards and auto loans will cost you far more in the long run than you can imagine. Besides getting you into the habit of spending money that you don't have, consumer credit usually comes with relatively high interest rates. (Using credit cards for a transaction and then paying your bill in full when it comes due is fine.) Another common and related mistake to buying consumer goods on credit is leasing cars. Many auto leasers fail to understand lease contracts, costs, and related issues. Extracting yourself from a lease takes enormous persistence and resolve, so it's better to avoid these expensive long-term car rentals in the first place.

17. **c)** Karl needs to make his personal financial education a priority now. He's earning money and on his own and is therefore responsible for all things financial in his life now. Feeling pressed for time is a common excuse for procrastinating. Some people continue to procrastinate and avoid thinking about and planning for their financial futures. One of the more common failures is not taking advantage of retirement plans offered by

employers, including those offering free matching money. Self-employed small business owners may fall behind on their taxes for similar reasons. Although this error is more common among self-employed people, plenty of other folks fail to file their tax returns and pay the taxes they owe.

18. **d)** Spending excessively on home and home improvements can be a problem. You've likely heard that home purchases (especially and including new construction) and home improvement projects inevitably take longer and cost more than you expected up front. (The same can hold true for habitual furniture buyers and those in love with endlessly making over their home decorating.) If your financial situation doesn't have much wiggle room and margin for error, sloppy planning can lead to unfinished projects and even personal bankruptcy.

19. **c)** The proximity to the preschool is nice, but the importance and value of that will be short lived. Buying and then selling property entails relatively enormous transaction costs. Buying this small home, which they will probably want out of once more kids arrive, is likely to be a mistake. Impatient and time-pressed buyers sometimes just want to "get it over with and get back to their lives." These buyers often make poor purchase decisions and soon find out that they either have to sell the house due to financial considerations or want to sell it based on other factors that could've been more thoroughly researched.

20. **a)** Jason has got to get on the stick and figure out how to invest his money. Keeping retirement money languishing in a money market fund for seven years is unacceptable and costly to his financial future. Although I am an advocate of taking your time when investing significant sums of money, a fair number of folks who need decent returns to accomplish their goals sit on cash for years due to fear of losing money, lack of education, and not researching good investments. Take, for example, one successful executive who confided to me that he kept all of his spare funds in low-interest bank accounts because his father had lost everything during the great stock market crash of 1929.

21. **c)** Jason needs to do his homework and more digging before making an investing decision. Some people too quickly toss their money into inappropriate or poorly researched investments. I see this happen quite often with people picking individual stocks, rolling over retirement money, and choosing a new

investment to replace maturing CDs. A related problem to this one is taking investment advice from poor or biased sources. Friends top the suppliers-of-bad-investing-ideas list, followed closely by the news media and columnists. Too often, insecure people rationalize acting on others' picks by thinking that others are far more in the know. Without a doubt, one of the biggest complaints I heard over the years was from clients concerned about investments they bought from brokers. Their dissatisfaction often stemmed from the fact that they bought these products without understanding the high fees and commissions associated with the broker-sold vehicles. Other common broker-related regrets are buying through friends and selling otherwise good investments solely on a broker's advice.

22. **d)** Richard may be unhappy with insurance spending but he is actually underinsured. (He should shop around for all of his existing coverages in order to be sure he's getting good value for his insurance dollars.) He doesn't have near enough life insurance given his income, and he is completely lacking disability coverage, which kicks in and replaces his employment income if he suffers a long-term disability. Every day, people without disability insurance end up with long-term disabilities, and people lacking life insurance pass away and leave their loved ones financially strapped. In addition to the danger of exposing yourself and dependents to catastrophic losses, if you fail to get necessary insurance, you may develop a medical problem (known by insurers as a pre-existing condition) that prevents you from getting future coverage. Richard is wasting money on his current life insurance. Over the years, I had many clients complain about misleading sales pitches and projections from life insurance brokers. In the worst cases, people funnel money into costly and low-return cash value plans that offer no up-front tax breaks instead of taking advantage of excellent retirement savings options through work.

23. **b)** Marva has too little invested overseas, and the fact that foreign stocks are underperforming allows her to invest more at what may be a quite favorable price. Looking to bail when the going gets tough is a natural human tendency. This mistake reminds me of the time my family was headed to a summer beach vacation. Along the way, we drove by an old van along the highway. Outside of the van, about half a dozen members of a

band stood and watched as their vehicle went up in flames. Clearly, these folks responded intelligently to the early signs of danger and got out while they still could. Thus, it makes sense that when an investment goes down in value, we want to hit the eject button before it completely vanishes before our eyes. However, even the best investments have their down periods, and your short-term pessimism could cause you to sell right before prices surge. Investors who dumped stocks, in general, after the 1987 crash and the early 2000s bear market missed out on enormous future gains.

People make mistakes with their money because of gaps in their knowledge. If you take the money lessons from this quiz and throughout this book to heart and commit to avoiding these same errors, you can sidestep a tremendous amount of misery and lost money—perhaps totaling into the hundreds of thousands and maybe even millions of dollars.

2

Getting Motivated

"Procrastination is one of the most common and deadliest of diseases and its toll on success and happiness is heavy."
—Wayne Gretzky

Just about everybody avoids dealing with some aspect of money. For some, it's as simple as avoiding balancing a checkbook or making decisions about where to invest saved money. Others neglect needed insurance coverage, perhaps out of fear of confronting their own mortality and vulnerabilities. Some people are plagued by broader problems such as feelings of guilt and shame about money or feeling that money seems dirty and evil.

The fact that money-related issues aren't always at the top of your priority list may well be a good sign. Perhaps you spent the past weekend with friends and family or were engrossed in a captivating book. But, continually avoiding money or some aspect of your finances can result in unnecessary long-term pain.

"I didn't open an investment statement for nearly two years. In the past when I reviewed my investments, my stomach got in knots and I felt tremendous anxiety and tension," Susan told me as we reviewed her investment portfolio. Much of Susan's money was sitting in a money market fund, and the remainder was in GNMA (Government National Mortgage Association—Ginnie Mae) mortgage-backed bonds that she didn't understand and felt intimated about. "My broker, who I inherited through a relative, rarely called…probably because he knew better! I never made decisions and was plagued by discomfort with just about any investment. I'm ashamed to say that I couldn't even tell you how much I have invested just now or where it all is," she sheepishly told me.

I confess to avoiding some aspects of dealing with money. Over the years, I've found it kind of humorous, actually, that many people assume that because I write financial advice books and columns and have worked as a financial counselor, I must maintain meticulous financial records, including regularly balancing my checkbook. The reality is that I abhor and despise the minutiae of balancing checkbooks and tracking other little, picky details.

I got a lot of mail from readers the first time I admitted to not balancing my checkbook. Such a confession didn't fit well with the image that some people wanted to have of me as this all-in-control, detail-oriented, financial-loving sort of guy. The fact is that I do enjoy numbers and analysis and thinking about financial strategy. But, I detest spending hours of my time on the tedium of making all the dollars and pennies balance precisely in my checking account register. I'm satisfied with the portion of income that I save each month and have low-cost overdraft protection. (This can be obtained through your bank if you have a traditional checking account. Some discount brokerage accounts offering unlimited check writing provide low-cost margin loans as overdraft protection.) That's more than good enough for me. But, this approach isn't for everyone. Some people face high fees if they bounce a check from overdrawing their account, or they're unable to keep a sufficient cushion in their account to ensure that they rarely face a situation in which overdrafts occur. I'm not recommending my approach for everyone; I'm simply demonstrating the fact that most of us avoid some aspect of dealing with our finances—and what I believe is a workable and healthy solution to what I don't enjoy spending my time doing! (If you live on a tight budget and keep low account balances, by all means regularly balance your checkbook register and keep a running total of your account balance.)

I've worked with plenty of money procrastinators. Some of these people hired me in the hopes of helping them get a grip on their financial situation. More often than not, avoiders didn't recognize their underlying problems but instead contacted me because of a pressing quandary— such as wanting to buy a home and not feeling comfortable with how much to spend. My challenge was to gently get folks to realize the larger issues and little details that were being ignored.

Some personal finance procrastinators can "get away" with their ways for a number of years. However, whether it's in the short-term or the long-term, eventually, problems do occur from avoiding dealing with money and related decisions, and sometimes the damage can be catastrophic.

George, in his mid-forties, was his family's provider. He had four children, and his wife didn't work outside the home. Although he was a good wage earner, he and his wife were hopelessly disorganized when it came to managing their money, and they consistently avoided financial decisions and planning. They didn't save for retirement, they lacked proper life and disability insurance, and they did not have an adequate emergency cash buffer. One spring morning, George collapsed in his office and was rushed to a nearby hospital, where he found out that he'd suffered a major heart attack. Six months later, he had another heart attack that, sadly, took his life and left his wife and children with a small life insurance policy that his employer provided as a basic benefit. The family was in financial and emotional turmoil from George's death and the resulting chaos caused by a lack of financial planning and their money avoidance. His widow lost their home in the next year. Due to cost considerations, the family was forced to move to another town; the kids then had to go through the difficult process of forging new friendships in a new school district on top of all the other emotional hardship that they were suffering through.

Some money avoiders don't plan ahead and save toward future goals. I've met with people in their forties, fifties, and even their sixties who are just beginning to comprehend the consequences of such behavior. Often, the reality hits home when they contact the Social Security Administration (SSA) or get a mailing from the SSA and learn what size benefit check they'll get at full retirement age (which is around age 66 for most people). By reality, I mean the realization that they'll have to continue working into their seventies in order to maintain the modest standard of living to which they've become accustomed.

Several issues typically cause a lack of retirement funds. Many money avoiders could save more money, but they typically aren't motivated and organized enough to do so. Generally, they haven't bothered to conduct even basic retirement analysis (covered in Chapter 4, "Developing Your Personal Financial Action Plan") to understand how much they should be saving to reach their retirement goal (or even think about when and if they wish to retire).

Because money avoiders dislike dealing with money, what they're able to save often gets "ignored" and languishes in low- or no-interest bank accounts. Avoiders also tend to fall prey to the worst salespeople, who push them into mediocre or poor investments with high fees. When avoiders choose their own investments, it's often done based on super-ficial research and analysis, which can lead to piling into frothy invest-ments when they're very popular. Discomfort causes avoiders to bail out when things look bleak.

Because insurance is an admittedly dreadful and unpalatable topic for most people, many folks avoid insurance-related issues. And, while well-intentioned and commission-hungry insurance agents get some people to plug insurance gaps, these salespeople may not direct you to the policy best suited to your needs. In fact, brokers might sell you costly insurance (e.g., cash value life insurance) that provides them with a higher take and you with less insurance than you need.

Insurance gaps come to light when a disability or a protracted illness occurs. Too often, we believe that these problems only happen to elderly people, but they don't. In fact, statistically, you are far more likely to miss work for an extended period of time due to a disability or lengthy illness than you are to pass away prematurely.

As we age, the percentage of people passing away gradually increases. The following table shows the mortality rate for various age ranges. You can see that while just 1 percent of those people between the ages of 25 and 34 pass away each decade, the portion approximately doubles with each passing decade. While 1 in 100 is a relatively small probability, it's a much greater probability than winning your local mega-millions jackpot. Nearly 1 in every 25 people passes away during the decade between the ages of 45 and 54.

Age	Percent of People Passing Away (During Decade)
25–34	1.0%
35–44	2.0%
45–54	4.3%
55–64	9.6%
65–74	23.5%
75–84	55.8%

Money avoiders, more often than not, lack wills and other legal documents that should specify to whom various assets shall pass and who is responsible for what (e.g., administering the estate, raising minor children) in the event of their untimely demise. When money is to pass to heirs through an estate, the absence of documents can lead to major legal and family battles.

Personal Finance Quiz III—Avoidance Behaviors

I often saw physical signs and symptoms that indicated I was dealing with someone who was a money procrastinator. Answer the following questions to see if any, and how many, apply to you:

1. Are you financially disorganized and prone to clutter? Because avoiders dislike dealing with money and related issues, they don't spend their free time keeping documents organized and easy to find.

2. Are you late with your bills and tax payments? Money avoiders often incur late fees and interest charges on various household bills. Those who are self-employed and responsible for quarterly

income tax filings are at additional risk for falling behind with tax payments, the negative financial consequences of which can be huge.

3. Do you have unopened financial account statements? We all get busy with life, but I was amazed at how many money avoiders I worked with who would have piles of unopened account statements, even during periods when their types of investments were doing fine, thus eliminating any reason for avoiding opening potentially bad news.

4. Do you have a sense of unease, and even shame and embarrassment, with having cash sitting around in low-interest accounts? Money avoiders who are able to save money may have a tendency to allow it to accumulate, for example, in bank accounts that pay little, if any, interest. Although they may know that they could and should do better with investing the money, they can't overcome the inertia.

5. Do you experience feelings of enormous stress and anxiety over money issues and decisions? One of the main reasons that avoiders relate to money in the way that they do is because for whatever historic reason(s), making financial decisions makes them feel uncomfortable and stressed. (In some cases, for example, growing up in a home where money was an ongoing source of unhappiness, conflicts, and problems can lead to avoidance behavior as an adult.) Other people believe that they lack the skills and knowledge necessary to take control of their finances. Finally, some folks believe, right or wrong, that their current financial picture isn't so bright, so they simply decide to avoid the bad news, even though ignoring the situation will only make things worse in the end.

6. Do you have a low level of interest over money issues and decisions? Although some avoiders shun financial decisions and responsibilities due to anxiety, others are imitating behavior learned from their parents or are rebelling against a parent who was financially or emotionally overbearing.

7. Do you have an absence of long-term financial planning and thinking? Many of the money avoiders I dealt with clearly hadn't thought much of what their personal and financial goals were for the years and decades ahead.

8. Do you have marriage problems relating to money? Money avoiders typically have conflicts over money with their spouses, and their avoidance may stem from or be exacerbated by that.

Understanding Why We Procrastinate

Understanding some of the common feelings and issues surrounding money-avoidance behavior can help in coming to acknowledge and productively change the habits. Here is a compilation of the common reasons I observed in my financial counseling work as to why some people are money avoiders:

➤ **Feelings of incompetence.** Some people have negative memories and associations from prior attempts, with parents or spouses, of dealing with money and making financial decisions. Many money avoiders have similar feelings of incompetence with math and mathematical analysis, which are certainly key abilities to possess for effective personal financial management. Lack of experience in making financial decisions certainly plays into feelings of incompetence as well.

➤ **Disorganization.** Money avoiders have a tendency to be generally disorganized people who avoid dealing with other facets of their lives as well. With only so many hours in the day, people who are poorly organized struggle just to deal with work and family responsibilities. Making financial decisions, especially involving longer-term issues (e.g., retirement planning, insurance), are easily postponed or never considered.

➤ **Marital friction.** As I will discuss in Chapter 5, "Love and Money," money is among the leading causes of marital discord. So, some spouses cope by avoiding the topic altogether in the hopes of keeping more harmony in their marriages. In the short-term, this avoidance strategy may reduce some stress and arguments. In the long-term, however, it doesn't work, as dissatisfaction gone underground doesn't go away (or get better).

➤ **Fear of future problems.** People who were abused growing up or lived with a loved one who was a substance abuser often worry about bad things occurring. Ditto for folks suffering from depression or with generalized anxiety disorders. Money troubles are often intertwined with abuse issues in homes, which leads to plenty of negative associations with money and simply not wanting to deal with the topic.

➤ **Perfectionism.** Although this is a less-common reason for people shunning money matters, some perfectionists continue putting off making decisions and taking action because they can always find flaws in or potential obstacles to their intended course of action. Or, they may feel that they might make a better decision with just a little more thinking and analysis. Of course, we can't predict the future, and we are limited in our time, money, and analysis.

➤ **Can get away with it.** Some people simply don't want to deal with money issues and decisions and are able to get along sufficiently well enough through good fortune and being surrounded by those who enable the avoiding behavior (perhaps through caregiving and taking responsibility). Unfortunately, life changes and unforeseen problems can expose gaps in poor financial management.

➤ **Enables us to avoid dealing with difficult issues like aging and death.** We procrastinate doing financial planning for retirement and buying life insurance for the same reason we don't have a will prepared—we'd rather not think about aging and dying and other difficult and unpleasant topics.

Conquering Money Avoidance and Disorganization

If you or someone you know is a money avoider, my goal isn't to turn you or them into someone who loves dealing with money. That's not going to happen. However, we can work together to ensure that you can accomplish common financial goals and won't suffer the ill effects that money avoiders so often do in their neglect of their finances.

Coming to terms with money avoidance takes time and patience. That statement isn't meant to provide you with a reason to continue to forgo making changes in your financial life. Instead, I'm relaying a fact and reminding you that change takes time and some steps forward interrupted by steps back.

The first and most important part in the process is to recognize the tendency and some of the biggest causes. Many people find it helpful to write down their feelings relating to money avoidance or to speak about their feelings and history with money with someone who is an empathic listener.

"I always felt stupid about math and wholly inadequate. I can't even bring myself to use a calculator out of fear I won't even know how to use that properly," says Heidi, a forty-something-year-old woman. It took Heidi about two years to make some major changes in how she handled her personal finances. She began to make progress when I was able to persuade her that she didn't have to be a math whiz to make positive financial changes. Heidi didn't have major spending problems, but she was sloppy and lazy about saving money and investing it well.

I had her sign up for her employer's retirement savings plan so that she could begin to save about 8 percent of her salary. We had the money withdrawn from her salary and directed into a handful of well-diversified mutual funds. "I can't believe how painless it is to do this, and there was virtually no math involved. All I had to do was complete a one-page enrollment form, which required me to say what funds and what percentage of my contribution went into each fund that I selected," said Heidi. With the meager amounts she had been saving that were languishing in a low-interest bank account, Heidi would've needed to work until her mid-seventies to achieve the standard of living in retirement that she desired. Now, she's on track to be able to stop working by her late fifties. Seeing these quantifiable changes in her retirement age and gaining a basic understanding of the steps she needs to take to reach her goals was a great motivating source to Heidi and has given her savings a purpose. Equally, if not more important, she feels in control of her life financially, and she has rid herself of that ever-constant underlying anxiety about not being on top of things.

I found that many avoiders felt overwhelmed with a laundry list of financial to-do's. That's why you should prioritize and only work on the top one or two items at a time. I'd tell clients that even though they might have a total of eight or ten things on their longer task lists, they shouldn't expect to complete those next week or even next month. It might take them six months to a year to work through the longer list. Here's how to get control of your money:

> **Pay your bills automatically.** People who are financially disorganized often are late paying bills. Late payments, particularly when it comes to paying taxes, are a problem that can lead to substantial late fees, interest, and penalties. Even if the fees and additional interest from individual late payments—$5 here and $30 dollars there—don't seem all that significant on their own, they can add up to a hefty total if you make paying bills late a habit. One of the best things that a money avoider can do with his bills is to set up each of them for automatic payment.

Whether it's your phone, utility, or monthly mortgage bill, you should be able to establish an automatic payment plan that doesn't require you to initiate payment. With just a little upfront work with each creditor or billing company—often not much more effort than paying a monthly bill—you can rid yourself of unnecessary fees and interest and save a little time each month. Many companies accept (and actually prefer) payment through an electronic transfer from your bank account. Some loan holders (such as the U.S. Department of Education) may even lessen your interest rate slightly in return for what amounts to a guarantee of an on-time payment every month. If not, you may be able to have the payment charged on your credit card, but be careful with this route if you sometimes don't pay that bill on time! (Another alternative is to use online bill paying through your bank.) If, for whatever reason, you're unable or unwilling to put your bills on an automatic payment system, you can put together an accordion-style folder and organize your bills according to when during the month they need to be paid. Please understand that I think that this system is second-rate (in terms of efficiency and likelihood for success) compared to an automatic payment system.

➤ **Develop a regular investment program.** Just as Heidi did, all money avoiders should make their investing automatic. If you work for an employer, doing so is usually easy. Often, the most daunting part of the process is wading through the wad of retirement plan and investment information and brochures your benefit's department may dump upon you when you tell them that you want to sign up for their payroll deduction savings program. Not only will your money grow faster inside a tax-deferred account, but your employer may also offer free matching money. The simplest way to navigate through the morass of paperwork is to look first for the specific form you must complete to sign up for the payroll investment program. Thoroughly read that form first so that you know what you need to focus upon and get smarter about as you review the other materials. If your earnings come from self-employment income, you'll need to establish your own retirement account. Learn about the different retirement account options and choose the one that best meets your needs. The two self-employed retirement account options that enable you to sock away the greatest amounts are SEP-IRAs and

Keoghs. With each of these plans, a self-employed person may contribute up to 20 percent of his business' net income, up to a maximum of $45,000 (for tax year 2007). These plans may be established through the major mutual fund companies that I like, such as Vanguard, Fidelity, and T. Rowe Price. And, you can generally set up these accounts so that a regular monthly amount is zapped electronically from your local bank account into your mutual fund investment account. (Be careful not to overfund your account, which may happen if you overestimate your business income prior to completing your tax return.)

➤ **Close insurance gaps.** Nearly every money avoider I've met over the years has had problematic gaps in insurance coverage. Solving this problem presents some challenges because understanding various policies and the coverage of each is complicated. Add on top of that the unfortunate fact that to buy most insurance policies, you must deal with a commission-based insurance agent. Talk about a recipe for headaches and conflicts of interest! But these are not acceptable excuses for avoiding this issue because so much is at stake. (Please examine Chapters 15 through 17 for helpful advice on filling in your insurance gaps.)

➤ **Hire financial help, carefully.** Money avoiders are clearly a group of people who could benefit from hiring a financial advisor. However, they're also among the people most likely to make a poor choice when hiring. It's difficult to evaluate or care enough to evaluate the financial expertise (and potential conflicts of interest) of a financial advisor if you're disinterested in (or suffer anxiety about) and actively avoid money issues. Your first step, if you're inclined to hire help, is to clearly define with what it is that you desire assistance. Do you need assistance with analyzing your budget and developing a plan to pay down consumer debt? If so, most financial advisors aren't really trained for or interested in helping you with that—there's far more money to be made selling investment and insurance products to the affluent. (If you're looking to wipe out debt and analyze your household budget, please see my suggestions in Chapters 9 and 10.) Advisors are best suited for folks who want to quantify how much they should be saving for specific goals and determining where to invest it. However, there's no getting around it: You do have to do a lot of digging to find a competent and ethical advisor who has reasonable fees. With that information in hand, you can confidently and strategically evaluate potential service providers who can help you overcome your inertia and get you on track managing your money. (See Chapter 19, "Hiring Financial Help," for how to hire the best help for your situation at an affordable price.)

3

Your Money Beliefs and Practices

"There is only one class in the community that thinks more about money than the rich, and that is the poor. The poor can think of nothing else. That is the misery of being poor."
—Oscar Wilde

Even if you are "well educated," you probably could learn more about how to make the most of your money and the time and energy that goes into making, spending, saving, investing, and protecting it. After all, the basics of good personal financial practice—spending less than you earn, investing your savings in proven vehicles for the long term, and securing adequate insurance coverage—are relatively simple. Many people, however, are unable to follow these rules for the same reasons people can't follow a diet: It's difficult, and it can be emotionally taxing. I've seen many people allow their individual fears, biases, mistaken beliefs, past experiences, and external pressures to color and sabotage their efforts to practice good financial habits.

Your Money History

In order to identify, accept, and overcome the money-related obstacles that are currently preventing you from reaching a place in life where you're satisfied with what you have—financially *and* personally—you need to start by getting a handle on what I'll call your "money history," particularly the influence of your parents, your childhood, and young adult environments.

Here's an example. Before she visited my office seeking financial advice, Eva had made repeated attempts at various times in her twenties and thirties to learn how to invest her retirement savings, which she kept in a low-interest bank account. She subscribed to *Money* magazine, read the business section of her city's newspaper, enrolled in an adult education course at a local college, and discussed investments with coworkers and friends. Every information-gathering initiative ended with the same result: Eva couldn't bring herself to move her money from her bank account into growth investments like stocks and bonds. Eva, a bright professional woman, wasn't able to realize the impact that her upbringing had on her adult views of the investing world until she was in her forties.

In recalling an incident that occurred at the tender age of seven during a discussion with me, Eva finally got to the bottom of her anxieties concerning investments. "My mom was always complaining about how my father lost money gambling in the stock market. My father was working with this broker who encouraged lots of trading. When the broker switched to a new firm, he mailed out an announcement letter to our home. After my mother opened it in front of me, she tore it into many pieces and vowed that my father wasn't going to squander any more of our needed money. We were always scraping by for money, so my mother got very angry at my father's investment losses." This wasn't an isolated scene. Eva realized that, as a child and young adult, she constantly received negative messages at home about investing.

Although the impact of such family tension could have been obvious to outside observers, for Eva, it didn't become clear until she met with me and discussed her financial history. Eva benefited from learning that stocks and investing weren't gambling and weren't that complicated. She came to understand that her father's broker was encouraging her father's excessive trading, which was detrimental to her dad's investing success.

Eva's story illustrates how one's family history can influence current views on personal finance. However, it's only one example. Other experiences can be even more difficult to interpret, even for outside observers. Taking a historical inventory isn't easy, but if you put in the time and want to challenge yourself and your beliefs, the process can be productive. Eva's story also illustrates the second part of examining your money mindset—examining your current views and behaviors.

Taking Stock of Your Money Background

Set aside time—about an hour should do—for some personal reflection, ideally in a place and at a time when you'll be free from distractions. Go to the library, the beach, a coffee shop, or some other place that's, ideally, away from your home. Reflect upon the following questions:

1. What personal experiences (good and bad) relating to money do you recall from your childhood? Did you work as a kid and teenager? What lessons did you take away from these experiences? If you didn't work, think about why you didn't and what your parents said to you (or implied) about working and making money.

2. What memories of your parents (or other guardians) do you have that relate to finances? Were your parents spenders or savers? What financial crises occurred, and how did your parents handle them? Did money cause tension and problems at home? If you don't have many explicit recollections about money with your caregivers, what implicit messages did you take away from how they led their lives and the role that money played in it?

3. What efforts did your mom and dad make to teach you about money? How much freedom and latitude did they give you with money? What lessons did you take away from this? If you had to summarize their philosophy and approach to money in a sentence or two, what would it be?

4. How important were financial considerations in what you chose to study and what jobs and career you sought? Did you pursue work based upon what interested you or what you believed you could make more money at? Were you pushed into your career by someone else for the supposed financial security you could achieve?

5. Thinking back to your childhood and young adult years, what significant events happened to you and your family that impacted how you felt about money? These events could include, for example, a major illness, a parent being laid off, volunteer work you did, and so on. You need not have a long laundry list of major events—the two or three most important and formative occurrences will do.

Having taken the time to ponder your background and how it colors how you relate to money, take the next step and spend some time reflecting on your current feelings and attitudes toward money. Can you identify with any of the following?

➤ What stresses you about money?

➤ Are you frequently juggling bills and trying to figure out whom to pay next?

➤ Do you watch your investments daily or not look at your investment statements out of fear? Why?

➤ Are you looking for a hot investment tip that could multiply your money quickly?

➤ What financial secrets are you keeping from your spouse (and others)? What would cause you feelings of humiliation and embarrassment?

Remember that there are no right or wrong answers to many of these questions. In working with clients, I've found that simply taking the time to think about and reflect upon one's history with money provides valuable insights that enable people to cultivate better financial habits. Quite often, people who go through this process say things like, "I never took the time to consider why I do what I do with money or even what I'm doing." Don't beat yourself up if you can't handle developing thoughtful responses all in one sitting. Some people find that these questions bring up strong memories and emotions, so you may need two or three sessions to complete this task.

> *"That man is richest whose pleasures are the cheapest."*
> —Henry David Thoreau

Your Friends and Money

Our peers may have a major influence over how we spend money and even deal with money overall. When I used to teach an adult education personal finance course at the University of California, I talked about consumer spending and our choice of cars. Over the years, a surprising number of students confided to me that they had been embarrassed by the shabbiness of their cars. One person said to me that office mates would get on him that his car was "trashing up" the parking lot. Sales professionals who call on clients and take out clients in their cars were especially self-conscious about their vehicles.

Here are some examples where money comes into play with others. Consider each and what lessons you can learn about how your friends and peers affect the way that you think about and spend and use your money:

➤ **Going out to eat or entertainment.** Do you go out to restaurants, bars, or entertainment venues? Do you go on trips or vacations with others? How do you choose the place? Do the folks you tend to hang out with discuss and care about the cost, or is it not discussed? How are things handled when it comes time to paying the bill?

➤ **Lending money.** Are you comfortable lending money to friends or family? Have you ever done so with bad results (for example, not being repaid)? If the loan extends over a lengthy period (years, not months), have you collected a reasonable level of interest?

➤ **Gift buying/exchanges.** In a typical year, how much do you spend on gifts for others? Do you feel obligated to buy many people gifts? Do you find yourself spending more than you can comfortably afford or giving more than you receive?

Exercise: Using the preceding topics as a guide, spend some time reflecting on your interactions with friends and other acquaintances relating to money:

Your Environment and Money

Another profound influence on how you deal with and relate to money is your environment. For example, how did you choose where you live? It's fine to want to live in a convenient and safe area, but if you select a location populated by the rich and famous, how able are you going to be to save money, especially with conspicuous consumption surrounding and tempting you?

In addition to where you live, consider the other circles in which you travel—your work environment, areas where you spend a lot of your free time, and so on.

Exercise: Write down your thoughts about your environment and how it may impact and reflect your views on money:

In the next chapter, you take a look at tailoring your own personal plan.

4

Developing Your Personal Financial Action Plan

"Keep away from people who try to belittle your ambitions. Small people always do that, but the really great make you feel that you, too, can become great."
—Mark Twain

"My problem lies in reconciling my gross habits with my net income."
—Errol Flynn

I n my work as an hourly-based personal financial planner, I developed and honed a process for working with clients at varying income levels to make practical and holistic financial improvements. This chapter will be the first of several that begin to walk you through that process with various questions, worksheets, and exercises to enable you to put your knowledge and insights into action.

In this chapter, you're going to do some (further) soul searching about your past financial experiences and your future goals, and you'll begin to organize some of your financial documents. Now's the time to begin developing a personalized plan. You may want or need to hire some experts to help you with portions of this, so along the way, I will highlight who might best assist you and refer you to Chapter 19, "Hiring Financial Help," for how to find competent professionals who have reasonable fees.

The financial goal of developing a personal action plan is to develop recommendations to help you to

- ➤ Improve earnings of assets
- ➤ Reduce cost of loans
- ➤ Achieve financial independence goals
- ➤ Reduce your taxes, especially regarding savings/investments
- ➤ Improve catastrophic insurance coverage
- ➤ Reduce insurance costs
- ➤ Save the time and hassle of financial research and shopping

My goal is to provide you with the information and insight needed to make informed financial decisions. I recommend "best value" providers—they not only offer lower prices, lower management expenses, and higher returns, but also offer high financial safety and good service.

Before we jump into this, I'd like to remind you of some important points about my approach and recommendations:

➤ I do not sell (nor have I ever sold) financial products (e.g., insurance, investments), nor do I receive compensation from financial institutions I recommend.

➤ I would like you to commit that you will not implement financial strategies and purchase financial products that you do not understand. I ask that you request and read the prospectus/contract prior to purchasing any and all financial products. Seek the services of a qualified attorney or accountant in the event that legal or tax expertise and advice are required.

➤ Investment success requires a multi-year time horizon, and investing in stocks and bonds will entail risk of share price declines.

➤ I cannot guarantee the financial service providers recommended or their products, service, and performance.

What follows are some questions to ponder and requests to retrieve various financial documents. If you have family, you may well find that discussing these topics raises sparks and conflicts. Chapters 5, "Love and Money," and 6, "Families and Money," can assist you with handling and solving money conflicts with others.

Background Information

List your sources of income:

_____ $ _____ / month

_____ $ _____ / month

_____ $ _____ / month

Are you likely to have a significant change in your income, assets, or liabilities in the next three years? If yes, consider please why and the likely dollar or percentage change:

Do you have health problems or disabilities?

Do you smoke?

Are you planning to have children/more children?

Do your children or any other relatives who may be dependent upon you have any major medical problems or disabilities?

Are your parents (or in-laws) likely to need your financial support?

What financial decisions have you made that displeased you or where you felt you lacked information and/or understanding?

What financial decisions have you made that pleased you?

How would you characterize your desire to take risks in investments (circle one)?

Conservative (Preserve Principal) Maximize Current Income			Aggressive (Long-Term Growth) Maximize Total Return	
1	2	3	4	5

Comments:

Why are your current savings/investments invested where they are?

Goals and Concerns

Please describe your personal and financial goals and concerns.

Short Term (next few years)

Long Term (7–10+ Years)

Assets

(NOTE: The first part of this section deals with non-retirement assets. Retirement savings are covered later in this section.)

For each of the following, please locate a copy of the most recent statement:

➤ Bank checking and savings accounts
➤ Other savings/CDs/money market accounts
➤ Brokerage accounts (stocks and bonds)
➤ Mutual fund accounts

OTHER ASSETS (list)   **$ Value**

Business owned: _____ _____

Gold/silver: _____ _____

Artwork/antiques: _____ _____

Other (specify): _____ _____

REAL ESTATE—RESIDENTIAL/OWNER OCCUPIED

Price paid: $ _____ Approximate current value: $ _____

Current annual property taxes: $ _____

Current mortgage balance: $ _____ Monthly payment: $ _____

Original length of mortgage: _____ years

Current interest rate: _____ %

Interest rate is: Fixed _____ Variable _____

If interest rate is "Variable":

How often does rate adjust? _____ months

Maximum rate change per adjustment period: _____ %

Maximum rate allowed over life of loan: _____ %

Upon which cost of funds index is the mortgage based? (check one):

_____ 11th district

_____ Treasury bills _____ months

_____ Other (specify) _____

What is the "margin" (amount added to cost of funds index to obtain rate)? _____ %

If you currently rent, do you desire to purchase real estate in the next 3–5 years?

If yes, will you have to accumulate the down payment yourself or will you receive assistance from others (for example, family)?

For each of the following, locate a copy of the most recent statement:

➤   IRA/Keogh accounts

➤   Employer-sponsored savings/retirement accounts

➤ Profit sharing

ESOPs

401(k)/403(b) (Annuity)

Pension

Other

➤ Social Security benefits statement—the government now annually sends these out to everyone at least 25 years old. Statements are generally mailed about two to three months before your birthday. If you haven't gotten a statement in the past year or have lost or thrown it away, here are two ways to get one:

Request one online at www.ssa.gov (click on the link for "Your Social Security Statement" on the right side of the home page).

Request form SSA-7004 by calling 800-772-1213.

Do you currently save a regular amount of your monthly income? If yes, into what type of account is the savings going (e.g., IRA, employer 401(k), regular savings)?

Account Type

You _____ % or $ _____ / month _____

_____ % or $ _____ / month _____

Spouse _____ % or $ _____ / month _____

_____ % or $ _____ / month _____

Have you contributed to an IRA this year?   Yes _____ No _____

Has your spouse?   Yes _____ No _____

Did you contribute to an IRA last year?   Yes _____ No _____

Did your spouse?   Yes _____ No _____

Studies have shown that "retirees" typically spend 65%–80% of their pre-retirement income during retirement years. Which of the following (percentages) descriptions best applies to you?

_____ (65%) I save a large portion of my annual earnings; will not have a mortgage by retirement; am a high-income earner and do not anticipate leading a lifestyle in retirement reflecting my current high-income.

_____ (70%)

_____ (75%)

_____ (80%) I save little of my current earnings; will have a significant mortgage or growing rent to pay in retirement; need virtually all current income to meet my current lifestyle, which I would like to maintain in retirement.

At what age do you desire to have sufficient savings and pensions so that you can retire or significantly reduce employment income?

You   age: _____ years

Spouse   age: _____ years

Do you plan on working for income past the age at which you will receive full Social Security benefits—ages 65 to 67? (If yes, until what age do you expect to work, and how much income do you anticipate earning annually?)

Do you wish to earmark a portion of your assets for your beneficiaries (for example, family member, charity)? If so, what is the approximate dollar amount and beneficiary?

Will you tap into the equity in your home to provide for retirement?

Yes _____   No _____   Only if necessary _____

If yes, how much equity would you utilize? $ _____

Does your employer have a pension plan, and if so, do you know your accumulated benefits? (Get a copy of your pension plan benefits description and a recent statement of your earned benefits.)

You   Yes _____ ($ ____/mo)   No _____

Spouse   Yes _____ ($ ____/mo)   No _____

Planning

Most people don't like to plan, unless we're talking about something really fun, like a vacation. Planning for your financial future is a little like planning a vacation. You're organizing your money and time so that you get to do all the great things you want when you get there.

Planning your finances doesn't have to be too long or involved. In the absence of financial goals and objectives, however, most people's finances simply reflect the history and disorganization of their lives.

Some people are put off by planning, particularly those who are younger or who have not taken an interest in finances. It's hard enough to know where you'd like to be next year, let alone a decade or more from now. But, you don't need to know exactly where and what you'll want to be doing. Sound financial planning is flexible and adaptable to change.

The first step with planning is setting some goals. Planning your finances can be sort of fun, not to mention profitable! You may be able to save thousands of dollars more per year and hundreds of thousands (if not millions) over your life with smart planning. How? By reducing your overall spending, taxes, borrowing, and insurance costs and boosting your rate of savings and investment returns.

Net Worth Calculation

Your net worth is the total of your financial assets (investment account, including retirement and non-retirement), minus your financial liabilities. Before we jump into this, please keep in mind some things I do and don't include in the calculations:

➤ **Your home.** I generally exclude this in the calculations (on both the asset as well as the liability side). If you plan to use the equity in your home toward retirement, however—for example, by trading down to a less-costly home or through a reverse mortgage— feel free to include your home in the calculations.

➤ **Pensions and Social Security.** These are absolutely assets and should be included in the calculations.

➤ **Personal property.** I do not include your car(s), furniture, and so on. These are consumer items that depreciate over time and are not assets that people typically sell to finance their financial goals.

In the next section, you will perform a net worth calculation in conjunction with your retirement planning.

Retirement Expectations Versus Means

A long-term financial goal that most people have is someday to retire. To some, this means leaving work for an income entirely. For others, simply cutting back on work or choosing to volunteer is most appealing. If you don't plan on continuing to work well into your golden years, you need a reasonable chunk of funds in order to maintain a particular lifestyle in the absence of your normal employment income.

If you're a typical person, you'll need less money to live on in retirement than you were earning during your working years. Good news! Otherwise, you'd need to save a lot more money to be able to retire. Remember, in retirement, you also won't need to be "saving" any of your income, and many of your work-related expenses (commuting, "work" clothes) will go away. With less income, your taxes should decrease as well.

Some people, however, need to have income in retirement that equals 80 percent or more of their pre-retirement income. This could occur if you expect many of your expenditures to remain the same. Perhaps you're a renter or will still have a significant mortgage in your senior years. Maybe you have expensive hobbies that you'll have more time to pursue.

What resources will you have to meet your retirement needs? In addition to government benefits such as Social Security, personal savings and company-provided pensions round out most people's retirement income sources.

Under current rules (which are subject to change), you're eligible to collect reduced Social Security benefits as early as age 62. The age at which you may collect full Social Security benefits depends on when you were born:

Date of Birth	Age for Full Social Security Benefits
Before 1938	65 years
1938	65 years, 2 months
1939	65 years, 4 months
1940	65 years, 6 months
1941	65 years, 8 months
1942	65 years, 10 months
1943–1954	66 years
1955	66 years, 2 months
1956	66 years, 4 months
1957	66 years, 6 months
1958	66 years, 8 months
1959	66 years, 10 months
After 1959	67 years

For retirees now beginning to receive full Social Security benefits, those who earned around $20,000 per year during their working years are receiving about $750 per month. Those who averaged $60,000 per year (today's dollars) during their working years are collecting about $1,470 per month, and averaging $100,000+ per year should lead to a maximum benefit of $2,000+ per month.

Social Security is intended to provide you with a subsistence level of income in retirement for the basic necessities of living, like food, shelter, and clothing. It is not intended to be your sole source of income and should and must be supplemented by personal savings and company pension plans.

Many people are concerned about collecting their Social Security. The most common fear is that it won't be there when they retire. Although theoretically possible, this is highly unlikely. First, politicians aren't likely to say as a group, "Sorry, the money is all gone, and you don't get any." They'd get run out of office!

It's possible that you may have to wait until a slightly older age to collect benefits or that more of your benefits might be taxed. However, the current mood in Congress is against tax increases on retirees.

For purposes of retirement planning, what matters is where you stand today as far as reaching your goal. You need to crunch some numbers to get a handle on this. My favorite web site tools and booklets come from Vanguard (www.vanguard.com) and T. Rowe Price (www.troweprice.com; 800-638-5660 for their work booklets). Using the data you gathered earlier in this chapter, these resources can walk you through the calculations needed to figure out how much you should be saving to reach your retirement goal.

The assumptions that you use are key factors in your retirement planning calculations. The assumed rate of return that you're earning on your investments and the assumed rate of inflation are both particularly critical. Over the past century, the rate of inflation has averaged about 3 percent per year. Growth-oriented investments, such as stocks, have returned about 10 percent per year historically. Bonds and other fixed income-oriented investments have returned about 5 to 6 percent per year.

Many people find when they perform the calculations for the first time that they need to be saving a lot more money to reach their retirement goal. Don't give up! There are a number of things that you can do to lessen the depressingly high savings you apparently need:

➤ Extend the number of years you are willing to work or consider working part-time for a few or more years past the age you were expecting to cease working.

➤ Get more aggressive with your investing. There's a risk in not taking enough risk: Your money won't grow quickly enough to keep you ahead of inflation and taxes and enable you to meet your goal.

➤ Reduce your spending. The more you spend today, the more years you'll have to work in order to meet your savings goal.

➤ Tap into your home equity. If you didn't factor using some of your home's equity into your retirement nest egg, consider doing so. Some people are willing or want to trade down into a less-costly property in retirement. It's also possible to take what's called a reverse mortgage to tap some of your property's equity (see the sidebar on reverse mortgages).

➤ Reduce your taxes while investing. Be sure to take advantage of retirement savings accounts, especially when you can gain free matching money from your employer or are eligible for the special tax credit from the government (see Chapter 9, "Your Spending Plan"). When investing money outside of retirement accounts, take care to minimize taxes (more on this in Chapter 14, "Your Investing Plan").

Even if you're young and can't think about when you'll have gray hair (or simply less hair!) or plan on working to a ripe old age, retirement "planning" makes great tax sense. That's because one of the best tax breaks is contributing to retirement accounts.

In the U.S., numerous types of retirement accounts exist. For-profit companies may offer 401(k) plans, whereas non-profit organizations can offer 403(b) plans. Self-employed people may establish a Keogh or SEP-IRA account. All of these accounts are similar in that contributions into them from your employment earnings are not taxed at either the federal or state level. In other words, these contributions are tax-deductible.

Living on the House: Reverse Mortgages

Reverse mortgages, which enable you, through a loan, to receive tax-free income on your home's equity while still living in the home, fill a void and are just beginning to tap into growing demand. The lender pays you (lump sum, monthly payments, or with a credit line), and the accumulated loan balance and interest is paid off when your home is sold or you pass away. The typical borrower: a 70-something widow who's running out of money, wants to stay in her home, and needs money for basic living expenses or to replace a leaky roof.

With their high up-front costs, though, the effective interest rate on most reverse mortgages easily jumps into the double-digit realm if you only stay a few years into the loan. And reverse mortgages can be complicated to understand and compare. Your effective interest rate varies greatly depending upon how long you're in the home and using the loan, the timing and size of payments you receive, and your home's value over time. One unknown that you can't control is if an extended nursing home stay forces the sale of your home if you're not there for 12 months. In such a situation, at least the proceeds from the sale could be used toward the nursing home costs.

To qualify for a reverse mortgage, all the home's owners (coop apartments generally aren't eligible) must be at least 62 years old and use the home as their principal residence. Any outstanding debts against the home must be extinguished.

Unlike a traditional mortgage, you need not have any income or even good credit to qualify for a reverse mortgage. And, unlike a conventional mortgage, reverse mortgages are non-recourse loans—you can't lose your home for failing to make payments since there are none.

Many retirees I speak with say that taking out a reverse mortgage was a good experience for them. Often cited are feeling that the extra income allowed keeping up a home's maintenance and paying medical and other costs, not having to scrimp so much on things like eating out sometimes, and provided peace of mind in not having to make payments.

Is a reverse mortgage for you? Start with the non-financial considerations—your desire to keep your current home and neighborhood and your comfort level with the size of your home and the associated upkeep. Consider if you wish to stay in your home for the foreseeable future, or if you would rather tap into your home's equity by moving and downsizing to a smaller home or simply renting.

According to Ken Scholen, Director of AARP's Reverse Mortgage Education Project, the federally insured Home Equity Conversion Mortgage (HECM) typically provides the most money at the best ongoing interest rates for all but the most expensive of homes.

Don't keep your situation and concerns a family secret. "Discuss within your family to get everybody thinking and talking about a range of options," advises Ken Scholen. You may also be able to enhance your monthly cash flow by taking advantage of local property tax deferral and relief programs for seniors—check with your local tax assessor's office for details.

Part of the appeal of a reverse mortgage is the lack of attractiveness of alternatives if you'd like to stay in your home. With a home equity loan, the big challenge is the required payments. Home equity loans are recourse loans, and if you're unable to keep up with payments later in retirement, the lender can foreclose. Also know that any money invested that generated investment income would be taxed. Given the lack of risk-taking desires of most seniors with their investments, invested home equity money would be unlikely to generate high enough returns to cover the loan's interest costs.

In addition to using AARP's useful web tools at www.aarp.org/revmort, take advantage of the increasing numbers of free, independent reverse mortgage counselors around the country—call 800-209-8085 and ask for counselors in your area.

The market for reverse mortgages is getting increasingly competitive as there are more lenders coming into the marketplace.

In the early to mid 2000s, retirement plan annual contribution limits increased substantially thanks to tax law changes. For tax year 2007, here are the annual contribution limits for various retirement accounts. (These amounts increase each year with the cost of living.)

➤ 401(k) plans—$15,500.

➤ 403(b) plans—The lesser of 20% of employee's salary to a maximum of $15,500.

➤ Simplified Employee Pension Plan, Individual Retirement Account (SEP-IRAs)—The lesser of 20% of your self-employment income to a maximum of $45,000.

➤ Keoghs—The lesser of 20% of your self-employment income to a maximum of $45,000.

➤ Individual Retirement Accounts (IRAs)—Up to $4,000 per year, so long as you have at least this much employment (or alimony) income. Those age 50 and older may contribute up to $5,000 annually. Up-front deductibility depends upon whether you participate in another plan through your employer. If you do, and your adjusted gross income on your tax return exceeds $50,000 if you file as a single person or $80,000 if you're married filing jointly, the tax deductibility of your IRA is reduced or eliminated. If you can't take the tax deduction for a regular IRA, consider the newer Roth IRAs, which allow for tax-free withdrawal of investment earnings in your later years. (See the section on non-deductible retirement accounts near the end of this section for more details.)

The main attraction of retirement accounts is the tax savings. Suppose that between federal and state taxes, you're paying about 35% in taxes on your last dollars of income. If you're able to contribute, say, $6,000 into a tax-deductible retirement savings plan ($500 per month), you should see your federal and state tax bills decrease by about $2,100. This immediate tax savings is usually a great incentive to encourage people to use retirement accounts to build wealth. But this benefit is only part of the value derived from using retirement accounts.

Because the money contributed to the retirement account is not taxed at either the federal or state level, your take-home pay shrinks by much less than the $500 contribution. (Note: Social Security and Medicare taxes are unaffected by a retirement contribution—these taxes are paid regardless.)

Self-Employed Retirement Savings Plans

One of the biggest benefits of earning self-employment income is the ability to establish a tax-sheltered retirement savings plan. These plans not only allow you to contribute more than you likely would be saving on a tax-deferred basis for an employer, but they can also be tailored to meet your specific needs.

As with other retirement savings plans, your contributions to these plans are excluded from your reported income and are thus exempt from current federal and state income taxes. The earnings that accumulate on your savings over time are also exempt from current income taxes.

You pay taxes on your contributions and earnings when you withdraw them, presumably in retirement, when you should be in a lower tax bracket.

An SEP-IRA plan cuts through much of a Keogh plan's red tape and is somewhat easier to set up and administer. As with a Keogh plan, when you as the employer establish a SEP, you must offer this as a benefit to employees if you have them.

In order to determine the exact maximum amount that you may contribute from self-employed income, you will have to have your completed Schedule C tax form. As with other tax-deferred retirement savings plans, there is a penalty of 10% imposed on distributions before you reach age 59 1/2. This penalty tax is in addition to the regular income tax that is due in the year you make the early withdrawal.

A Keogh plan must be established by the end of the tax year (usually December 31st), although you have until the filing of your federal tax return to make your actual contribution to the plan.

The drawback to a Keogh plan is that it requires slightly more paperwork than a SEP-IRA plan to set up and administer (although the no-load mutual fund "prototype" plans greatly simplify the administrative burden).

Owners who have employees to be covered by a plan may be more interested in a Keogh plan, as you may be able to contribute more relative to your employees. Speak with a tax advisor or investment management company for more information.

Once you contribute money into a retirement account, the profits on that contribution are not taxed. So, in addition to slashing your taxes when you make your contribution, you save from this tax-deferred compounding of your investment over time. In other words, all of the taxes you would have owed over the years compound in your account and make your money grow faster. You pay tax on this retirement account money only when you make withdrawals.

Here's an example to illustrate the incredible value over the long term of making modest contributions to retirement accounts now. Assume that you are able to save and invest $6,000 in a year. If this money is not contributed to a retirement account, then $2,100 in taxes is owed. The following chart assumes the money is invested at an 8% return. After each period in the example, money in the retirement account is withdrawn and taxes are paid at the assumed rate of 35%. For the scenario where the money is invested outside a tax-sheltered retirement account, the same tax rate of 35% is assumed.

The Power of Tax-Deferred Retirement Accounts

Year	Using Retirement Account	Not Using Retirement Account
0	$6,000	$3,900
10	$8,420	$6,474
20	$18,178	$10,750
30	$39,244	$17,846
40	$84,726	$29,628

Because you start with much less to invest when you don't contribute to retirement accounts since money is immediately siphoned off to pay taxes, you end up with less. The longer the money is invested, the more you profit by investing inside a retirement account.

If your employer matches or contributes additional money to your account, you'll be even better off. It's free money, so don't miss out! Some employers, for example, might match your contributions at 25 cents (or more) on the dollar you contribute. Even if you unexpectedly need to withdraw your contribution, you should still come out ahead—the penalties for early withdrawal are only 10 percent federal tax and whatever nominal amount, if any, your state charges.

Some people are concerned that if their tax rate in retirement is higher than it is during their working and saving years, then funding retirement accounts could lead to higher taxes. While possible, this is unlikely. Because of the tax-deferred compounding, you should come out ahead by funding your retirement accounts. In fact, your retirement tax rate could increase and you'd still come out ahead.

How high does your retirement tax rate need to be in order to negate the tax-deferred compounding benefits of a retirement account? The following chart shows the same example that we just looked at, with a new twist. You can now see how high a tax rate needs to be applied in retirement so as to eliminate all of the tax-deferred compounding of the retirement account. (Remember that the assumed tax rate of the person contributing to the retirement account was 35%.)

Your Tax Rate Needs to Rise Tremendously in Retirement to Eliminate Tax-Deferral Benefits

Year	Using Retirement Account	Not Using Retirement Account	Retirement Tax Rate to Eliminate Retirement Account Benefits
0	$6,000	$3,900	n/a
10	$8,420	$6,474	50%
20	$18,178	$10,750	61%
30	$39,244	$17,846	70%
40	$84,726	$29,628	77%

As you can see, the longer the money is invested, the higher your tax rate would have to rise to wipe out the tax-deferred compounding benefits.

Retirement accounts that you establish, such as a SEP-IRA or Keogh (if you're self-employed) and IRAs, can be set up through most major financial institutions, such as mutual fund companies, brokerage firms, and banks. (I provide details about investment options in Chapters 11 through 14.) These accounts can be transferred to different firms at your discretion. Simply call the company that you want to move your account into and ask it to send you its account application and transfer forms.

For retirement accounts that your employer maintains, such as a 401(k) plan, you are limited to the investment options that the plan offers. When you leave this employer, you can "roll over" your account balance into an Individual Retirement Account (IRA). Simply contact the investment company that you'd like to use for the IRA and have it send you its account application forms. Instruct your previous employer where you'd like your money sent—don't take possession of it; otherwise, you'll get hit with a 20 percent federal income tax withholding.

Retirement Account Accessibility

Some people contribute very little—or not at all—to retirement accounts because of worries about having access to their money. You should know that generally speaking, you may incur a tax penalty for withdrawing money from a retirement account prior to reaching age 59 1/2. The penalty is 10 percent of the taxable amount withdrawn in federal taxes, plus whatever penalty your state assesses.

There are exceptions, however, that allow you to withdraw retirement account money before age 59 1/2 without penalty. First, you may withdraw before this magic age so long as you make withdrawals for at least five consecutive years or until age 59 1/2, whichever is greater. The size of the withdrawals must also be based on your life expectancy according to IRS assumptions.

If you suffer a disability or incur significant medical expenses, this may also allow you to withdraw money from your retirement account without penalty.

But what if you have a short-term need for money? The best solution is to ensure that you maintain an emergency reserve of money outside your retirement account. Your employer's retirement plan may also allow borrowing. It's also possible that you may be able to borrow money from other sources, such as a family member or through a line of credit or lower-interest credit card.

Not all retirement accounts offer tax-deductible contributions. In fact, if you work for an employer that does not offer a retirement savings plan such as a 401(k) or 403(b), you're limited to making, at most, a $4,000 contribution ($5,000 if you're age 50 or older) to an Individual Retirement Account (IRA).

Your ability to take a tax deduction for an IRA contribution depends on several factors. First, you may contribute to an IRA only to the extent that you have employment income. (Alimony is the only exception.) If, for example, you work just a little during the year and make $2,000, that's the maximum you may contribute to an IRA. If you earn more, you may contribute up to the amount of your employment earnings to a maximum of $4,000.

However, if you are a high-enough income earner, and you are covered by some sort of pension or other retirement plan at your employer, you may be limited in your IRA deduction. You are allowed full deductibility of your IRA contribution if you are an active participant in a retirement plan and your modified gross adjusted income (AGI) is $83,000 or less (joint tax filers) or $52,000 or less (for single tax payers).

A Roth IRA does not offer an up-front tax break, but it does offer ongoing tax shelter as well as tax-free withdrawals of investment earnings post age 59 1/2. You may contribute up to maximum limits, which are the same as on a regular IRA, so long as your modified AGI does not exceed $99,000 if you're a single taxpayer or $156,000 for married couples filing jointly. If you can't take the tax deduction for a regular IRA, a Roth IRA makes complete sense.

If you want to invest more of your money so that it grows without the burden of high taxation, other options do exist. Investments that are more growth oriented—for example, such as stocks and real estate—may make sense for you (see Chapter 10, "Borrowing and Debt Management").

Pension Decisions

Some employees, especially those who work for larger organizations, earn pension benefits. With such a plan, the employer is putting away money on your behalf and investing it on your behalf. Pension plans certainly simplify "saving" for retirement. Slowly but surely, such plans are being phased out and replaced by plans discussed earlier, like 401(k) plans, where employees must elect to save their own money from their paycheck and direct the investment of it over the years.

With pension plans, employees typically face two sets of important decisions. The first is whether to take the pension as a monthly retirement payment or a lump sum distribution. For those who want the monthly pension payment, there is usually a second decision among several payment plan options. Let's deal with each of these in turn, starting with the first and biggest issue—lump sum or monthly payments.

Like the sticker price on a house, a lump sum, instead of a monthly pension, sounds like a big number. However, pension plans offering a lump sum option are generally structured to provide about the same expected value to employees. That's why it's usually hard to decide on financial factors, and the decision hinges more on qualitative considerations.

An important factor to start with is where you are with retirement planning (see the section earlier in this chapter) and how much "risk" you can take with this pension money. As an example, consider the case of Walter and Susan. When I reviewed their situation, Walter was 56 years old and ready to retire from his employer of the past 27 years. He had to decide whether to take a $20,000 annual pension, with no cost of living allowance (COLA) and a 50 percent survivor's annuity, or a lump sum of $265,000.

They seemingly had quite a bit earmarked for retirement already: expected Social Security benefits totaling $2,650 per month at age 62, Susan's pension of $1,500 monthly (with a COLA), and traditional retirement savings plans—his was worth $255,000, and she had about $70,000 in hers. However, the standard of living that these assets could provide was only about 50 percent of their annual combined salaries of $130,000.

Prospective retirees should conduct retirement analysis to determine how the standard of living likely to be provided by their assets compares with their expected retirement expenses. Walter did an analysis through the investment company managing his firm's 401(k), and this suggested they had enough to retire. However, this presumed he worked to age 60, and Walter didn't recall specific numbers detailing how much wiggle room he might have. Because he was trying to call it quits by age 56, he needed to update the analysis.

The bottom line was that the income from Walter's pension was of great importance. If they took the lump sum and managed it badly or simply had bad investment luck, it would affect their living standard. The good news: They didn't live lavishly. Their modest ranch home had no mortgage, and Walter's long and costly commute would vanish when he retired.

According to El Cajon, CA-based financial advisor Bill Bengen, Walter's $20,000 annual pension payment is greater than the expected income from the lump sum would be for about the first 18 years of Walter's retirement, when he reached age 74.

Some additional key considerations when weighing a pension versus a lump sum are as follows:

➤ **How adept are you with managing money?** A major benefit of the pension is that the investment responsibility rests with professional pension managers who are far less likely to make dramatic moves. The best way to answer this question is to reflect upon your historic experience managing money. If it's problematic or you simply lack such experience, it's better to lean toward the pension and steer clear of the lump sum. Walter's investment management history showed evidence of being emotionally driven—in the spring of 2006, he sold most of his stock holdings when he was worried about the economy and gas prices. "I do get jumpy the closer I get to retiring," he admits. (And, they already had $300,000+ that they're managing.)

➤ **What is your health situation and family longevity record?** If you have a major medical problem or reason to believe your genes destine you to fewer golden years, one advantage of the lump sum is that you get all of the money to use and use sooner if you choose and/or can leave the remainder to your heirs. The pension only lasts as long as you do (and reduced benefits as long as your spouse does).

➤ **How comfortable will you be tapping into principal?** Many retirees are fine with living off of investment income, but it's psychologically difficult for most to use principal. Thus, pension checks, which are more comfortably spent, can indeed provide a higher standard of living.

➤ **What is the safety of your pension benefits?** Retirees often fear that a pension benefit also may only last as long as a company does. Pensions are backed by the Pension Benefit Guaranty Corporation (PBGC), an independent government agency, up to a monthly amount of $3,574, so Walter is well covered. (Pessimists who feel PBGC is woefully underfunded would argue he might take a haircut should his employer fail in the years ahead.)

PBGC Maximum Monthly Guarantees for Plans Terminating in 2007

Age	2007 Straight-Life Annuity	2007 Joint and 50% Survivor Annuity
65	$4,125.00	$3,712.50
64	$3,836.25	$3,452.63
63	$3,547.50	$3,192.75
62	$3,258.75	$2,932.88
61	$2,970.00	$2,673.00
60	$2,681.25	$2,413.13
59	$2,516.25	$2,264.63
58	$2,351.25	$2,116.13
57	$2,186.25	$1,967.63
56	$2,021.25	$1,819.13
55	$1,856.25	$1,670.63
54	$1,773.75	$1,596.38
53	$1,691.25	$1,522.13
52	$1,608.75	$1,447.88
51	$1,526.25	$1,373.63
50	$1,443.75	$1,299.38
49	$1,361.25	$1,225.13
48	$1,278.75	$1,150.88
47	$1,196.25	$1,076.63
46	$1,113.75	$1,002.38
45	$1,031.25	$928.13

In making this important decision, beware of financial planners and brokers' advice. If you take a pension, there's no lump sum for them to manage.

If you opt for a monthly check, some plans offer different options that basically differ from one another the way that investments do in terms of risk and return. The "safest" option, with the lowest payment, would be a 100 percent joint and survivor option. This payment continues as long as either the pensioner *or* the pensioner's spouse is still living and makes sense for risk-averse retirees who are dependent on the pension check (and perhaps are not in the best of health). Intermediate in risk and payment amount would be an option such as the two-thirds joint and survivor plan, whereby after the death of the pensioner, the survivor receives two-thirds of the pension amount paid to the pensioner before his or her passing. The riskiest option, but the one that maximizes payments now, is the single life option, which only makes payments so long as the pensioner is living. I would only advocate selecting this option if you are in good health, have plenty of assets, and your spouse could afford to live without the pension check.

Major Purchase Planning

Unfortunately, many of the things that you purchase over the course of your life cost a hefty chunk of money. In some cases, you're not going to have sufficient cash on hand to buy what you want when you want. So what should you do?

The answer really depends on what it is you're buying. If, for example, you're buying a home, the purchase price will likely preclude a cash purchase unless you live in a low-cost area or you are fortunate in having flush finances and relatively simple wants. Financing most of a home purchase via a mortgage can make good financial sense in the long run. Why? First, mortgage rates are quite competitive, and the interest on your home loan (as well as property taxes) is generally tax-deductible. Second, because homes are assets, they usually appreciate in value over the long haul. This doesn't mean that they go up in value every year.

I don't advise using credit for other major expenditures. Borrowing for purchases such as a car or vacations, for example, can be financially dangerous. The difference here is that you're buying items that lack "investment" value. In other words, these are consumption purchases.

Although vacations, a new wardrobe, or living room furniture may enhance the quality of your life and make you feel good, these aren't investments. You could live without these purchases, and they won't enhance your long-term financial health.

What's more, borrowing to make these types of consumption purchases is costly. You'll pay a higher rate of interest than, say, when you are buying a home. The interest on consumer debt such as credit card and auto loan debt is also not tax-deductible.

A good test for making a consumption purchase is whether you have the money on hand to pay in cash. For example, if you want to buy new furniture that will cost $2,000, can you pay cash for it? You don't literally have to pay in cash if you find it more convenient to use your credit card at the store and then promptly pay the credit card bill in full. The point is that you're not carrying this debt for months on end.

Avoiding the financing of consumption purchases forces you to live within your means. If you're buying new cars and other items by carrying debt month to month, you'll have a difficult time saving money in the future. More of your future income will already be claimed and will be gobbled up by debt repayment. And don't forget that these purchases are costing you more the longer you carry the debt.

Buy what you can afford by saving for it in advance or setting your sights lower.

To simply calculate how much to save per month for a major purchase, first determine the approximate cost of the item in question and over what time period you'd like to save the money. For example, let's suppose you would like to buy a good-quality used car that goes for about $18,000, and you'd like to complete the purchase in 24 months. Simply dividing $18,000 by 24 yields about $750 per month. If you can't do that—the solution(s) are pretty simple—cut the expenditure amount and/or save over a longer period.

College Cost Planning

No doubt, raising a family is a challenge to most budgets. Barring an unlikely fully paid academic, athletic, or other scholarship, paying for a college education is likely to be the largest expenditure you'll make for your children. Here are the current *average* costs per year for higher education:

Four-year private college	$35,000
Four-year public college	$18,000
Two-year community college	$14,000

Most parents are frightened by such numbers. Try not to be. There's a price, but what you buy should extend benefits for decades. And unless you're affluent, you're not going to have to shoulder all this financial responsibility yourself.

A variety of loan and grant programs exist, some of which are not based on "financial need." Unless you are wealthy, you're not going to be able to pay for the full cost yourself. Most parents shouldn't even try because they really can't afford it, and doing so may cause them other money troubles. Guide books and other information sources for loans, grants, and scholarships can be found in your child's school counseling office, local public libraries, and college financial aid offices. Start your search early—your child's junior year is a good time to think seriously about colleges and aid sources.

Be aware that your best intentions could create financial problems. Wanting to save money to provide for your children's college costs is a good instinct. However, if you do so at the expense of, for example, contributing to retirement accounts, you'll increase your tax bill, both short and long-term.

Be particularly careful about investing money in your children's names through so-called custodial accounts. Money that is in a custodial account is legally theirs when they reach the age of majority, which varies from 18 to 21 years depending on which state you live in.

The other problem with saving in custodial accounts is that the college financial aid system greatly penalizes you for doing so. Money in your child's name is assumed available and earmarked for college costs. If, on the other hand, you invested the money in your own retirement account(s), the financial aid system completely ignores it. (Just keeping it in your own non-retirement accounts is far better than putting it in junior's name.) All other factors being equal, your children will qualify for less financial aid the more money is in their names.

The benefits of custodial accounts are twofold. First, many parents like the fact that this money is clearly earmarked for the child's educational costs. A second perk is that there are some tax savings from the interest earned in the money in custodial accounts. Past the age of 17, all of the earnings produced by the money in your child's name is taxed at the child's rate. Before age 18, the first $1,700 is taxed at the child's rate, with everything above $1,700 taxed at your rate.

Invest in your name, especially your retirement accounts, first and foremost. As detailed in the retirement planning section earlier in this chapter, doing so will minimize your tax burden. And, you will be better positioned to finance your retirement and be able to help your kids financially if you're on stronger financial footing.

The financial aid treatment of 529 savings plans and (Coverdell) education savings accounts (ESAs) has been unclear over time. (Some states do offer modest tax benefits for contributing to 529s, but don't let the tax tail wag the dog in your decision making.) When such accounts are held with the parents as owners, the assets are treated as parental (non-retirement) assets. Although such accounts are not considered as children's assets on the federal financial aid forms, a number of schools are asking parents to disclose such assets and treating them as children's assets for college. Therefore, beware that while you may derive some tax benefits from using such accounts, those benefits may be negated if it harms your children's financial aid package. Utilizing these accounts is more of a no-brainer if you're affluent and reasonably expect no financial aid.

Prioritizing Different Goals

Most of the time, various potential purchases and financial goals will be competing for your limited income. Deciding what purchases and goals are more important to you is, of course, a personal decision. However, consider the tax and long-term planning implications as you make trade-offs.

An important issue to weigh is your ability to take advantage of the tax benefits from funding retirement accounts. Assuming you do wish to someday retire, the sooner you start to save, the less painful it will be.

A common dilemma is whether to save for a home down payment versus funding a retirement account. The advantage of doing the retirement account is that it provides immediate tax relief. The drawback is that the money is inaccessible under current tax laws without incurring a penalty.

In order to buy a home, you will need cash for a down payment and other closing costs. If you want to buy a home and save for retirement, you can try putting away some money monthly for each. However, if you're eager to get on with the home purchase, you could focus on that in the shorter-term and plan on saving more for retirement after you buy the property. Just be careful to buy a home well within your financial means that gives you the slack in your budget to save money as well as pay the mortgage.

5

Love and Money

"With money in your pocket, you are wise and handsome, and you sing well too."
—Yiddish saying

I t should come as no surprise, since many people don't learn good personal financial habits growing up and how to negotiate the range of money problems likely to come our way as adults, that two adults entering a relationship are virtually guaranteed to have issues relating to each other on the topic of money. Relationships are challenging. Opportunities for differences and conflict abound, from child rearing to sex to recapping the toothpaste, but money issues can set off the some of the largest fireworks (and produce plenty of smoldering hot spots just under the surface) in a relationship.

If couples don't disagree and fight about money, at least occasionally, it's probably because they don't talk about the subject at all rather than because they're always in agreement on financial issues. Couples also hide money issues from one another. Married Americans were surveyed by the research firm Ipsos-NPD to learn what secrets they keep from their spouses. On the list were the usual suspects such as extramarital affairs. Failures at work and personal dreams and aspirations were other commonly concealed topics. However, the number-one issue married couples covered up was how much they spend! One woman told the market research firm conducting the survey, "I don't like to tell him how much I spend when I go shopping. I'm afraid he'll cut back on the budget." But this pattern of secrecy didn't rest solely with wives—husbands hid details of their purchases from their wives about as often as the women duped the men in their lives.

Andy and Joanne's marriage was, in many ways, a classic example of opposites attracting. The differences extended into many facets of their lives and often seemed to strengthen their bond, but when it came to money, the differences created conflict. Joanne loved saving it, while Andy enjoyed spending it. Joanne clipped coupons, rarely treated herself to any indulgences, and took great pride in saving the maximum in her retirement plans. Andy, meanwhile, spent lots of money on his hobbies, motorcycles and sports, and he occasionally accumulated credit card debt due to overspending.

The friction and fights grew over the years, as did the insults. On one particular day in my office, Joanne fired the first salvo, "You spend irresponsibly and only think of yourself," which prompted Andy to retort, "You may die with more money, but you don't know how to have fun and enjoy life!" Like many couples, they repeatedly had the same fights over the same issues.

Fortunately, over the years of working with them, I helped Andy and Joanne realize that they must compromise and be more accepting of the other's differing money personality. They instituted a budget/spending limit for Andy that allowed him to spend a modest amount as he chose, while he also began a regular savings program. Joanne agreed to save a little less money than she had before and splurge from time to time.

Almost without exception, when I ask couples to recount their dating days, it's clear that they rarely, if ever, seriously talked about money issues. Most people are raised to believe that it's impolite and inappropriate to discuss money with others—it's a private, personal, and confidential matter. During courtship, most couples are in denial about the importance of all things financial, even though it's a huge issue looming on the horizon for the relationship.

Marriage takes place, the couple might enjoy a honeymoon period when all is right with the world and their relationship, and then over time, personality differences relating to personal financial management slowly emerge and cause friction. (Please note that I've seen plenty of cases where money friction existed during the dating and courtship days too.) Although arguments and disagreements about money often stem from other, broader relationship issues, the communication that does take place typically fails to improve the situation. "Couples get locked into accusatory, judgmental patterns of conversing with one another. In order to handle money well, couples need to communicate, negotiate, and compromise," says divorce attorney Violet Woodhouse, author of *Divorce and Money*.

How Men and Women Handle Money Differently

I've long been fascinated about the differences between men and women and how they think about and relate to each other regarding money. A lot has been written about gender differences and money, but much of it is frankly dopey and not empirical or based on research. Consider, for example, some of these gems, which come from a leading financial magazine quiz entitled, "Do You Manage Your Money Like a Boy or Girl?"

Q: You buy a lottery ticket and win $2,000. Most likely, you use the windfall to:

    a. Put money in your kid's college fund.

    b. Pay bills.

    c. Buy yourself an expensive present.

Option "a" is considered the female response, whereas option "b" is deemed the male response. Choice "c" is the gender-neutral answer. So men don't plan for their children's future while women do.

Q: A grandparent recently died and left you a valuable watch. You:

    a. Sell the watch and invest the money.

    b. Wear the watch.

    c. Put it in a drawer as a keepsake.

Option "a" was deemed the male response; option "c" the female response; "b" the gender-neutral reply. So women are sentimental and men aren't.

In my years of work as a financial counselor and columnist, I had many interactions with couples as well as opportunities to collect information from them. I can confidently make some generalizations about how men and women differ in relating to money in relationships, but please remember that these are simply generalizations, not hard and fast statements that apply to every man or woman. The value and point in being aware of these generalizations is that it may help you to help yourself and can help you in relationships where such problems surface.

For sure, women, as a group, are far, far more likely to ask for help and admit gaps in their knowledge than are men. I saw this tendency repeatedly in my work with couples. Men's egos more often get in the way of seeking assistance and education. Men are much more likely to plow ahead, even when they lack sufficient information and background on a money topic. My psychologist friends tell me that men, in our society, are more conditioned to view asking for help as a sign of weakness.

When it comes to investing, men are more willing to take risks. Although they may get themselves into trouble by relying too heavily on the investment vehicles that occupy the highest ends of the risk/return spectrum or leveraging themselves with borrowed money, for example, men are more likely to take the necessary risks to generate healthy long-term returns. However, as I discuss in Chapter 12, "Cultivating Good Investing Habits," researchers have found that men actually earn lower long-term investing returns than do women because men tend to trade too much. Although women may to be more conservative in their investment decisions, they do well long-term because they are far more likely to do their homework to identify and then hold onto good investments.

Generational issues and trends play a role in explaining common financial differences between men and women. Prior to the rise of the feminist/women's movement, many women were raised to view managing money as a man's job, with the belief that being financially dependent upon a man was the default state of affairs. In more recent generations, women have generally been raised to think and act independently, including taking responsibility for making financial decisions. Men and women are both more apt to view a marriage as a true partnership between equals, which certainly has some benefits. However, I've observed at least one downside: There is more *competition* within couples and marriages over money (among other issues). "There is far less 'we' thinking going on with couples today and far more 'me' thinking," says divorce attorney Violet Woodhouse.

On this same topic of "me" thinking instead of "we" thinking, I've been surprised over the years by how many people have stashes of money hidden from their spouses. I first encountered this issue early in my career as a financial counselor when a physician client, who never met me with his wife present, volunteered the fact that he had hid accounts from her. He justified this practice by saying that, "She has a wooden head."

If you think that your spouse does have a wooden head, hiding money isn't likely to be the best strategy! Many people fail to think about the implications should they unexpectedly pass away and how their surviving spouse would handle finances in such a case. The surviving spouse needs to know where to find important financial documents (investments, insurance, etc.), how to understand all of the arrangements, and how to handle matters going forward. Your spouse certainly won't be able to handle these responsibilities if assets are hidden and you don't discuss the details of your households' financial situation.

Worse-case scenario aside, the broader issues of marital trust come into play. When I've pressed clients on why they hide assets, more often than not, the reasons boil down to an overall lack of trust within the marriage that needs addressing. Some version of the following is commonly used to explain. With each, I've presented an alternative way to think about the situation that is both more constructive and ethical:

"I don't want my spouse to know how much we really have saved because then he/she will pressure/expect me to spend more."

In many cases, I've found that education and knowledge about the amount of assets truly needed for goals the couple share, such as retirement, go a long way to helping both sides to be more realistic and honest with one another.

"My spouse doesn't deserve what he/she will get if we divorce, so I'll take what I really deserve for myself by hiding assets."

The spouse from whom the assets are being hidden usually has an inkling that something is afoot, especially after the realities of a divorce are settling in. Divorce attorneys have a variety of ways of ferreting out assets, and judges have been known to financially penalize those who hide assets.

"I'm worried that my spouse will prevent me from accessing money during a divorce, so I need to have a stash of safety money to tide me over."

This is a harder one to reason with. The lack of marital trust embedded in such a mindset should be dealt with first and foremost.

"I've cheated on taxes (or in some other way) and need to hide my money."

I once had a counseling client who was a waiter and had been paid "under the table" for years. He had tens of thousands of dollars in his apartment! He was terrified to place this money in any investment account out of fear that it would be a red flag for the IRS. I advised him to get his money invested and physically safe (a fire or theft would've left him without a nest egg) and to then start properly and legally filing his taxes. He was even more horrified to learn that his tax evasion could land him in jail, in addition to huge accumulating penalties he faced.

Finding Financial Peace as a Couple

As I discussed earlier, couples rarely delve into their financial philosophies and differences during the courtship and honeymoon phase of their relationship. Then, as problems and tensions arise and busy work schedules and other commitments get in the way of communication, issues fester and tend to worsen.

If you're currently in what looks to be a long-term relationship, don't keep putting money talks on the back burner. Take the risk to discuss your feelings, attitudes, and beliefs about money and be ready to respectfully listen to your partner's approach. More important than seeking a multi-page written agreement to specify how you will handle everything, work at understanding your differences and decide on a process for negotiating agreements when conflicts inevitably arise. This will help minimize small problems mushrooming into big ones but, of course, doesn't guarantee a lifetime of trouble-free financial bliss.

Men and women who enter marriage with significant assets sometimes are concerned about protecting those assets for themselves and other family members, especially if they have children from a prior relationship. Enter the prenuptial agreement, a legal document that spells out who gets what in the event of divorce. Think of it as planning a financial divorce before you even get married.

Although it may seem painfully obvious, you'd be surprised by the number of people who overlook the fact that prenuptial agreements are an extremely sensitive topic to bring up. If you're considering broaching the subject, I can't stress enough the importance of the timing and approach. I've witnessed some engagements broken off as a result of proposed prenuptial agreements. That said, many couples successfully navigate these tricky waters.

The first common-sense piece of advice I can offer you on this topic is to not spring the discussion or proposed agreement on your partner at the eleventh hour. In fact, a prenuptial signed too close to a wedding (e.g., the day before the wedding) may not stand up to legal challenges if the argument can be made that the other spouse felt pressured into signing for fear of the wedding being called off at the last minute.

Bring up the topic as many months in advance of the proposed wedding date as possible. In fact, I wouldn't do any wedding planning at all until the topic is discussed and harmoniously resolved. Otherwise, you run the risk of having to call off a wedding should the agreement provoke problems. Schedule some time to discuss the subject. Don't just bring it up out of the blue or, even worse, during a time of conflict. Both parties should have their own attorney for review and counsel concerning the legal agreement. Last but not least, be sure to fully disclose your financial situation so that the agreement holds up legally.

Ultimately, the best reason to have a prenuptial agreement is being realistic and simply understanding that people change. Just because your fiancée verbally states that he or she doesn't want any of your money (or home equity, or portfolio, or...) as you stare lovingly into each others eyes on a warm moonlit evening two months before your marriage doesn't guarantee that's how he or she will behave in a lawyer's office in the thick of an emotional divorce. If you'd like to learn more about prenuptial agreements before meeting with an attorney, I recommend the book *Prenuptial Agreements: How to Write a Fair & Lasting Contract* by Katherine Stoner, attorney-mediator, and Shae Irving, J.D.

Regardless of what point in your relationship, or whether tension and disagreements have surfaced, it's vital to schedule a good time to talk. Talks should always be private and out of earshot of children, relatives, friends, and others.

When discussion is needed to resolve a problem, it helps to not only talk about concerns but also to share compliments, especially before you get to the issues you'd like to see changed. When concerns are raised, you dramatically increase the likelihood of your partner hearing, listening to, respecting, and positively responding to your point of view if you present it as your feelings on a topic rather than a criticism of the other person's financial habits. For example, instead of introducing a point of contention with, "You're a reckless over-spender," phrase the issue as, "I'm concerned about having enough saved for retirement so that I don't feel chained to my job." Try, "I'm really stressed that we haven't been saving enough to buy a home. Having a place of our own is important to me. Can we talk about it?" not, "It's time for you to grow up and act like a responsible adult."

No matter what the topic is that you're at odds over, acknowledging, respecting, and even appreciating your partner's money personality differences from yours is vital. Try to think openly about the situation for a minute. If you're a miser, be grateful if you didn't marry another miser. If you'd married another miser, you'd likely never enjoy the fruits of your hard work! Yes, a miser/spender marriage may produce fireworks on financial issues, but with open minds and communication, such a pairing can also produce positive results, as both partners move away from their extreme polar behaviors to a more balanced and fulfilling position. Misers can learn that they can spend some money "frivolously," enjoy the experience, and not end up in financial ruin. Chronic over-spenders can experience how good the sense of financial security feels that accompanies living more within one's means, paying down consumer debt, and beginning to see growing investment balances.

This give-and-take process and emphasis on compromise also works, of course, when other financial differences come into play. An aggressive, risk-loving investor paired with a conservative bank-account-adoring partner can agree to take some reasonable and calculated risks with a portion of the money and be more careful with the rest of it.

The root of successfully and happily managing money as a couple is to compromise. You must remember that there's not just one "right" answer.

Also, realize that conflict over money issues happens, and constructively deal with it. Disagreements and differing points of view shouldn't be buried or viewed as a sign that your relationship is doomed or abnormal.

Also, it's not healthy for one person to simply suck it up and give in all the time to the partner (building up resentment along the way). I've seen numerous couples in which divergent points of view were simply ignored, including one particular pairing of a spender and miser. The miser woman in one relationship kept plenty of her own money separate from the spender, but the spender husband was able to spend excessively using credit cards and other forms of consumer debt. As a result, the problems and differences didn't get addressed, while the debt balances grew and grew to dangerous levels. The reality of the situation wasn't acknowledged and confronted until I sat with the couple in my office and went through their assets and liabilities and showed them how little net worth was left due to the debts that were piling up. They had ignored the issue and, frankly, were in denial about it. It actually took me several meetings to get them to accept the reality of the situation.

I then helped them come to an agreement by focusing them on their shared goal of saving for retirement. They agreed to save about 12 percent of their incomes in tax-sheltered retirement accounts. The harder issue for the couple to deal with was what to do about the consumer debt the husband had amassed. The wife agreed to pay off about half of it because a sizable portion of the spending went toward the couple's home expenses and purchases. The husband agreed to cut up the credit cards and pay down the other half of the debt, a task which was accomplished within about 18 months. (The couple delayed saving the 12 percent monthly until all the consumer debt was gone.)

All couples have plenty of financial tasks to take care of, so encourage open communication and shared responsibilities, while taking advantage of each partner's talents by matching tasks based upon interests and skills. Start by developing a list of responsibilities, such as paying bills, shopping for and managing insurance issues, handling investments, and so on. Decide who will take care of each task, the level of consultation you're both comfortable with for that assignment, and how often the task will be performed. Put it all on paper so that you both know who's supposed to do what and when and to minimize the potential for misunderstandings down the road.

In addition to divvying up financial responsibilities, all couples should actively decide whether to keep money in separate or joint accounts or some of both. I'm not a fan of "his versus hers" money and completely separate accounts. (If you've been divorced and are getting remarried, you might consider, as an alternative, a prenuptial agreement, which is covered earlier in this chapter.) Marriage is a partnership, after all, and, legally, state divorce laws generally treat a married couple's assets as pooled and divide them up upon divorce accordingly, even when they're in separately titled accounts. For many couples, pooling and sharing of accounts works fine, especially when communication is open and problems are productively addressed. Separate accounts and finances often create friction, especially if one person cuts back on work outside the home to be with the kids or if wide pay differences exist between the partners. I've also observed a tendency toward increased secrecy and related problems with separate accounts if spouses keep much of their spending habits private. That said, a combination of joint and separate accounts is a workable compromise for some couples. The key to making this arrangement work is setting a discretionary spending limit. For example, you must consult your spouse on purchases of more than say $50 or $100.

When all else fails, you can turn to other sources for assistance. Unfortunately, in my financial-counseling experience, I've found that most therapists and marriage counselors are ill prepared to help with financial issues. (You may be able to find a competent and ethical financial advisor who also has expertise in the psychological realm dealing with couples.) If you do go in search for a couples' counselor to help you navigate and mediate your money differences, here are some specific issues that I advise you to investigate and interview questions that I suggest you ask:

- ➤ **Professional experience.** How many years have you done couples counseling? What portion of your current practice is devoted to couples? You want a therapist who has plenty of expertise and experience dealing with couples, not someone who just dabbles in such work.

- ➤ **Personal experiences.** Are you happily married? For how long have you been married? Is this your first marriage? Do you have children?

Some therapists may not care for these more personal questions, and some will get defensive. Such responses can be telling. While I respect everyone's right to privacy, I think that all of these questions are in bounds. Getting to the issue of whether the counselor is able to practice what he or she preaches isn't "prying." If you want to work on resolving your marital differences, you need to know up front if you're dealing with a therapist who is on her fourth marriage.

- ➤ **Approach to money.** Please describe your philosophy on money management. How do you resolve financial disagreements in your family? What techniques do you recommend to your clients? Asking these questions will help you determine if you and your prospective therapist are on the same wavelength and can communicate about such important issues.

There are a number of books on the market purporting to help couples improve their relationships. Although a few titles hone in on financial matters, most don't; they cover money along with other common issues that cause problems with couples. Among my favorite couples' book authors are the following:

- ➤ **Dr. Leo Buscaglia.** I first saw Dr. Buscaglia years ago when he made regular PBS appearances. Unfortunately, Dr. Buscaglia, who was a professor at the University of Southern California, died of a heart attack in 1998. However, you can still find Dr. Buscaglia's many excellent and inspirational books, such as *Living, Loving & Learning* and *Loving Each Other: The Challenge of Human Relationships*, at bookstores, especially online retailers.

- ➤ **Dr. John Gottman.** Dr. Gottman is a psychology professor who has extensively tracked and studied thousands of married couples. Among his many books are *The Seven Principles for Making Marriage Work*, *Why Marriages Succeed or Fail*, and the *Relationship Cure*.

> **Dr. Phil McGraw.** The famous television psychologist has written numerous critically acclaimed books, including *Relationship Rescue* (and a separate *Relationship Rescue Workbook*).

Money and Divorce

Having worked with many divorced clients, I can tell you that the problems relating to money may get magnified post-divorce. Money is intimately connected with divorce. Within the marriage, arguments over household finances can push the marriage to its breaking point or serve as a symptom of a larger set of conflicts and hostilities. During a divorce, couples often argue over how to equitably divide the assets. After the divorce, the newly single often find that they must adjust to a lower household income and reconfigure financial plans.

Divorced spouses often are forced to undergo a crash course in personal finances and divorce law while trying to deal with one of the most emotionally charged and draining episodes an individual can face. According to the Holmes and Rahe Social Readjustment Scale, developed by Thomas Holmes and Richard Rahe, going through a divorce is one of life's most stressful events.

As difficult as it may be, perhaps the most important step that you can take to ensure a "financially successful" divorce is to consciously separate your financial issues from your legal issues and emotional struggles. Both your emotional well-being and financial well-being are important, but if you let your emotions interfere with the financial decisions that you must make in the process of a divorce, neither party "wins" as legal bills will wreak greater havoc with your finances and further fray your nerves.

Everyone who goes through divorce suffers emotionally, especially in the short-term. But a Yale University School of Medicine Study found that divorce causes and leads to about three times as many cases of clinical depression in men as in women. The National Center for Health Statistics found that divorced white men have a three times higher suicide rate as married men. One of the explanations for these numbers is that women are more likely to seek help with emotional and psychological issues (and sooner) and to share their feelings with friends. Men, unfortunately, are more likely to turn to drugs and alcohol for solace and to over invest at work and become workaholics.

Last but not least are the children, on whom divorce is often the hardest. A common source of conflict in marriages with children is parents fighting about differing parenting styles. It's sad to see parents sabotaging each other using their children and not putting the best interest of the child (which is being on the same page, whether married or divorced) first. Psychologists recommend that parents take classes on co-parenting.

Victoria Felton-Collins, who has a background in psychology and runs a money-management firm that specializes in serving the needs of divorcees, says that divorce does not have to be "messy and expensive." She cites the case of one couple that had $5 million in assets, yet only spent $5,000 in legal fees. On the other end the spectrum, a couple with assets of $100,000 spent a whopping $20,000 on legal fees. In another case documented in the *Washington Post*, developer Richard Kramer was ordered by pay more than $800,000 to help his wife pay *half* of her legal bills in divorce court. The Kramers weren't fighting over custody of the children. They were haggling solely over money (the fortune was estimated to be in the tens of millions of dollars). "The time spent in this litigation by all of the involved attorneys and the bills resulting from them are obscene. This is one divorce, and it is costing millions of dollars," argued the judge. By separating their emotional life from their financial life, a divorcing couple may very well be able to settle out of court. Collins says that few divorce participants are happy with what judges decide, while negotiated settlements are usually "more palatable." In order to fight the irrationality of emotions, paralysis, and that overwhelmed feeling, she advises that participants break down the big undertaking into small, manageable tasks.

In addition to keeping your emotions at bay, educate yourself financially. I've found that many people report feeling less overwhelmed with the fallout from divorce and more empowered when they begin to improve their knowledge base. Sign up for a personal-finance course and pick up a few good books. You might also consider seeking financial advice, but be careful. Attorneys generally lack the training and related perspective to adequately analyze your entire financial picture. Most financial advisors sell products, not their time and service. Plus, most have little experience dealing with divorce-specific issues. Consulting with a good tax advisor is worthwhile in some cases, as tax considerations weigh heavily in some divorce situations. For example, if you have the choice between paying more in alimony or child support, it's useful to know that payments for the former are tax-deductible, while payments for the latter are not.

Planning for life financially post-divorce is also important. Most divorcees are faced with lower incomes and higher costs of living because living together as a family is usually cheaper per person than maintaining separate households. One of the most important exercises for soon-to-be divorced individuals is to analyze their individual spending. Lower-income earning spouses, who are typically women, face the biggest reduction in standard of living post-divorce. Your "new" budget will help justify requests for alimony or child support during the divorce and serve as a guide to adjust to a new financial life after the divorce. Other financial issues must be rethought as well after divorce. For example, your insurance needs may change, you may need to consider revising your retirement plan, and you may want to alter your investment strategy.

If you're not committed to divorcing, perhaps all this talk of consulting lawyers and transforming yourself into a financial and tax expert is daunting. To a certain extent, I say "good." I'm not being callous. It's just that if there's a way to work things out, especially when minor children are involved, the best way to successfully deal with divorce is to work on your prevent defense. Work at making your marriage work so that you can keep both halves of the whole intact. Consider seeking help from the resources I recommend earlier in this chapter (see the earlier section entitled "Finding Financial Peace as a Couple") as well as a marriage counselor/psychologist if you just can't talk things out yourselves.

Money Passed Down: Estates and Inheritances

In my work as a financial counselor, I was often amazed at the dramas played out and the issues raised over the passing of money and wealth between the generations when someone died and left assets to relatives and others. Inherited money almost always came with some strings attached. This important section will help you deal with this often prickly issue.

Retirees often worry about depleting their assets due to chronic health problems and either running out of money or not having anything left over for their heirs. These folks may be reluctant to enjoy their wealth in their golden years. However, most retirees don't end up with pro-tracted nursing home stays, so people tend to die with more money than they anticipated. If you're currently considering such issues, you can determine the sufficiency of your assets and gain some peace of mind. T. Rowe Price has some excellent resources on its web site (www.troweprice.com) and in printed booklets (800-638-5660) for helping determine if you have enough assets to support your desired lifestyle through retirement and what you may have left over for future generations, if that's your goal. Alternatively, you could engage the services of a good financial advisor. (See Chapter 19, "Hiring Financial Help.")

Most parents prefer to pass along some wealth and associated financial security to their offspring. Problems come into play, though, when too much wealth may be passed along. John Levy, a "wealth counselor," says that expectations of a substantial inheritance can delay ones' offspring from growing up and maturing. His advice to parents is to make sure that kids work while growing up and post college, which leads to self-esteem, self-reliance, and independence. That's great advice.

If you have children who you'd like to pass your money on to, to make sure that your kids get some money from your estate, but not too much, I recommend giving your money away gradually, while you're still alive. Especially if you have enough assets to know that your heirs will be receiving at least modest sums, consider giving away some money each year. Under current tax laws, you may annually give up to $12,000 (free of federal taxation) in assets to each of as many people as you desire. If you're married, your spouse may give an additional $12,000 per year. The advantage of giving money gradually is that you can see how your heirs are using (or abusing) their new-found wealth, a perspective that you obviously won't have if you wait to pass along your entire estate when you pass away.

Taking this approach does come with a few potential pitfalls. It's the rare parent who is able to give money to his kids and say nothing about how they should or should not use or manage it. Offering some guidance and advice is fine and to be expected, but don't try and set restrictions (more on this topic in Chapter 6, "Families and Money"). You did your best raising your kids, providing them with a fine education, and teaching them about life. Let them make the most of *their* opportunities and show you how much they've learned. Likewise, don't use periodic distributions of your estate or the promise of an inheritance to get your kids or their spouses to do what you want them to do in other aspects of their lives (starting a family, moving closer to home, or buying a house, for example). Now, if your son or daughter or his or her spouse has an addiction, that's another matter. In that case, withholding the money until the problem is properly addressed is a legitimate course of action.

Handling Sudden Wealth

The biggest irony in regard to people pursuing large sums of money is that, more often than not, those who come into substantial money discover that life isn't "better" for them. Folks who come by their wealth suddenly, such as through an inheritance, their company going public, or winning the lottery, are often surprised at the stress and problems that accompany their new-found riches. Sudden wealth doesn't make one's days blissful and free of worry— quite the opposite in many cases.

For starters, people who've fretted about money and believed that their having more money will make their lives so much better typically find that their lives don't magically improve when they have greater financial assets. Interestingly, people who experience windfalls find dissatis-faction with the rest of their lives.

The key to making the most of your wealth is to keep in mind what money can buy—choices, freedom, and options, but only if you recognize that and take advantage of it. For example, most parents wish they had more time for their kids and themselves. If you have come into a financial windfall, you can work less and have more time, yet few people take advantage of this opportunity.

Take your time with handling a lump sum of money. I think it's a wise move to park the money in a money market fund and get, say, 5 percent over the next year while you get smarter about your options. Don't rush to invest the money and lose a lot of it due to inadequate research and poor decisions.

6

Families and Money

"You may not have saved a lot of money in your life, but if you have saved a lot of heartaches for other folks, you are a pretty rich man."

—Seth Parker

Our consumer-driven culture and the importance that we place on careers and workplace success are harming ourselves and our families. We are increasingly relying upon institutions like our schools to raise our children. Kids, especially young ones, benefit from parental time. But the more we work to support car and house payments and all those toys and activities, the less time we have to be with them. And the more we neglect our personal health and our relationships.

Parenting responsibilities, especially in more affluent communities (where many aspire to live), are widely viewed as something to be delegated and avoided. Popular columnists like Anna Quindlen freely disparage parenthood. In a column entitled "Playing God On No Sleep: Isn't motherhood grand? Do you want the real answer or the official Hallmark-card version?," Quindlen discusses her feelings of disgust upon visiting a doctor's office with her sick child and seeing a cross-stitched sampler on the wall that said, "God could not be everywhere so he made mothers." She wrote this column in part, she said, out of her own "fascination" with the story of Andrea Yates, who drowned her five children in a bathtub. Quindlen concludes her piece by reasoning, "If God made mothers because he couldn't be everywhere, maybe he could meet us halfway and eradicate vomiting, and colic too, and the hideous sugarcoating of what we are and what we do that leads to false cheer, easy lies, and maybe sometimes something much, much worse, almost unimaginable."

Quindlen's problem—which I have observed in both men and women—stems from people who started families believing that they could do it all: excel in their career, raise kids, and have a life. But raising children is an enormous and time-consuming responsibility, and it's completely unrealistic and unhealthy to think that you can spend as much time at your job and career after having kids as you did before bringing kids into the picture. And, if you view your children as an impediment to your career, you are unlikely to savor the experience of having and raising kids.

In *The Time Bind: When Work Becomes Home and Home Becomes Work*, sociologist Arlie Russell Hochschild presented her discoveries about how some employees actually prefer being at work and away from their domestic responsibilities and challenges. The real eye-openers in Hochschild's research were the choices some employees made: Wealthier employees were actually the least interested in being at home, and few employees who could afford to do so took advantage of opportunities offered by employers (e.g., paternity and maternity leave, working part-time) to spend more time at home.

Although men have generally become more involved at home in recent decades, there has been little, if any, give on the work-front. Few men are taking advantage of working part-time, leaving the workforce for a few years, or taking paternity leave.

The most surprising and unsettling factor to consider is that, often, a second income (from full-time work) doesn't really financially benefit a family much—if at all—when you factor in all of the extra expenses involved, a fact I've confirmed time and again when reviewing budgets of families in which both spouses are working full-time. In addition to the additional services (e.g., child care, meals out, household repairs and maintenance) bought when a couple is starved for time due to work, taxes can hit two-income couples hard. The largest expenditure for most families is their tax bill. Many families find that their second income ends up being taxed at a high rate when federal, state, and local taxes are tallied.

Priorities: Work Versus Family

When people overinvest in work, there are consequences. Kids don't get enough of their parents' time; physical, emotional, and mental health problems develop among all members of the family; and divorce (and even suicide) happens. I personally know several people who had nervous breakdowns as a result of the pressures they faced at work. And I know others whose spouses (usually the wives) walked out (most often on the husbands) after feeling that the job had become more important than the marriage.

Dr. Bryan Robinson, author of *Chained to the Desk: A Guidebook for Workaholics, Their Partners and Children, and the Clinicians Who Treat Them*, provides quantifiable proof of what should be intuitive—putting in long hours may provide financial riches, but it can leave workaholics and their families in rags emotionally. Robinson's research found that the children of workaholics suffer many of the same ills—depression, anxiety, and other emotional disorders—as do the children of alcoholics. His study also found that spouses married to a workaholic felt more estranged in their marriages and less in control of their lives. In Robinson's study, just 45 percent of spouses married to workaholics remained married, compared to 84 percent in marriages where no one was a workaholic.

With parents working so much, our kids are increasingly being raised by nannies, babysitters, teenage camp counselors, and the mass media—especially television. Most of us spend more and work more than we need to. This state of affairs has long puzzled me because my best days at work don't even come close to the best days I've had with my kids.

Increasingly, children are spending more time with an electronic babysitter, filling their free time with video games, television, and the Internet, among other multimedia activities. Back in the mid-1960s, parents, on average, spent about *30 hours* per week with their kids. By the turn of the century, that number was almost cut in half to *17 hours* weekly, according to surveys conducted by the University of Maryland. These same kids are spending in excess of *40 hours* per week watching television, playing video and computer games, and listening to pop, rock, and rap music. James Steyer, author of *The Other Parent: The Inside Story of the Media's Effect on Our Children*, provided a welcome dose of perspective to the situation when he says, "If another adult spent five or six hours a day with your kids, regularly exposing them to sex, violence, and rampantly commercial values, you would probably forbid that person to have further contact with them."

Psychology professor Tim Kasser, who is also the author of the book, *The High Price of Materialism*, has found in his research that "time affluence" has a significant influence on people's happiness. "What makes people happier is more time to pursue intrinsic activities and goals such as health, personal growth, spending time with family and friends," says Kasser. In his research, Kasser also found that time-affluent people are more mindful—that is, being "there in the moment" and "in the flow"—and that this too leads to greater happiness.

John de Graaf has published an excellent book of essays on the topic of time affluence and time poverty: *Take Back Your Time: Fighting Overwork & Time Poverty In America*. "Our passion for spending and the levels of debt that some people take on forces them to work longer and harder and has severe consequences for personal health, family time, community life, and the environment. Many people would like to work less but it's hard to do so. People fear losing their jobs and important benefits like health care if they push for less than full-time work," says de Graaf.

Balancing Family and Work: Spend Less, Work Less

Over the years, I've gotten lots of questions, e-mail, and snail mail about stocks, mutual funds, home buying, and other money topics. Without a doubt, however, I've received the most mail when I've written about balancing work with the rest of one's life.

You should spend plenty of time and energy outside of work enjoying your other interests, your friends, and your family. Your kids are only young once, and you don't get any do-overs.

Parents say that they do, indeed, want to spend more time with their children. In a survey done for the Boys & Girls Clubs of America and KidsPeace, a whopping 94 percent of parents said that they see a positive relationship between the amount of meaningful time adults spend with children and the manner in which those kids deal with big issues like drugs, alcohol, and discipline. The majority of parents (54 percent), however, said that they had little or no time to spend engaged in activities (physical and educational) with their children. The major impediment that parents cited was their work schedules.

Many people find that working hard pays great dividends, especially when they're fortunate to work in a field that they enjoy. Gaining a sense of mastery in a given field and adding to one's knowledge base and list of accomplishments over time feels great. And who among us doesn't revel in a promotion and pay raise? But therein lies the problem in setting limits and maintaining a balance.

You can reach a tipping point with work—a point of diminishing returns. How much do you value free time to engage in your favorite activities like reading a good book, watching a movie, having dinner with friends, gardening, or exercising?

Please don't get me wrong. There's nothing inherently wrong with working hard at something. But what about your other priorities and keeping balance in your life? At what expense are you building your wealth?

America is the world's most affluent society. So, why are we working so many hours to buy all the "best things?" The best things in life—love, attention, strong family relations, friends—really can't be bought. Some folks, especially if they're single parents earning modest incomes, can't afford to work less. But many people can find ways to spend less and work less. In this section, I'm going to show you how.

One of the continuing sources of stress that pressures us to keep working so hard is the rate at which we spend. So, take a hard look at your expenditures over the past six months. Get out your checkbook register, credit card statement, and anything else that documents your spending. Determine your spending on clothes, restaurants, childcare, cars, vacations, and so on. Ask yourself what non-essential spending you could trim. Be sure to recognize that even though a particular category like clothing is a necessity, a portion of it can be discretionary.

You and only you can make the final decision as to what expenses you are most willing and able to cut. Perhaps you'd rather eat out less instead of giving up the occasional ski outing. Discussing how, where, and why your family spends will naturally bring up work-related topics. For example, maybe you're buying so many meals out because no one is home at a reasonable hour to start cooking dinner. The pressure to keep working is intertwined with spending.

If you're part of a dual-career household, take a hard look at the taxes you're racking up each year as well as the additional expenses you're incurring from both people working full-time. The additional costs and hassles of that second full-time job may well outweigh the increased income, and the extra earnings may be far smaller than you thought. (Please see the worksheets and suggestions for reducing your spending and taxes in Chapter 9, "Your Spending Plan.")

Consider cutting back on your work hours or switching to a more family-friendly employer—especially if you have youngsters at home. If you want to consider your employment options, ask people you know for advice on good employers. You can peruse the increasing number of lists published by various magazines and web sites of supposedly family-friendly employers. For example, *Working Mother* magazine (www.workingmother.com) publishes a useful annual list of family-friendly employers. The definition of "family-friendly" differs among lists but is often based upon the comprehensiveness of a cost-effective benefits' package. Most lists give preference to companies offering flextime. For more employer recommendations, you can also contact a local chapter of the Society for Human Resource Management. Visit their web site at www.shrm.org to obtain contact information for local chapters.

Do You (or Does Someone You Know) Work Too Much?

Conquering the urge to overwork begins where denial ends. Below are a series of 20 questions from Workaholics Anonymous. If you answer "yes" to most of these questions, you probably are a workaholic.

1. Do you get more excited about your work than about family or anything else?
2. Are there times when you can charge through your work and other times when you can't?
3. Do you take work with you to bed? On weekends? On vacation?
4. Is work the activity you like to do best and talk about most?
5. Do you work more than 40 hours a week?
6. Do you turn your hobbies into money-making ventures?
7. Do you take complete responsibility for the outcome of your work efforts?
8. Have your family or friends given up expecting you on time?
9. Do you take on extra work because you are concerned that it won't otherwise get done?
10. Do you underestimate how long a project will take and then rush to complete it?
11. Do you believe that it is okay to work long hours if you love what you are doing?
12. Do you get impatient with people who have other priorities besides work?
13. Are you afraid that if you don't work hard, you will lose your job or be a failure?
14. Is the future a constant worry for you, even when things are going very well?
15. Do you do things energetically and competitively, including play?
16. Do you get irritated when people ask you to stop doing your work in order to do something else?
17. Have your long hours hurt your family or other relationships?

18. Do you think about your work while driving, falling asleep, or when others are talking?

19. Do you work or read during meals?

20. Do you believe that more money will solve the other problems in your life?

Source: Workaholic's Anonymous

Workaholics Anonymous has few local meetings taking place around the country—perhaps because its members are so busy! However, you may be near a town or city with a local chapter; check their web site, www.workaholics-anonymous.org, for a list of current meeting locations.

Weigh your priorities and take appropriate action, including switching to an employer that doesn't encourage and reward workaholics. Start your assessment of your current employer by considering the people near the top of organization chart:

➤ Are these "leaders" leading balanced lives?

➤ Do they have happy and fulfilling home lives, as best you can tell?

➤ Would you dare to call them role models?

Some people find more peace of mind with working part-time if they pay off or reduce the size of their mortgage. I've encouraged some parents to downsize to a more modest home, for example, to reduce the pressure for both people to work full-time, after assessing their financial status and their goals, both professionally and personally. Keith and Mary, for example, realized they were in over their heads once they had their third child, around the same time Keith's income dropped significantly. Even though Keith's income went back up, they decided to move to a smaller, less expensive home in the same community. "We felt a little ashamed, like we had failed in moving down, but we're less stressed by being able to spend less time working and thinking about work …others we know are considering doing what we did."

If your family currently consists of you and your spouse, and you don't yet have children but would like to in the future, I have two words of advice for you—plan ahead. Adding children to the family equation is an enormous change that places all sorts of stressors on a couple. Planning ahead can go a long way to helping you to keep your heads above water financially and emotionally. Try to structure your financial situation and obligations so that you won't both be forced to work long hours. By keeping your expenses low and saving a large portion of your incomes when you are both working, you will be better able financially (and psychologically) with scaling back on work once you start your family.

Hiring Household Help

Raising kids and running a household are huge responsibilities and involve tremendous time commitments, if you want to do things well. If your budget and your other financial commitments and priorities allow it, by all means, consider hiring some help. I suggest that you make a list of the tasks that you least enjoy doing. My list would include such tasks as oil changes on cars, general housecleaning every other week, and cleaning my home's gutters. After you make your initial list, go through it and cross off those items that you're least comfortable delegating to someone else and the tasks that involve too much hassle or cost to delegate.

Where I see some families with children get into trouble is when they make sweeping decisions, such as "we need a full-time, live-in nanny." When that happens, numerous important aspects of childcare get delegated so that parents have more time for work and non-essential activities outside the home. Think about it: Would you rather have someone do a sloppy job cleaning your garage or raising your child?

Take the case of Bruce Cozadd and how he and his wife have structured their childcare schedules. Bruce searched for a company that was "not full of workaholics." But, he confesses, "Those bad genes took over, and I started climbing the ladder because it was there." Cozadd rose to the position of chief financial officer and then chief operating officer at a pharmaceutical company. In order to spend more time with his family, he finally called it quits when his company was acquired and his position had him traveling much more.

Bruce and his wife, Sharon, finally set limits on the amount of childcare they hire—their nanny's day ends no later than 3 p.m. They also sit down each month, in advance, and coordinate their schedules to maximize the time they spend

---

with their kids and each other. I like their idea of setting limits and coordinating schedules.

One final and very important point: If you're going to hire a nanny, spend the necessary time and money and get someone who loves children and truly wants to be with your kids. You don't want someone who's going to ditch you and your kids for another job next month or next year. Take a hard look at the applicants' resumes and see what experience and interests they have in working with children. Ask applicants how long they envision staying in the job for which you're considering them. Initially, don't explain why you're asking such questions or what you're looking for, exactly. You want honest, off-the-top-of-their-head answers. Listen closely to these answers and thoroughly check references for recent work positions applicants have held. Lastly, pay household help legally and withhold taxes. In addition to complying with the law, your payments for the nanny into Social Security also provide her with needed disability and survivor's insurance.

Teaching Kids About Money

Listen in to children talking today, and you will find that money frequently comes up. Lots of time is spent discussing the latest consumer products and clothing and what things cost. Kids are also surprisingly aware of what the snazziest sports cars sell for and how much professional athletes make and spend on homes and other things. This actually should be no great surprise, given the extent to which such topics are covered in the media and the amount of media that many kids are exposed to these days.

Although most of the parents I know want their children to have the best education possible and give reasonable thought and effort to teaching their kids various real-world skills, most parents that I know unfortunately neglect to educate their kids about personal financial matters. I don't think this is a conscious decision. In the rush of day-to-day life, most folks probably don't even think about the issue. In addition, many parents may not understand or know how to teach personal finance, or they may have their own problems and issues with the topic.

Some parents assume that personal-finance skills are covered in school, but that assumption is wrong. Schools are increasingly incorporating money issues into the existing curriculum (e.g., math lessons), yet the broader concepts of personal financial management still aren't taught in the vast majority of schools. When schools do attempt to touch on such issues, many (especially budget-strapped schools) rely far too heavily on "free" "educational" materials from the likes of VISA and MasterCard. These credit card titans provide materials that implicitly and explicitly support carrying consumer debt (on credit cards, auto loans, etc.) as a sound way to finance significant purchases and living expenses. In fact, VISA and MasterCard school-supplied resources endorse spending upwards of 15 to 20 percent of one's monthly take-home income to pay credit card and other consumer debts!

What (and How) Kids Learn About Money

In the absence of financial education, kids are still "learning" about scores of product-buying opportunities on a daily basis from the many marketers and purveyors of popular culture. Advertisers only teach children to value their products. Without parental involvement, children rarely learn how to thoughtfully spend, save, and invest money.

Unbelievably, the average American child sees about 40,000 commercials per year, according to the American Academy of Pediatrics. Since 1983, the annual amount of television advertising directed at kids has skyrocketed from just $100 million to more than $15 billion (a 150-fold increase) according to Juliet Schor, author of *Born to Buy: The Commercialized Child and the New Consumer Culture*. Companies spend gobs of money promoting their products and brands to kids for one simple reason: It works. Kids can hum and sing along with commercial jingles at startling early ages. By first grade, children easily recognize many companies' advertising logos and brand names. Kid's preferences drive billions of dollars of spending, both their own purchases, and more importantly, their parents' buying decisions. In a study published in the Journal of the American Medical Association, 6-year-olds at schools were given the task of matching advertising logos with specific products pictured on a game board. An unbelievable 91 percent of 6-year-olds correctly matched Old Joe, a cartoon character promoting Camel cigarettes, with a picture of a cigarette. As the studies' authors concluded, "Very young children see, understand, and remember advertising."

According to a survey commissioned by the Center for a New American Dream, American teens will ask their parents an average of nine times for a particular item they have seen advertised before the parents give in to the purchase. Not only are kids nagging and getting their parents to spend more money, but children's health is being harmed (increased obesity and diabetes) through the marketing of junk food. When children are bombarded with ads from fast food outlets, soda companies, and candy bar companies, not surprisingly, they end up eating at McDonald's, Wendy's, Burger King, and KFC; drinking Coca-Cola, Pepsi, and Mountain Dew; and eating Hershey's, Nestle, and Snickers!

Surrounded by constant advertising messages, it's no wonder, then, that coupled with the lack of school-based and parent-initiated personal financial education for children, kids know all too well how to borrow and spend but know little about investing and saving. According to a survey by the Jump Start Coalition, only 14 percent of high school seniors knew that stocks provide better long-term returns than bonds or savings accounts. Amazingly, one in seven of those seeking credit-counseling help are college students. This latter figure is less shocking and more understandable when you consider that one in three college students has four or more credit cards and that many colleges and universities today receive hundreds of thousands of dollars annually from credit card companies for on-campus promotion access.

While working with clients and answering questions from many readers, it has become clear to me that personal financial habits are largely formed during childhood, and those habits that we adopt often mirror the financial practices of our parents. Although some children reject the examples that their parents' provide, far more often, kids mirror the personal financial habits they observe at home. Adults who live it up now, borrow on credit cards and auto loans, and don't save for the future tend to raise children who are accomplished spenders and poor savers.

Children, of course, learn from the example set by their parents (and others), both in words and actions. While it's bad enough that kids are bombarded with promotions and temptations to spend their money, some parents exacerbate that problem by acquiescing to too many requests and demands that their children make. This reinforces a mindset focused on spending and consumption to the detriment of saving and investing.

William Damon, professor of education and director of the Center on Adolescence at Stanford University, has reviewed and compiled the results of many studies that examined indulging children. These studies tracked kids into adulthood. Damon found that, when given too much too soon, indulged kids grow up into adults who have difficulty coping with life's disappointments and end up with a distorted sense of entitlement that gets in the way of success at work and in personal relationships. He also found that indulging children causes them to grow up into adults with a more egocentric, self-centered perspective, which raises mental health risks for depression, anxiety, and greater risks for alcohol and substance abuse.

Getting Children on the Right Financial Path

If you don't teach your kids about money realities and issues, you're setting them up for unnecessary and easily avoidable problems when they go out into the real world. So, I'm going to help you navigate the role money plays in parent-child relationships and understand how to raise money-smart kids. The bulk of this section is devoted to specific, action-oriented steps that you can take to properly teach your kids about personal finance.

One of the great challenges in raising kids among our country's relative economic abundance is fulfilling the natural parental desire to provide children with opportunities for personal growth and development without spoiling them into dependency.

As I discussed in the previous section, regularly overindulging kids can result in long-term damage to their well-being, but you surely don't want to deprive them either. Suppose your daughter seems to have a talent and passion for music. Should you not enroll her in music classes or get her private lessons outside of school simply because doing so may seem extravagant—especially if you didn't grow up with such opportunities? And, where do you draw the line with such expenditures, especially when money is tight or you and your spouse have different philosophies and beliefs about such spending?

Of course, you should provide for your kids. The great danger, especially in more affluent families or in less affluent families willing to spend beyond their means, is engaging in continuous and excessive spending on our kids with the implicit belief that more is better. Being a good parent requires some hard work. Although saying "yes" is more fun and makes you more popular, especially in the short-term, psychologists universally agree on the importance of setting limits and saying "no." Explaining and enforcing limits creates feelings of security for children and actually demonstrates to them that you care. And, it teaches them that, indeed, money doesn't grow on trees or come in unlimited supplies from credit cards. Kids benefit immensely from learning to work for things—saving, making choices, sacrificing, and contributing to their families and households through chores. After all, isn't that what the real world is all about?

Alternatives to Buying Things for Kids

Parents who buy too much for their kids, in my observations, have difficulty changing that habit. The key is to learn new ways to show that you love and care for your children rather than buying so much. Here are some ideas. They may seem like no-brainers when you read them, but the challenge is actually following through on the suggestions:

➤ **Rededicate yourself to hugs and kisses.** The busier we get, the less affection we tend to give our kids. Like work, raising children can become a series of tasks to accomplish, activities to complete, and deadlines to meet. We can all benefit by slowing down and giving affection to our kids.

➤ **Play a game together.** Here's a warning: After you make the decision to spend some time playing games with your kids, you may have to free up their time and, quite honestly, provide some "encouragement" to win them over to the idea. To facilitate the process, it helps to have electronic-free days in your home. In our family, we set aside two weekdays each week where there's no television, computer, or video games. (On other days, we have time-usage restrictions in place.) We imposed this digital moratorium to make time for other things that were increasingly being crowded out.

➤ **Go for a walk and talk.** Although many kids will resist, taking a walk with one of your kids can be a great way to get some fresh air and exercise while taking a few minutes to connect and have fun. Just try not to have unrealistic expectations for lengthy, deep, and profound conversations. Just take a walk and see what happens.

➤ **Catch them doing something good.** In many parents' efforts to teach their children good habits and extinguish poor practices, we can focus too much on correcting the negative. Praise and compliments increasingly get crowded out and overlooked. Don't let that happen in your family—catch your child doing something well several times every day!

➤ **Get involved in their world.** Whether you build something, do an art project, or play catch in the yard, don't always be a spectator. Get down and dirty, have some fun, and enjoy being a kid again! All those to-do lists around the house and at work that keep you from lending a hand or joining the fun more often will always be there waiting for you, but, before you know it, your kids will be grown and out of the house.

➤ **Go out for a meal with one child.** Okay, so this one does involve some spending. However, many parents find that, when they think about it, they don't have much one-on-one time with individual kids, especially in families with multiple children. Make it a habit to grab lunch or dinner with one of the kids on a regular basis.

According to a survey conducted by the National Bureau for Economic Research, children who get personal-finance education in high school save 5 percent more of their incomes than kids who aren't exposed to such education. Five percent may not sound like a lot, but, when you consider that most adults should be saving about 10 percent annually to accomplish their financial goals and actually save less, saving 5 percent more is a huge difference.

While high school is a terrific time to teach kids key personal financial concepts before they're nudged out of the family nest, you can and should begin to teach kids about money much sooner. The elementary school years, when kids are learning math concepts and getting comfortable with numbers, are an excellent time to lay a solid knowledge base.

An allowance is a terrific way to introduce children to a whole host of personal-finance lessons. In fact, a well-implemented allowance program can mimic many money matters that adults face every day throughout their lives. From recognizing the need to earn the green stuff to learning how to responsibly and intelligently spend, save, and invest their allowance, children can gain a solid financial footing from a young age.

Consider beginning a regular allowance when your kids reach the five-to-seven age range, around the time that a child is learning to read and master basic math skills like simple addition and subtraction. As for a dollar amount, consider a weekly allowance of $0.50 to $1.00 per year of age. So, for example, a six-year-old child would earn between $3 and $6 per week. Of course, the size of the allowance should depend, in part, on what sorts of expenditures and savings you expect your child to engage in and, perhaps, the amount of "work" you expect your child to perform around the house.

I believe that allowances should be earned—children shouldn't just get one for "showing up." That's not to say that kids should get paid for all their work around the house—some things should be done for being part of the family.

The tasks required of children to earn the allowance can vary. For younger children, they can be as simple as making their bed daily and carrying their dishes from the table after a meal. As kids grow older, you can assign other household chores, such as cleaning their room, taking care of the family pets, or mowing the lawn. This approach demonstrates that increased responsibilities and harder work are often accompanied by additional rewards. Also, if you have children close in age, consider rotating the various tasks to keep things interesting and avoid "fairness"-based grievances from the younger set.

Have kids save a significant portion (up to half) of their allowance money toward longer-term goals, such as college. The allowance system that I personally prefer is for children to reserve about one third of their weekly take for savings.

After they've earmarked their savings money, you can take the opportunity to pass along the importance of charity to your kids. They could also put a portion of their allowance into a box earmarked for charity. (This can also provide an opportunity to teach them about how to evaluate potential worthy causes.)

The amount that can be spent should by and large go toward "discretionary" purchases, especially when kids are younger. You want kids to learn how to make purchasing decisions and learn from their mistakes, including running out of money until their next allowance payment if they overspend. (I don't agree with the philosophy of giving kids a larger allowance and then having them, for example, buy their school lunches and other required purchases with that money. Do you really want your eight-year-old to go hungry on Thursday and Friday because he spent too much earlier in the week?)

I've long cautioned my own kids about viewing all forms of advertising with a skeptical eye, but a single purchasing decision provided a more powerful lesson for them than all my warnings and reminders combined, when they ran into some used Pokemon cards on eBay. They thought they were getting the deal of a lifetime because they'd heard of single Pokemon cards being "worth" $40, yet here they were buying dozens of cards for less than $10! As I expected, they were quite disappointed with their purchase because they ended up with a bunch of mediocre cards that were likely "worth" less than they paid. (One obvious caution when allowing kids to make their own mistakes is that you need to be involved sufficiently to keep them from buying or accessing inappropriate items and material and to keep them from committing to a transaction that is more costly than they can afford. The Internet is particularly problematic in this regard.)

For larger desired purchases, kids can learn to save the portion of their weekly allowance earmarked for purchases over weeks and even months. For example, a family I know has a boy who wanted a more expensive bike than his parents were willing to pay for. So, the boy saved the extra $75 he needed, and it took him nearly six months to accomplish his goal. Besides learning how to save toward a larger purchase and not getting in the bad habit of borrowing for consumption, this experience provided some additional benefits that surprised the parents. "I've never seen my son take such good care of a bike as the new one he bought partly with his own money," said his father.

As kids accumulate more significant savings as the weeks turn into months and the months turn into years, you can introduce the concept of investing. Rather than trekking down to the boring old local bank and putting the money into a sleepy, low-interest bank account, I prefer having kids invest in mutual funds (which you can do through the mail or online). Although stocks returning an average of 10 percent per year sounds attractive to most grown ups, young kids may not be able to comprehend what that kind of return really means or the long-term power of compounding returns. Most kids can better understand these mathematical concepts beginning in late elementary school when they're comfortable with more complicated multiplication. I have two useful ways to illustrate to kids how small regular investments can grow into substantial amounts over time through modest returns from sound investments. One is to work out on paper how money grows over the years. The second approach is to show kids with play money.

Rather than investing in stocks through mutual funds, another option for kids is to buy individual stocks. In Chapters 11 to 14, I advocate adults investing in funds. That said, kids can learn more about how the financial markets work and understand stocks better by sometimes picking individual stocks rather than using funds. Just be careful to keep transaction fees to a minimum and teach your kids how to evaluate a stock and its valuation and not simply buy companies that they've heard of or that make products they like. One investing game that I've reviewed and tested with kids is Mr. BigShot (www.mrbigshot.com). It's fun, educational, and entertaining.

Although allowances are an awesome way to teach kids about money, there are numerous other steps you can take to make your kids financially savvy. Among my favorites are the following:

➤ **Reduce their exposure to ads.** The primary path to reduced exposure to ads is to cut down on TV time. When kids are in front of the tube, have them watch prerecorded material. You can direct the television viewing of younger children, in particular, toward videos and DVDs. And for older kids, if you use digital video recorders (DVRs), such as TiVO, you can easily zap ads.

➤ **Teach your kids about the realities of advertising and marketing.** Invest the necessary time to teach and explain to your kids that the point of advertising is to motivate consumers to buy the product by making it sound more wonderful or necessary than it really is. Also explain that advertising is costly and that the most heavily promoted and popular products include the cost of all that advertising, so they're paying for it when they buy those items.

➤ **Read good books on the topic with your child.** The Berenstain Bears series has some terrific titles such as *The Berenstain Bears Get the Gimmies*. For late-elementary-school age kids, *Quest for the Pillars of Wealth* by J. J. Pritchard is a chapter book that teaches the major personal-finance concepts through an engaging adventure story. Consumer Union, publishers of *Consumer Reports*, also publishes a kids' magazine called *Zillions* that covers money and buying topics.

➤ **Play games that teach good money habits.** Games that I've played with kids that I think are fun and teach good financial habits include The Allowance Game, Monopoly, and Life.

➤ **Teach them how to shop wisely.** Being a smart consumer requires doing your homework, especially when buying more costly products. Teach your kids the value of product research (including using sources like *Consumer Reports* for product reviews) and comparison shopping. Demonstrate how to identify overpriced and shoddy merchandise. Finally, show them how to voice a complaint when returning defective products and go to bat for better treatment in service environments, two additional tasks that are part of being a savvy consumer.

➤ **Introduce the right and wrong ways to use credit and debit cards.** Those plastic cards in your wallet offer a convenient way to conduct purchases in stores, by phone, and over the Internet. Credit cards, unfortunately, offer temptation for overspending and carrying debt from month to month. Teach your kids how a checking account works, explaining that debit cards are connected to your checking account and thus prevent you from overspending as you can on a credit card.

➤ **Be mindful of your statements and attitudes about money.** Kids are little sponges. They learn a lot from what you say and how you say it and your actions. Do you encourage shopping or gambling as a form of recreation and entertainment? If you're critical or judgmental of people with money, your kids may learn envy or that having money is somehow wrong.

➤ **Encourage them to get a job.** Your child's initial exposure to the work-for-pay world can start with something as simple as a lemonade stand. I had an extensive newspaper route for a number of years, and I cut lawns and did other yard work during high-school and college summers. By holding down such jobs, kids can learn about working, earning, saving, and investing money. (Beware, though, that your kid's employment income could lead to a smaller college financial aid package.) It also provides welcome relief for parents to not continually be the source of spending money. Working outside the home does raise some safety issues. By all means, be involved in ensuring that your child has a safe work environment.

A colleague of mine recently shared his childhood work experiences with me, and I think they further highlight the value of work-related experiences for kids. "When I was young, my Dad wrote up contracts for me when I wanted something, like a new baseball glove. I would be paid modest amounts for various chores, and once I had accumulated enough for the item, we would go and buy it. Once a year, the town fair came and I would get paid a penny for every dandelion that I pulled from the yard. I usually pulled 500 to 1,000 and had 5 or 10 bucks to blow on rides and cotton candy at the fair. In about fifth grade, I realized that there was far better cash to be made outside the confines of my extortionist family. I began to hire myself out to the neighbors for shoveling snow and yard work. I took great pride in my work, and I loved being my own boss and setting my own schedule."

7

Valuing Saving and Spending

"Men are divided between those who are thrifty as if they would live forever, and those who are as extravagant as if they were going to die the next day"
—Aristotle, 360 B.C.

"What is the difference whether you squander all you have, or you never use your savings?"
—Horace, 35 B.C.

A t all income levels, you can find folks who live well within their means and those who live beyond their means. While overspending is a problem in many countries, especially in America, oversaving is problematic as well. This chapter discusses how to strike the right balance between spending and saving.

Everyone should evaluate the balance that they strike between spending money and saving and the amount of time and energy that they put into earning, spending, and saving money. I find that even people who are "on track" with their savings and are not overspending or oversaving may be putting way too much energy on their consumption and purchases.

Why Most People Have Trouble Saving Enough

With the onslaught of new technology and gadgets, temptation and opportunity to spend money abound. It's not enough that shopping malls and strip malls have taken over the suburban landscape and retails stores are everywhere. Following the deluge of mail-order catalogs cramming people's home mailboxes, now the Internet offers endless 24/7 shopping temptation. Add in easy credit and you've got a surefire recipe for people to overspend and shop too much. This holds true no matter your income level.

Plenty of celebrities with millions pouring in end up in financial trouble because they spend it as fast—or faster—than they earn it. Best-selling author Patricia Cornwell was not accustomed to having so much money flowing her way and, by her own admission, went on "impulsive shopping sprees." In addition to fighting spending problems, Cornwell also ended up in alcohol rehab after smashing her car. Mike Tyson, the former heavyweight boxing champion, filed bankruptcy despite having earned more than $300 million during his career. Hard as it is to believe, Tyson's out-of-control spending on mansions, cars, jewelry, exotic animals, and extravagant gifts consumed his gargantuan paydays. Michael

Jackson, the famous pop singer, has had similar problems. Celebrity spendaholics underscore the important lesson that it's not what you make, but what you're able to save and keep.

Consumer debt is how most people buy things that they often don't really need. Examples of consumer debt include auto loans, credit card debt, and finance company loans. The *majority* of Americans carry consumer debt. If you have credit card debt or auto loans, take some solace in the fact that you're far from alone and that many others have overcome these hurdles. But, being in the majority doesn't make these habits healthy. So don't think that consumer debt is a fine thing— because it's not.

One of my first assignments as a management consultant in the financial services industry was doing a product-line profitability study for a regional bank. Consultants got paid a lot of money to do this type of analysis, which basically helped a company figure out how much (or little) profit it made on its various products and services. It was no great surprise to our team that the bank's credit card business was much, much more profitable than its other lines of business. We found that banks, in general, routinely had a profit margin that was five to six times higher, despite charge-offs (loan losses) from credit cards, compared with their other lines of business.

Banks committed to the credit card business are quite sophisticated in identifying consumers likely to borrow a lot on their credit cards and thus be profitable to the bank. For example, Shailesh Mehta, the long-time CEO of Providian Financial (since acquired by Washington Mutual), a major player in the credit card business, routinely pocketed more than $10 million annually in compensation. How does one get to such a lofty position and garner such incredible paydays? In part, by making credit cards so profitable. Mehta, a "mathematical genius," developed the computer models used by Providian to identify middle- and lower-income consumers likely to borrow a lot. He was hailed by a former MasterCard president as one of the brightest and most able people in the business. In a *New York Times* article about his banks' credit card strategies, Mehta said, "Credit is very important to people; it is the ability to acquire things. We want to grant people the maximum possible credit line, and we get compensated for taking that risk."

Not surprisingly, lower-income households carry the heaviest burden of credit card debt in relation to their incomes. Among households with annual incomes below $40,000, the average credit-card debt carried amounts to more than 10 percent of their household income. Banks target and push high-limit credit cards to those people most likely to get hooked on them. The banks then add insult to injury by hitting them with poorly disclosed and outrageous interest rates and fees. Major credit card purveyors, which have heavily promoted supposed low interest rate cards, really whack you if you make a couple of late payments. A nine percent interest rate can quickly mushroom to 25+ percent! You may also be hit with $35 late fees, which raise your effective interest rate even higher.

In a speech to the American Community Bankers in Washington, former Federal Reserve chairman Alan Greenspan discussed, among other topics, the high levels of debt carried by American consumers. As quoted by Bloomberg Business News, Greenspan said, "Credit card debt has risen in large part because households prefer the convenience of cards as a method of payment, and hence, the increase does not necessarily indicate greater financial stress." Greenspan, who was a political appointee as the Fed chairman, clearly didn't understand or wasn't willing to admit the problem facing many Americans. While some Americans are in hock due to devastating events beyond their control, such as large medical expenses or job loss, many people with consumer debt end up in that position because their spending exceeds their income, and consumer borrowings close that gap. Jay Westbrook, a law professor, conducted an extensive study of people who filed personal bankruptcy and found that the typical filers were well-educated, middle-class baby boomers who overconsumed with credit cards. The *fact* is that the majority of American households carries a significant amount of debt on cards and is not simply using credit cards as a convenient payment method!

Another venue in which using consumer debt is now totally accepted as normal and common place is the car lot. Auto salespeople are trained to sell new cars through auto loans or leasing by focusing the prospective buyer's attention on the monthly payment (e.g., $399, $499, etc.) and diverting attention away from the sticker price of the vehicle ($20,000, $25,000, etc.) or the total cost, including financing costs. Auto dealer ads on television and radio barely mention the sticker price anymore, and it's usually buried in the fine print in the newspaper. The monthly leasing or loan cost, however, is HUGE and won't be missed or forgotten.

When I wrote my first book, *Personal Finance For Dummies*, the editors at that book's publishing company were incredulous that I was advising readers to *not* borrow and *not* take out a lease to buy a car. How, my editors, asked, did I expect people to buy expensive new cars with cash only? I replied that if someone doesn't have enough saved to buy a new car without a hefty loan or a lease, he shouldn't be buying such an expensive car—or a *new* car! We spoiled Americans don't stop to consider that most people around the globe don't own a car, let alone a brand-spanking new one fresh off the assembly line. What about buying a good-quality used auto?

You can give yourself a world of perspective without even leaving your own state or city: Go visit a soup kitchen, shelter for the homeless, or another place frequented by the poor. Spend some time in a small town or section of a city where middle class and poor people live. You won't see many new, expensive cars during these visits.

The average new car today costs about $30,000! Over the years, auto prices have risen faster than incomes, so auto makers and dealers have developed plenty of ways to keep monthly loan or lease payments seemingly reasonable enough to entice consumers to buy such costly cars. Loan terms have been stretched from three years to five years, and now to as many as seven or eight years. But there's an additional upside (for the auto makers and dealers) to stretching out loan terms so people can "afford" costlier cars. Auto manufacturers have been happily pushing longer-term loans to develop another route to your pocketbook—by enriching their financing subsidiaries that originate most auto loans. Those increasingly common no- or low-money down deals aren't public service campaigns.

And neither are low- or no-interest rate loans manufacturers and dealers provide to get you behind the wheel of a new car that's over your head financially. Those terms are nothing more than gimmicks that lack the following important disclosure: "If you take this loan at the ridiculously low advertised interest rate, you might as well forget getting a competitive price on the car because we will have to soak you." Don't be fooled by the low advertised interest rates: The two largest U.S. automakers (General Motors and Ford) make more money from their financing divisions than they do from selling cars! Rather than thinking of GM and Ford as auto makers, investment analysts think of these companies as banks that happen to sell cars as an inducement to get people to take out loans!

Not only does financing auto purchases lead people to buy more expensive cars than they can truly afford, increasing numbers of American families are buying second, third, and even fourth cars they don't truly need and can't afford.

I've long called consumer debt "bad debt" because it carries relatively high interest rates and you get no tax breaks on the interest paid. Easy access to consumer debt is one of the leading reasons that consumers overspend, buy things that they don't need, and spend money that they don't have. Consumer debt is the financial equivalent of cancer. Once it starts growing, it can easily get out of control as the high interest charges pile up on top of the debt. And, of course, there's the temptation to keep spending and taking on even more debt. Overspending leads to a plethora of long-term personal and financial consequences:

➤ **Feeling trapped in unfulfilling work.** If you're always looking forward to and dependent upon that next paycheck to meet your minimum monthly consumer debt payments, you're highly unlikely to feel like taking the risk of changing jobs.

➤ **Lost investing opportunities you could be taking advantage of with the money currently going to pay the accumulating interest and service the debt.** The thousands or even tens of thousands in consumer debt is ugly enough. Even uglier, though, is the missed opportunities—decades from now, money invested rather than spent on this debt could have mushroomed into hundreds of thousands of dollars.

➤ **Delayed retirement.** Having to make interest payments on consumer debt will add years if not decades to how long it will take you to accomplish saving enough to retire.

➤ **Divorce.** Stress, overspending, and too much consumer debt places great strain on even the best of marriages.

➤ **Increased taxes.** Many consumer purchases are taxed at the state and/or local level, and the more you spend, the less able you are to fund retirement accounts and gain the accompanying tax breaks.

➤ **Bankruptcy.** You may think that bankruptcy can't happen to you and that you can handle servicing your debt (for example, by meeting the minimum payment requirements every month). However, an unexpectedly long period of unemployment, major family medical issue, or some other unanticipated problem can tilt the balance and make the debt unmanageable. And with some consumer debt, such as credit card debt, it may take you decades to pay it off if you simply make the minimum payment!

> "The man who will live above his present circumstances is in great danger of living, in a little time, much beneath them."
>
> —Joseph Addison

The simple truth is that credit cards and other consumer debt enable you to spend money that you don't have. Many people have a warped sense of what they "need" because so many of us base our expectations on what we see and hear around us. We see others driving newer, costlier cars, so we think and believe that we "need" one (or two or three) of those as well. We think that to be viewed as successful, attractive, and with it, we "need" to buy the things that advertisers endlessly bombard us with.

Buying Things You Don't Need

Whether the products are option-packed cars, "high-end" home appliances, or the latest designer clothing, marketers motivate consumers to buy on emotion rather than need. Marketers play on insecurities, fears, and guilt and suggest that you can feel better about yourself and loved ones by buying their products. (This pattern begins at a young age— more than 6 in 10 teenagers say that buying certain products made them feel better about themselves, according to a study conducted for the non-profit Center for a New American Dream.) You won't be able to overcome overspending and consumer debt until you recognize these pressures and how they corrupt your buying decisions.

The appeal to emotional fulfillment rather than need fulfillment isn't limited to the marketing of products. Personal services are increasingly being sold on this basis. Witness the number of television shows that do extreme makeovers on people's bodies. A cosmetic surgeon in *Forbes* magazine was quoted as saying, "If someone comes in to see you and you are fat and a little sloppy, right away you put them off, and you're probably not going to get a second chance. People think that this person does not take care of himself, so he won't be conscientious in the workplace."

Why People Buy Things That They Don't Need

An eye-opening book to read is Pamela Danzinger's *Why People Buy Things That They Don't Need*. Ms. Danzinger runs a consulting firm that advises large consumer product companies on how to design products and convince consumers to buy them. Danzinger points out that much of American consumer purchases are discretionary. "The simple fact is that the contemporary American lives so far above subsistence, we have lost touch with the basic needs of life: food for nutrition, basic clothing, and shelter for warmth and protection," she writes.

The central thesis of Danzinger's book is that consumer product companies can induce consumers to buy costly products they don't really need by appealing to the consumer's desires and emotions. "In today's consumer driven society, satisfying consumer needs has less to do with the practical meeting of physical needs and everything to do with gratifying desires based upon emotions. The act of consuming, rather than the item being consumed, satisfies the need," she states.

Danzinger and her consulting firm identify 14 so-called justifiers (I'd call them rationalizations) that consumers employ when making discretionary purchases. Improving the quality of your life, buying on impulse, replacing an existing item (e.g., an older sofa), which leads to purchasing numerous related items (arm chairs and end tables), and purchasing certain goods for status are examples of justifiers. The goal of consumer product companies and their marketing staff is to persuade and cajole you into buying what they're selling even if you don't really need it. Remember this the next time the thought goes through your mind that you want or need to buy something that isn't a necessity.

Excess Spending and Its Consequences

All of the temptations, expectations, and pressures too often add up to big consumer debt problems, which eventually tip people over the brink financially. This section highlights some real-life cases that ended up in bankruptcy and will show you the kinds of people that this can happen to, how they ended up in trouble, and most importantly, what the consequences were, including the non-financial results.

Sara grew up in a family where she and the other children got fabulous presents at the holidays even though her family was poor. "I picked up my parents' habit of living in the moment and spending money as soon as you earn it," she says. Sara is a self-employed consultant with a Master's degree from an Ivy League university. She asked that her real name not be used because she's ashamed of her financial habits and worried about how her colleagues at work will view her. However, like many people in her situation, Sara doesn't know how common over-spending and living in debt is among her peers.

In her sixth year of marriage, Sara left her job at a large corporation to start her own company. Sara was doing what she loved; everything seemed to be going right for her. In the early months of her business, she earned little income. Sara carried credit card debt before starting her business. However, her outstanding balances grew as she developed her business and continued spending money as before when she was working for an employer offering a generous salary with benefits.

Meanwhile, Sara's husband was growing increasingly upset with her spending. He was a saver and disliked her carrying credit card balances at double-digit interest rates. Sometimes, he'd pay Sara's outstanding debt, just to relieve his own anxieties. Upon starting her own business, Sara used the increased flexibility in her schedule to indulge in one of her passions—dance. But her husband grew resentful of the time she spent with the dance troupe given her spending, debt, and low business income. He worked hard at his job and felt that he was carrying far too much of the household's financial burden.

Rather than scaling back on her purchases to compensate for her reduced income, Sara's wallet full of plastic tempted her like a stocked liquor cabinet tempts an alcoholic. She was addicted to her multiple credit lines, which gave her the ability to live a lifestyle beyond her means. Sara says that her excessive spending was ultimately unsustainable and contributed heavily to the failure of her marriage.

After her divorce, with her husband's income and belongings gone, Sara's spending actually increased because she had to repurchase items that she and her husband had jointly owned, such as her car, which she bought on credit. Meanwhile, "My mailbox was brimming with credit card offers," says Sara, adding, "The pleasure from spending became more necessary given the personal loss I suffered." Sara's debt mushroomed.

Within four years, Sara was drowning in more than $30,000 of credit card and credit line debts. She was often short on cash, so she began charging necessities such as groceries and using credit-card cash advance checks to pay her rent. Meanwhile, the initial "teaser" interest rates on her credit cards went from 9 percent to 18+ percent. With an annual income of just $35,000, Sara could barely keep up with the mounting interest payments. Paying down the debt balance seemed impossible.

An unexpected six-figure consulting contract provided hope for finally ridding herself of the high-interest consumer debt. However, fulfilling the contract was more expensive than she had expected due to high costs in hiring subcontractors. Stressed, exhausted, and unable to come up with her required quarterly income tax payments on her business income, Sara filed personal bankruptcy. Following on the heels of the failure of her marriage, Sara was now bankrupt financially as well as emotionally.

Duane Garrett hosted a radio show I sometimes listened to. He was a popular talk show host and attorney, the campaign chairman for Diane Feinstein's senatorial races, and friend of Vice President Al Gore. Garrett introduced Ted Kennedy at a Democratic National Convention and was the president of a sports memorabilia auction house he owned with two other partners. He was married with two daughters and owned a hilltop home in much-sought-after Tiburon, Marin County, near San Francisco. As the *San Francisco Chronicle* said, "Garrett appeared to have everything in life—fame, money, family."

One day, when I happened to be listening to his program, I was struck by Garrett lamenting that he was having trouble losing weight and he needed solutions. I called his show for the first time, got on the air, and offered him some words of encouragement. I told him that it seemed to me that he needed to exercise regularly. He quickly cut me off, his voice sounding almost panicked, saying that he didn't have time to mess around with exercise. I tried relaying my experiences—that I found myself far more productive at work and other endeavors when I was refreshed from exercise—but it was clear he wasn't interested.

A few weeks later, I heard on the local news that Garrett's body had been found floating near the Golden Gate Bridge. Garrett, the family man, supposedly successful entrepreneur, and mingler with political heavyweights, had sadly chosen to end his own life after leaping to his death from the bridge. In the subsequent weeks and months, it came out that his business was in trouble. He had accumulated more than $11 million in debts, including having heavily mortgaged his home, and had just $600,000 in assets. He'd been borrowing extensively from friends and business associates to pay off debts.

"Ultimately the scheme became so frenetic that Garrett took his own life rather than go through what he perceived as the humiliation of bankruptcy…" reported the *San Francisco Chronicle* after interviewing Garrett's friends. Interestingly, that same paper had written an article in the aftermath of his suicide in which it stated that Garrett "…was so entangled in a web of debt and deceit that he routinely bilked investors who were his friends and associates…" It further referred to his borrowing from Peter to pay Paul as a "Ponzi-type scheme." So, even in death, Garrett was humiliated, perhaps unfairly.

Like so many baby boomers, Garrett chased after the "good life." He bought the expensive home in an exclusive neighborhood; owned a large fishing boat, collected costly art, and drove luxury automobiles. His business failed. Failure is part of the small business world. Because he was so burdened with debt, it became clear to him that he couldn't dig himself out of the situation. The shame of his personal financial condition, debts, and failure is what led Garrett to kill himself.

Can You Save Too Much?

Evidence abounds for spending and consumption. However, I've come across people who may be saving "too much" and are overly concerned with forever amassing a bigger nest egg. (If you don't have this problem, and you think that this is like hearing about someone complaining that they have too much caviar, please read on—you may have loved ones, friends, or other contacts who suffer this problematic issue!) Just as some people think that their financial problems will be solved if only they could earn a higher income, oversavers typically believe that if they could reach a certain level of assets, they'd be more relaxed and could do what they really want with their lives. The bar, however, continually gets raised, and the level of "enough" is rarely attained. For this reason, some of the best savers also have the most difficulty spending money, even in retirement.

These super savers tend to have great insecurities relating to money. Specifically, they view amassing financial assets as providing them with safety and security that extends far beyond the financial realm. While having more financial assets, in theory, provides greater financial peace of mind, these riches don't necessarily provide more of the other types of security for which hoarders are searching. Plenty of money amassers I've known over the years tend to be lonely, isolated people. They typically have few friends and passions.

"She had few friends...she was an unhappy person, totally consumed by her securities accounts and her money," reported an article about Anne Scheiber in the *Washington Post*. Scheiber saved for the sake of saving without a goal or plan in mind and, frankly, without any benefit to herself. Despite earning modest wages during her working years as a government employee (IRS auditor), she passed away at the age of 101 with more than $20 million in assets. She did it through practicing the good financial habits of saving, starting at a young age, and investing in and holding onto a diversified portfolio of stocks.

Scheiber chose to live in a cramped studio apartment and never lived off of her investments, not even their income. In retirement, she only used her small Social Security check and modest pension from her employer. Scheiber was extreme in her frugality and obsessed with her savings.

Her stockbroker, William Fay, was quoted in a *Time* magazine article about Scheiber as saying, "Her world was limited to watching over her investments." Even Norman Lamm, the president of the university to which she left her estate, said, "She was obviously very intelligent and very unhappy."

While somewhat extreme in her excessive saving, Scheiber is far from unique in my observations as a financial counselor. In fact, I've come across a surprising number of people who have a "problem" with saving too much and spending too little.

When money hoarders marry people with significantly different money personalities, fireworks ensue and divorce is often the result. Financial security doesn't translate into emotional security and contentment.

Achieving a certain level of affluence can provide for greater access to quality healthcare in the United States. However, once one reaches the point at which quality healthcare is the norm, the incessant pursuit of more money can have a negative impact on the individual's long-term health and quality of life. For example, super savers often believe that they will be better protected as seniors and better able to enjoy their retirement years with hefty account balances. But the pursuit of more money, which typically entails longer work hours and greater stress, can lead to more health problems before and in retirement.

Many super savers, who also tend to be overobsessed with work, come from homes and families where they felt on the edge economically and emotionally. Although there are so many things that we can't control in the world, money amassers typically derive a sense of both economic and emotional security from saving a lot of money. And, they love watching their money grow, although they may have trouble with investing in volatile wealth-building investments like stocks because they generally abhor losing money.

Super savers have an amazing ability to selectively hear particular stories that reinforce rather than question their tendencies and beliefs. For example, stories periodically surface about how the legions of baby boomers retiring will bankrupt Social Security and cause a stock market collapse. Super savers batten down the hatches, save more, and invest even more conservatively when such stories worry them. News stories about stock market declines, corporate layoffs, budget deficits, terrorism risks, rising energy prices, and conflicts in the Middle East and elsewhere cause super savers to close their wallets, clutch their investments, and worry and save more. The lion's share of phone calls I fielded from my financial counseling clients came from worried super savers who often found something on the evening news, in print, or online to worry about. And, as any regular news junkie knows, there's plenty of negative, bad news available.

Too many financial planners have a tendency to heighten the anxieties of hoarders. One silly and inappropriate method I've seen some advisors use when creating a retirement plan is to tell their high-income clients that they need to save enough to replace, say, 90 percent of their current income throughout their retirement. A much lower percentage, which would necessitate saving a lot less money, may suit the client's long-term desires. Ultimately, the desired or needed percentage should be determined through retirement analysis of one's individual situation. I continue to be amazed at how often people refuse to question the perceived wisdom that they should amass enough assets to replace such a large percentage of their income. Such advice can be self-serving for the advisor, as it creates even greater dependency on the part of the client for their continued counsel.

The following are some case studies of typical super savers I've worked with over the years. I've chosen these people because each one illustrates different issues, challenges, and solutions for money amassers. In the next chapter, I'll also present additional advice for super savers and those who love them—or have to deal with them!

Postponing Achievable Dreams

Dee got out of debt quickly after medical school. When she came to me for advice at the age of 40, she had only $16,000 remaining to be paid off on her home mortgage and had accumulated a hefty investment portfolio. She described herself as "frugal and prudent to the level of paranoia." After reading some of my books, she came to ask herself, and then me, an excellent question: "Am I saving too much?"

Dee came to this point of introspection about her life and work because she was considering taking an extended leave to perform volunteer medical work overseas. As she put it, "I don't want to die with $15 million in the bank and miss out on life-expanding opportunities." Financially speaking, what perplexed her was whether she could take a hiatus from saving money. She felt very uncomfortable doing so until she came across some of my writings. At the time, her financial assets totaled about $1 million.

You can find plenty of financial advisors, affluent people, as well as others, who think one million dollars isn't "enough" and not worth nearly what it used to be. However, one million dollars in financial assets is a heck of a lot of money to have accumulated, especially by age 40 and especially for someone like Dee who lived in an area of the country that offers a relatively moderate cost of living. I know plenty of retired folks who live quite happily with that amount of money or less.

Like many super savers I've come to know, Dee didn't know how much new money she was actually saving annually. She was focused on her career and rarely set aside time to consider the bigger-picture financial issues. We were both surprised when she and I analyzed her finances to find that Dee was socking away about 40 percent of her yearly salary. Given her relatively high tax bracket, Dee's savings rate was even more astounding. She actually was saving about two-thirds of her after-tax take-home pay—that's huge! (Dee's monthly mortgage payment was a mere $400, and her total expenditures came to less than $50,000 per year.)

Although she enjoyed her chosen work as a physician, Dee was drained. She didn't like her current boss, worked 12-hour days, and often worked evenings and weekends at home. She estimated that she put in 70 hours per week but was quick to point out that she got a lot of joy from work, so she didn't feel like a workaholic.

She said that she would love to take a couple of years off but had been reluctant to do so because, "I've been a security-first person and want to have enough saved and be able to return to the same job, income, and ability to save more money." One of the reasons she continued to postpone her dream of doing overseas volunteer activities is that she'll likely never be guaranteed the same income and job upon her return. In speaking with her over time, however, she came to agree with me that she didn't know any unemployed physicians and that she wouldn't have much trouble replicating her current job, elements of which she didn't love anyway.

Dee's family background and upbringing is interesting and revealing. Her parents divorced when she was 12 years old. "My father had been a meticulous record keeper and financial manager. I needed to help my mom manage the household finances. I was doing the taxes for my mom at age 14. We balanced the checkbook together. Mom really needed my help. The thing that saved us was having a small mortgage— $108 per month," says Dee. Reflecting upon her childhood, she feels that these early years imparted a sense of insecurity and lack of control that she still wrestles with in adulthood, "...not because we got creditor calls or because I was deprived. We had no buffer for disasters or security." Dee was emotionally as well as financially deprived, and she missed out on a lot of childhood happiness. Now, as an adult, she seeks to exert control over her life through amassing a large nest egg, which can't provide emotional happiness and security.

My advice to Dee was that she shouldn't postpone what she really wanted to do. She was saving a lot and had very low expenditures in relation to her income. She worked in a high-demand, secure profession and would surely find comparable work upon her return from overseas. I also helped Dee do some basic retirement analysis, which enabled her to see how well off she was simply on the basis of what she'd saved already at the tender age of 40. When I last spoke with her, she commented, "I need to loosen up and see the world and enjoy myself and the planet. Thou shalt travel!"

> *"It is very well to be thrifty, but don't amass a hoard of regrets."*
> —*French poet, Charles D'Orleans*

When Enough Never Is

When I first met James, he was a highly successful executive in his late thirties. He was earning well into the six-figures annually and had already piled up a multi-million dollar net worth. James worked very long hours and, as a result, was developing some related health problems. When we began discussing his situation, he reported that he had never made a financial decision that he was pleased with. He rarely dated and, by his own admission, had few friends.

When we discussed his short-term and long-term financial and personal goals, James stated that he wanted to maximize the potential return of his portfolio without losing money. It wasn't obvious to James that these two conflicting objectives weren't really possible to achieve. James' feelings on this issue highlight a common problem that super savers have with investing. Many of them have great difficulty placing even modest portions of their money into the more conservative of vehicles that offer growth potential, such as stock mutual funds. If they do take the plunge into slightly volatile waters, they quickly bail when prices go down.

After working with James for a period of time, I came to learn that he had more than one million dollars in one bank account! In addition to the low returns this account provided, he hadn't realized the risk to which he was exposed. The FDIC insurance on one bank account is just $100,000. Thus, if his bank happened to fail (and banks do fail), he was at risk of losing all the money in the account in excess of $100,000.

One of James' longer-term goals was to achieve "financial freedom" by the age of 50 by accumulating about $10 million. He did indeed accomplish this goal, and, no surprise to me, it wasn't enough to satiate his desire to work and accumulate greater savings. He then turned to new worries after reaching the $10 million mark. He's now concerned about news reports of higher than expected oil prices and outliving his money. The bar keeps getting set higher and higher. So, James continues to work hard, save a lot, and not spend.

In my initial years working with James, I wasn't really able to help him with his problem of oversaving, and the reasons behind that fact are interesting and thought provoking. I had very limited interactions with him during this period. When he first consulted with me, I was frankly unaware of this problem that he had. In retrospect, I can see that part of the problem was that he did a masterful job of concealing some of his savings! He originally engaged my services simply to provide some investment advice on a retirement account. He wanted to invest the money in better-returning vehicles than a bank account, but he was fearful of moving out of the bank account.

James really needed the kind of professional counseling assistance that a sharp psychologist could provide. In his late forties, his lifelong financial habits were quite ingrained. I took the risk in suggesting to James that he work with a psychologist after he provided me an opening one day when he lamented his lack of a romantic relationship and the historic problems that he had with women. After working with a counselor for about a year, James arrived back on my doorstep, and we finally began to make some headway with his saving obsession and resistance to investing more aggressively. The biggest contribution from his counseling was that it enabled him to "see" how his long work hours and unrelenting focus on amassing money was causing him to be unhappy and fail at interpersonal relationships.

After I was finally able to get him to sit down with an open mind to work with me in reviewing the current state of his retirement planning, James became far more comfortable that he had already accumulated a lot of money to provide a nice standard of living down the road. Paying off his home mortgage, which was easy for him to do, also made him feel at greater ease with his financial situation. As he learned about different investments and the risks (including exposure to inflation and taxes) that he was incurring by keeping so much of his cash in bank accounts, he was far more receptive to diversify with some growth investments like stock and real estate.

> *"The advantages of wealth are greatly exaggerated."*
> *—Leland Stanford*

Hoarding and Cheating

I was initially struck by Michelle's assertive, take-no-prisoners manner. (Her personality reminded me somewhat of Martha Stewart.) Michelle was doing very well in her career and was saving a lot of money. She was quite proud of her burgeoning investment balances and she wanted a lot more future growth. She hinted that she was "aggressive" in preparing her personal income tax returns. Over the years, I began to learn what Michelle meant by that phrase: She inflated her deductions and didn't report all of her self-employment income. In other words, she was cheating. Ultimately, she landed in trouble with the IRS, got audited, incurred some stiff penalties, and was lucky not to do jail time given the amount of cheating she had done.

Michelle was well educated and accomplished in her profession. She certainly didn't "need" to cheat to make ends meet. Michelle cheated, it seemed, mostly from insecurities about her future. She worried that she may not be as employable or that her income would drop substantially in the future. She resented how much she had to pay in taxes and didn't want to have to work longer hours to make and save more money.

Her desires to amass more money also led her to bend the truth about other aspects in her life that had a financial component, such as product returns and orders that she made. She admitted to me on several occasions to returning products outside of their warranty periods and lying about when she bought them. I also found in my interactions with her that she often angled to get something for nothing and not pay for all of the services rendered.

Michelle was a sad and empty person who didn't connect with people. She was devoted to her career and accumulating money and not much else. She never raised topics that would've naturally led me into a discussion with her about recognizing and dealing with her problems. Although I'm no psychologist, it was pretty obvious to me that Michelle needed some enjoyable activities outside of her work that would enable her to meet and connect with others.

Gaining Appreciation for What You Have

Rick and Debby were in an adult education class that I used to teach for University of California at Berkeley. They were an energetic and attentive couple. When I told the class that, as a matter of policy, I did not want to have students calling me at the end of the course to engage my services as a financial counselor, Rick and Debby promptly dropped out of the class and called my office. (I feel that it is an enormous conflict of interest when "teachers" teach for the purpose of cultivating financial-advisory clients.) Despite my best efforts to convince them to stay in the class and learn how to better manage their money through completing the course, they became clients.

Rick and Debby both worked as full-time professionals in their chosen fields and were high-income earners. In their late forties, they had foregone the opportunity to have children partly because of their devotion to their careers. They were able to save large portions of their annual combined incomes—on the order of 35+ percent. While they were leery of the stock market, Rick and Debby owned a number of real-estate investment properties. Despite owning a half-dozen well-located and modest-sized single-family homes in northern California to accompany their near million dollars in other financial assets, Rick and Debby felt far from financially secure.

This couple had an amazing ability to see the glass as half empty rather than half full. Despite the hundreds of thousands of dollars in equity in all of the properties they owned, they dwelled on their feelings that they had bought several of them "near the top of the market." And despite their blue chip educational credentials and successful careers, they worried incessantly about being laid off and never being rehired. The better I got to know Rick and Debby, the more disturbed I became that, like Michelle, they cheated on their taxes. They seemed somewhat embarrassed to admit this but were comfortable enough with this behavior (and me) to discuss the situation.

Over time, I was able to show Ricky and Debby how well off they were with their investments. As the years passed, I kept reminding them how well their investments were appreciating and that the mortgages on their rental properties were being paid down while the homes were gaining in value. Performing a thorough retirement analysis and periodically updating the information helped them feel much better about the standard of living that their assets would provide. Debby scaled back her work responsibilities, and they eventually ended up adopting two children. They found that they loved being parents and working less.

Balancing Spending and Saving

Most people don't wish to work their entire adulthood. And, even if they do enjoy working for pay that much, who wants to live on the edge economically, always dependent upon the next paycheck to be able to pay the monthly bills?

That's why you should avoid the extremes of overspending and over-saving. Consider the analogy to eating food: eat too little or not enough of the right kinds of foods, and you go hungry and possibly suffer deficiencies of energy and nutrition; too much leads to obesity and other health problems. Overspending and undersaving hampers your ability to accomplish future personal and financial goals and in the worst cases, can lead to bankruptcy. Oversaving can lead to not living in the moment and for today and constantly postponing for tomorrows that we may not live to enjoy. Remember Goldilocks and her quest at the bear's home for the bowl of porridge that was not too hot and not too cold and a bed to rest in that was not too hard and not too soft. Everyone should save money as a cushion and to accomplish important personal and financial goals.

8

Establishing a Savings Foundation

"The saving man becomes the free man."
—Chinese proverb

"The only reason to have money is to tell any s.o.b. in the world to go to hell."
—Humphrey Bogart

All good hiking expeditions begin with proper preparation, and so it is with your personal finances. Unless you inherit vast sums of money, you'll need to build your base of assets largely from scratch. Even if you come to the journey with lots of existing resources, you should be able to improve how you spend and save money. This chapter will show you how.

Giving Yourself an Unfair Advantage

Before you begin your journey, you should make sure that you're not encumbered or held back unnecessarily. Carrying high-cost consumer debt—such as that on credit cards and auto loans—is like climbing a mountain with one arm tied behind your back. Perhaps it can be done, but if you can perform your climb with both arms, it will be safer and more enjoyable. Borrowing through consumer loans encourages you to live beyond your means and do the opposite of saving—call it deficit financing, as those in Washington do.

Just as you need reserves of food to power your trip up the mountain, you need to build up reserves of money to help fund your future financial goals. If you want to purchase a home or other real estate, deal with an emergency, pay for educational expenses, or retire, you need money.

Jeremy went house hunting and soon fell in love with a home. Unfortunately, after he found his dream home, he soon discovered all the loan documentation requirements and the extra fees and penalties he needed to pay for having such a small down payment. Ultimately, he couldn't afford to buy the home that he desired because he hadn't saved enough. "If I had known, I would have started saving much sooner—I thought saving for the future was something you did when you became middle-aged," he told me.

Melissa and Henry felt the same way about retirement planning. When they hit their 50s, they came to the painful realization that retirement was a long way off because they were still paying off consumer debts and trying to initiate a regular savings program. Now, they are faced with having to work into their 70s to achieve their retirement goals and/or living a greatly reduced lifestyle in retirement.

Those who are able to save can do so because of their smart and disciplined spending habits. I see this time and time again whenever I meet someone with a modest income, non-six-figure income paying job, and who has accumulated a substantial nest egg. Of course, this doesn't happen overnight and without sacrifice and some bumps along the way.

Here are the common traits among those who are able to consistently save a healthy portion of their income:

➤ **Understand needs versus wants.** Americans often have the most difficulty with this one. Too many people define necessities by what those around them have. A new $30,000 car is not a necessity, although some people try to argue that it is by saying, "I need a way to get to work." Transportation is a necessity, not a new $30,000 car! I'm not going to tell anyone exactly how they should spend their money. But, I will tell you that if you take out an auto loan to buy a car that you really can't afford, and you take a similar approach with other consumer items you don't truly need, you're going to have great difficulty saving money and accomplishing your goals and will probably feel stressed.

➤ **Spending is routinely questioned, and research is valued.** Prior to going shopping for necessities that aren't everyday purchases, make a list of the items you're looking for and do some research first. (*Consumer Reports* is a good resource.) After you're sure that you want an item, your research has helped you identify brands, models, and so on that are good values, and you've checked in with your bank/money market account to ensure that you can afford it, check in with various retailers and compare prices. When you set out to make a purchase, only buy what's on your list. The Internet can be a time-efficient tool for performing research and price comparisons, but be careful of common online problems. The first is advertising that masquerades as informative articles. The second problem is online retailers that may be here today and gone tomorrow or who may be unresponsive after the purchase. Of course, this latter problem occurs with traditional bricks and mortar retailers, too. Finally, Internet retailers are adept at pushing additional items that they have good reason to believe will appeal to you given your other purchases.

➤ **Always look for the best values for products that you buy.** By *value*, I mean the level of quality given the price you'd pay for the item. Don't assume that a more expensive product is better because you often don't get what you pay for. That said, you can sometimes get a significantly better-quality product by paying a modest amount more. Don't waste money on brand names. If you're like most folks, you've bought products for the status you thought they conveyed or because you simply assumed that a given brand-name product was superior to the alternative choices—without properly researching the issue before making the purchase. But thanks to advertising costs, brand-name products are frequently more expensive than comparable quality but less well-known brands.

➤ **Reducing time spent on earning and spending money.** The saddest part about being on the work and consumption treadmill is how much of your time and life you may fritter away earning and then spending money. Consider in a typical week how many hours you spend working and shopping. In addition to the time actually spent at work, consider commute time and time spent getting dressed and prepared for work. Now add in all of the time that you spent shopping and buying things. Compare the grand total of time spent on work- and shopping-related activities to time spent on the things you really enjoy in life.

➤ **Saving money is a learned and practiced habit.** Just as with changing what you eat or your exercise routine (or lack thereof), modifying your spending and savings habits is easier said than done. The information that follows can help you get on the path to consistently saving and then investing your money wisely to achieve your desired goals.

Getting your finances in shape to save is much like exercising in advance of your mountain climb. The best way to make your budget lean and mean and to save more of what you're earning is to examine where and on what you are currently spending your money.

Deals That Seem Too Good to Be True

Retailers run all sorts of specials to induce consumers to buy now. For example, consider that some Kia auto dealers offered free gas for one year (when gas prices pierced $3 per gallon), along with the buyer's being able to delay car payments for a year. Does this sound too good to be true?

Well, the attorney general in Oregon thought so and investigated one dealer's claims made in newspaper ads to "buy a new Kia; get gas for a year," with individual cars being promoted as coming with "gas for a year." According to the attorney general's office in Oregon, "In 'mice' type under each offer, the company stated that the deal was a 'combination offer.' Consumers were told in barely readable type to 'make your best deal on a package price...Gas offer is a $500 gas card.'" Not surprisingly, the government investigators found the ads, "...to not be clear and conspicuous, and $500 would not cover gas for a year for a typical driver."

Furniture retailers also frequently offer that if you buy now, you don't have to pay a thing for a year, and you might even get free delivery. This sort of "push" marketing does make it harder for some people to say no. Always remember that free financing, for say a year, is not a huge cost to the dealer, but it is a cost, and if you forgo it, you should be able to negotiate a lower purchase price. Retailers find that buyers are less likely to negotiate the price if they are getting a short-term financing break.

What you need to do is to assemble information that shows you what you typically spend your money on. Get out your checkbook register, credit and charge card bills, and your paystub and recent tax return. (Keep a notebook handy or use your PDA to track cash purchases, or try conducting all transactions on a debit card.) Collect your spending data for at least a three-month span to determine how much you spend in a typical month on various things—such as clothing, rent or mortgage, income taxes, haircuts, and everything else. If your spending fluctuates greatly throughout the year, you may need to analyze six- or even twelve-months worth of spending. (I walk you through this exercise in Chapter 9, "Your Spending Plan.")

Tabulating your spending is only half the battle on the path to fiscal fitness. (Our federal government, after all, knows where it spends its/our money, yet it hasn't come near to closing its deficit and reducing its debt.) Now, you must do something with the personal spending information that you collected. Specifically, you must decide where to make reductions or cutbacks if you want to save more.

Everybody's budget has fat, some much more than others. In order for most people to reach their financial goals, they must save at least 10 percent of their pre-tax income. Suppose that you're currently spending all of your income (a very American thing to do) and that you would like to be able to save 10 percent of your income. If you are able to cut your spending just 7.5 percent and put that savings into a tax-deductible retirement account, you'll actually be able to reach your 10 percent target. How? From the tax savings you'll net from funding your retirement account.

Money that you contribute into employer-based retirement plans, such as a 401(k) and 403(b), or self-employed plans, such as SEP-IRAs and Keoghs, reduces your current year's taxable income. Your contributions are typically free from both federal and state income taxes in the year for which the contribution is made. Additionally, all of your money compounds over time inside these accounts without taxation.

These tax reduction accounts are one of the best ways to save and make your money grow—here's a quick example to show you how. Take the case of Margaret, age 40, who is in a moderate tax bracket (paying approximately 35 percent in Federal and State income tax during her working years). She can afford to contribute $4,000 per year to her retirement account. In 25 years, when she turns 65, Margaret's retirement account balance would have grown to $393,388. Assuming she is paying taxes on this balance at the same rate in retirement (35 percent) leaves $255,702. Contrast this with having just $153,108 if Margaret had instead saved outside her tax-sheltered retirement account and paid taxes annually. In order for Margaret to be worse off saving in the retirement account, her retirement tax rate would have to exceed 61 percent. (This example assumes a 10-percent annual investment return.)

In order to come up with the money to invest, most people need to reduce their spending. (Increasing your income is another, but more difficult strategy.) It's a matter of personal preference where you will make cuts in your budget.

The biggest problem with overspending is consumer debt and its availability. So, if you tend to spend too much using credit cards and consumer loans, you have to remove the root of the problem. Cut up and rid yourself of your credit cards. Believe it or not, you don't "need" a credit card to function in modern society. Cash and checks worked just fine before credit cards were commonplace, and they still do. Get yourself a VISA or MasterCard *debit card*. These cards are connected to your checking account or money market fund and thus prevent you from spending money that you don't have. Check with your current bank and others in the area.

The larger mutual fund companies, such as Fidelity, T. Rowe Price, and Vanguard, offer asset management accounts that come with unlimited check writing and debit cards, although more of these accounts are available for higher-balance customers.

If you want to keep one credit card for, say, an occasional car rental, how about putting it in a water-filled plastic container in your freezer and thawing it out only for one-time usage? The approach may seem a bit extreme, but the simple fact that you have to make an effort to thaw out the plastic will introduce an added barrier to spur-of-the-moment spending decisions. The time that it takes for you to access the card provides additional time to reconsider your impending purchase. Don't keep any credit cards that are specific to one merchant (such as department stores). These cards are completely unnecessary, typically have the highest interest rates, and will tempt overspending.

> *"Before buying anything, it is well to ask if one could do without it."*
> —John Lubbock

To improve your consumption habits, you must first change your mindset about shopping. Typically, this involves changing shopping from a source of entertainment, a distraction from other problems, and/or an impulse decision to a simple means to an end—acquiring a product that you feel you need and want.

Observe friends and relatives who are thrifty and try learning some of their better spending habits. Don't shop with people who share your spending problems or who've often accompanied you on shopping sprees in the past.

If you're tempted to buy something you hadn't planned upon once you're in a store, make a note of the item and the store's price—and then go home without it! Do some thinking and research the product, returning to the steps I suggested previously. If you're sure you still want the item, and you can afford it, then shop around.

Eliminate temptations to shop and spend more. Toss out mail-order catalogs that clutter your mailbox, and don't click on ads or browse for products online. *Never* watch shopping channels or infomercials on television. Visit the web site www.dmaconsumers.org/consumerassistance.html and follow the directions for getting off mailing and telemarketing lists. Also visit the web site www.donotcall.gov to register for the National Do Not Call Registry. Finally, to reduce the mailings you receive caused by credit bureau information on file about your household, call 888-5OPTOUT.

Get your money back when products and services aren't up to snuff or when you realize you really don't need something you recently bought. The process of returning items will get you to think harder before making future purchases and pay some financial dividends.

Don't begin a regular savings program until you've zeroed out all consumer debt. (Work at paying off the highest interest rate debt first.) You're unlikely to earn an investment return, after taxes, that exceeds the relatively high interest costs on credit cards and other common consumer debt.

When you can afford to set some money aside in savings, make your saving automatic by setting up a direct-deposit payroll deduction with your employer (or using automatic checking account transfers to an investment account if you're self-employed). That way, you're free to spend what's left over, and you don't need to drive yourself and other family members crazy tracking every expenditure.

For tax advantages and protection from your own spending temptations, save inside retirement (tax-sheltered) accounts where possible. Employers offering retirement accounts can set you up with automatic payroll deduction. If you're funding your own retirement accounts (such as an IRA or Keogh), mutual fund and other investment companies can help you with establishing automatic investment plans as well.

Establishing a regular savings program and living within your means provides long-term financial benefits and peace of mind and satisfaction.

Keeping Money Accumulation in Proper Perspective

As with any good habit, you can get too much of a good thing. Washing your hands and maintaining proper hygiene is worthwhile, but it becomes problematic when you obsess over cleanliness, and it interferes with your life and personal relationships.

I've had the opportunity and enjoyment of helping numerous "over-savers" overcome their excessive ways. Conquering oversaving and an obsession with money typically requires a mix of education and specific incremental behavioral changes. Substantive change typically comes over months and years, not days and weeks.

The vast majority of super savers whom I've worked with and observed work too many hours and neglect their loved ones and themselves. They typically need to work less and lead more balanced lives. That may involve changing jobs or careers or simply coming up with a "stop doing list," the opposite of a "to-do list."

Money amassers also usually need to better learn how to loosen the purse strings. Learning to spend more and save less is a problem more Americans wish they had, so consider yourself lucky in that regard! Try the following strategies to enable you to give yourself permission to spend more:

➤ **Understand the standard of living that can be provided by the assets you've already accumulated.** This is one of my favorite exercises to use with super savers. Many people who I've worked with have been pleasantly surprised by this analysis. There are numerous useful retirement planning worksheets and analytic tools you can use to assess where you currently stand in terms of saving for retirement. My favorites are the printed work booklets offered by T. Rowe Price (800-638-5660) and their online tools (www.troweprice.com), along with the web tools available at www.vanguard.com. (See Chapter 4, "Developing Your Personal Financial Action Plan," for more about planning for your retirement.)

➤ **Get smart about investing your money.** Super savers often have trouble moving into growth-oriented investments and sticking with them because they abhor losing money. Chapters 11 through 14 are all about investing, including how to overcome these and other common fears and anxieties.

➤ **Go on a news diet.** Minimize and even avoid news programs that dwell on the negative, which will only reinforce your fears about never having enough money. One justification that super savers use for their actions that constantly resurfaces in the news is the litany of fears surrounding the tens of millions of baby boomers hitting retirement age around the same time. The story goes that retiring boomers will cause a mammoth collapse of the stock market as they sell out to finance their golden years. Real estate prices are supposed to plummet as well, as everyone sells their larger homes and retires to small condominiums in the Sun Belt. Such doom saying about the future of financial and real estate markets is unfounded. The fear that boomers will suddenly sell everything when they hit retirement is bogus. Nobody sells off his entire nest egg the day after he stops working; retirement can last up to 30 years, and assets are depleted quite gradually. On top of that, boomers vary in age by up to 16 years and, thus, will be retiring at different times. The wealthiest (who hold the bulk of real estate and stocks) won't even sell most of their holdings but will, like the wealthy of previous generations, pass on many of their assets.

➤ **Regularly buy something that you historically have viewed as frivolous but which you can truly afford.** Once a week or once a month, treat yourself! By all means, spend the money on something that brings you the most joy, whether it's eating out occasionally at a pricey restaurant or taking an extra vacation during the year.

➤ **Buy more gifts for the people you love.** Money hoarders actually tend to be more generous with loved ones than they are with themselves. However, oversavers still tend to squelch their desires to buy gifts or help out those they care about.

➤ **Go easier on yourself and family when it comes to everyday expenses.** How would you like it if a family member or close friend followed you around all day and totaled up the number of calories that you consume? Well, then, why would you expect your family to happily accept your daily, weekly, and monthly tracking of their expenditures? In some families, super savers who habitually track their spending drive everyone else crazy with their money monitoring. Personal finances become a constant source of unnecessary stress and anxiety. Especially if you're automatically saving money from each paycheck or saving on a monthly basis, does it really matter where the rest of it goes? (Of course, none of us wants family members to engage in illegal or harmful behaviors. But other than that, enjoy life.) Work at establishing guidelines and a culture of spending money that everyone can agree and live with. For example, some couples I know only discuss larger purchases, which are defined as exceeding a certain dollar limit such as $100 or $200. Parents who teach their children about spending wisely pass along far more valuable financial lessons than do elders who nag and complain about specific purchases.

9

Your Spending Plan

*"Beware of little expenses.
A small leak will sink a great ship."*
—Benjamin Franklin

*"It is easier to make money than to save it;
one is exertion, the other self-denial."*
—Thomas Halliburton

Most people can think of 101 things they'd rather do than track their spending. However, just a little bit of effort can pay big dividends that last a lifetime. Knowing where your money is going will empower you to make changes in your life and help you reach your financial and personal goals.

Different people have different ways to track and manage their spending. What works for one person won't necessarily work for another, simply because each person approaches spending, budgeting, and saving differently.

Rather than seeing this exercise as drudgery, look upon it as the first step toward using your money more efficiently—more powerfully—to maximize your satisfaction. Along the way, you'll also see how budgeting and expense control can lead to extra benefits, such as reducing your tax bill.

To start taking charge of your spending habits, it helps to have some concrete "evidence" of where your money is currently being spent. While you may have a guess of where most of your money goes each month, having the facts can be a real eye-opening experience.

Tracking Your Spending

Where does it all go?

You work hard for your money, so you owe it to yourself to make the most of what you are earning. Part of making the most of your money is to be careful not to let so much of it slip out of your hands after you earn it.

In order to track your spending easily, you should separate it into categories into which you separate your spending information. Within categories, there may be subcategories that allow further detailing of how you are spending your money. The following are some examples of categories and subcategories:

Housing	Food
Rent	Groceries
Mortgage	Meals Out
Property Taxes	Clothing
Utilities	Insurance
Gas & Electric	Health
Water	Auto
Cable & Internet	Home
Taxes	Life
Federal	Disability
State	And so on
Social Security	Subscriptions and Memberships
Entertainment	

To track your spending accurately, make sure that you capture all the different ways that you spend your money. That's why you need your checkbook register, credit card statement, and anything else that documents where you're spending your money.

Transactions that you do with cash present another challenge. Suppose you typically spend cash to buy lunch out, as well as a few bucks here and there on a magazine or coffee. How do you collect this data and mesh it with your other spending? One option is to estimate. This is quick but suffers from the selectivity and accuracy of your memory. Another option is to be more systematic and keep a little notebook (or PDA) with you for a week or two and record every cash purchase and what it was for. It is more time consuming and you risk odd stares from strangers and friends, but it is much more precise. Furthermore, the process of tracking your every financial move may cause you to change your normal spending habits. Remember, the point is to get an accurate snapshot of how you generally spend your money.

Don't get too bogged down in the details.

Having the data on where your monthly income is being spent is powerful information. But don't sweat it if you aren't able to track every last penny. In fact, to get 100 percent of the details letter perfect, you're likely to spend far too many hours that you won't enjoy (time you probably can't spare in your busy schedule).

This is a case where the 80/20 rule works well. This says that 20 percent of the work or data provides 80 percent of the value. In some endeavors, such as the construction of an airplane, every detail counts and could lead to disaster if it's not letter-perfect. The good news with your money matters is that this is not the case. Forever tracking every last dollar and cent you spend could lead to a boring existence and would probably drive you and your family crazy!

Necessities Versus Luxuries

One major financial danger is that what used to be thought of as a luxury, over time, becomes thought of as a necessity. Automobiles, when they were first built in the early 1900s, were a luxury. Most people got around through other, less-costly methods. Televisions arrived on the scene a few decades later and went through a similar adoption process.

Today, cars and televisions, including multiple ones, are considered necessities. In some households, there's almost one car and one television per person! Are cars and televisions necessities? Of course not. You can live without both. Besides the money you could save on the purchase and upkeep of these devices, some would argue that not having these trappings of modern life could improve the quality of your life. Consider the benefits of not having a car: No more insurance premiums, no more parking hassles, and increased exercise and sunshine from walking.

You may not be willing or easily able to give up your car. If you're part of a two-income household with kids, your commutes and other commitments may require a car. That's fine. However, you should question all the things you spend your money on, to prioritize what's most important and reduce spending on those items that are not. These are personal choices, but all choices come down to making tradeoffs. This includes where you live, where you shop, as well as what you buy. Although some people will tell you how they think you should be spending your money, ultimately, only you can decide.

Is the second car more or less important than a vacation abroad? Are you willing to give up regular clothing purchases, or would you rather quit your gym membership and start exercising in other ways?

Remember, if you're not saving enough to accomplish your personal and financial goals, either you have to spend less or earn more. For most people, spending less is more realistic. Once you're able consistently to save the amount you desire, how you spend the rest becomes less relevant.

Most people have some difficulty saving as much of their income as they'd like or need to in order to achieve their financial goals. A relatively easy way to fix this problem is to be more realistic with your goals. Many people, for example, aren't able to retire by age 55 by saving just 5 percent of their annual earnings. You might need to work a little longer, save more, and perhaps reduce the lifestyle expectations you have for retirement.

Budgeting Strategies

Once you know where your money is going in a typical month, you're in a position to start making some changes. One of those changes could be to plan ahead with your spending—a process called "budgeting."

Some people budget for the same reason that businesses do—so that the difference between the amount of money coming in and going out is not left to chance. Suppose that you analyze your past six months' worth of spending and realize that you're saving just 5 percent of your income. Perhaps you set as a goal saving 10 percent of your income. How do you accomplish that? You can go through the various spending categories and set targets that cut your spending enough so that your rate of savings increases to 10 percent. That's what budgeting is all about.

Here's an example. Suppose that your annual income is $40,000 and that you're currently spending $38,000 per year and saving $2,000 per year (5 percent of your income). You'd like to be saving 10 percent of your income, or $4,000 per year. So, you only need to come up with $167 more per month to reach your higher saving's goal. After reviewing your recent spending, you determine that you can make cuts in the following categories:

	Monthly Average	Budget	Difference
Dining (Meals Out)	$250	$175	$75
Entertainment	$170	$120	$50
Taxes	$1000	$958	$42
		Total	$167

By cutting your spending on meals out and entertainment by a total of $125 per month, you can funnel that savings into your employer's tax-deductible retirement savings plan. This tax break—assumed for this person to be worth about one-third of the retirement plan contribution—reduces the taxes and gets the person to her goal. Saving $2,000 more per year wasn't so difficult after all!

Budgeting is not perfect, and it offers no guarantees. All a budget represents is a plan or set of targets. You may plan to cut your spending on meals out by $75 per month, but whether or not you do in actuality is another matter. Don't let temptation get the better of you!

There are two common ways to develop a budget. The first method involves examining each of the spending categories and developing your best estimate for how much to reduce in each. Most people will cut more in some categories than others. As discussed in the "Necessities Versus Luxuries" section, you must decide which expenditures provide you with the most value. It involves trade-offs, and it is rarely easy.

The other method of budgeting is to start from scratch. Rather than looking at changes to your existing spending, you figure out how much you would like to be spending in the different categories. You start with a clean slate so to speak—you're not constrained by starting with or examining what you're currently spending. The advantage of this approach is that it allows for a more significant change. The disadvantage is that the estimates can be unrealistic.

Almost everything is fair game for change in the long haul. In the short-term, some expenses are easier to reduce than others. People who have difficulty saving money have a tendency to think of everything in their budget as a necessity. The reality is that there are opportunities to spend less on many items that seem like necessities, or are things we spend money on mostly out of habit.

Develop a plan and check back periodically to see how you're doing. You may go over a little in one category, but you might be able to make up for it by staying "under budget" in another.

Part of smart spending and budgeting involves keeping an emergency cushion for unexpected expenses. What if you lose your job or your roof springs a leak? What if both of these unfortunate events happen at the same time! How would you stay afloat?

Ideally, you should have an emergency reserve of at least three months' worth of living expenses in an account that is liquid and accessible without penalty. The "riskier" and more volatile your income is, the greater the reserve you should have. If your job is unstable and you have no other family members to turn to for financial help, you may want to keep as much as a year's worth of money in your emergency reserve. (See Chapter 14, "Your Investing Plan," for ideas on where to invest your emergency reserve money.)

Ways to Reduce Your Expenditures

It's one thing to want to reduce your spending and quite another to actually do it.

Whenever you make a purchase (on a product or service), it pays to shop around and make sure that you're getting value for your money. Remember that you don't always get what you pay for. Sometimes less-costly items are better.

Also, don't assume that reducing your spending has to entail great sacrifices. Often, simple changes in behavior can go a long way toward reducing your spending. For example, buying things in bulk typically reduces the cost per item purchased.

Other ways to reduce spending are more challenging. Keep in mind that what you're willing and able to reduce will be different from what your neighbor is able to do. The following sections highlight proven ways to trim spending and boost your savings.

Housing Expenses

For most people, the money that they spend on shelter is their single largest expenditure (or second biggest behind taxes). Everyone needs to have a roof over their heads. A common mistake is making housing decisions in a financial vacuum and not considering how these decisions affect your ability to achieve important financial goals. When you're thinking about purchasing a home (the term "home" is used here generically to refer to all types of housing, such as single family homes, condominiums, townhouses, etc.), you should look at your whole financial situation. Some people spend too much on a home, which then handicaps their ability, for example, to enjoy a particular lifestyle (such as more vacations, or scaling back on work) or to comfortably accomplish important certain goals, such as saving sufficiently toward retirement.

Doing a budget that factors in the housing costs of the home you're considering buying is a step in the right direction. The fundamental question is: Can you accomplish your other financial goals given the expenditures you're going to make on a home?

In addition to your monthly mortgage payment, property taxes, and insurance, consider other important costs such as maintenance of the home, commuting costs, and educational and other expenses for your children given the amenities and services of the community.

There are various strategies to reduce your home ownership expenses. The first is obvious: spend less on a home. What do you do if you already own a home that is stretching your finances thin? Many people think of their housing expenses as fixed. It's not true in the vast majority of cases. After weighing the costs of selling and buying, including taxes, you may want to consider a move to a less-expensive area or residence.

Another way to reduce your current ownership expense is to keep an eye on interest rates, and if they fall at least one percent from the level at which you bought, consider the costs and benefits of refinancing (see Chapter 10, "Borrowing and Debt Management"). If property prices in your area have been falling, you may be able to appeal to lower your property's assessed value and reduce your property taxes.

If you're a renter, you might move to a less-expensive rental or move into a shared rental. Living alone certainly has its advantages, but it is expensive. Also, consider buying a property. It may seem counterintuitive, but being a renter can be quite expensive. Think long-term: As a property owner, someday your mortgage will eventually be paid off. In the mean time, a fixed-rate mortgage payment doesn't increase over the years. Your rent, on the other hand, does increase with the cost of living or inflation.

Taxes

So you pay a lot of money in taxes. What can you do about it? Quite a bit, actually, if you get your finances organized and take advantage of the legally allowed tax breaks in our tax laws.

Reducing your taxes generally requires some advance planning. Making sound financial decisions involves considering tax and other financial ramifications *before* you make a decision. Don't wait until you're ready to file your tax return to learn how to reduce your tax burden. Please see the complete section on taxes later in this chapter.

Food and Dining

Eating in restaurants is costly, particularly if you're not careful where and what you eat. If you are busy, eating out can be a real time saver, and if you can afford it, certainly do so. Some people eat out a lot because they don't know how to cook, so why not learn? Cooking is a valuable and fun life-long skill and can pay big dividends.

When you do eat out, to keep costs down, try going out more for lunch rather than dinner, which is usually more expensive for a similar menu. Also minimize the alcohol, appetizers, and desserts, which can greatly increase the cost of a meal.

Regarding groceries, try to keep a healthy inventory of things at home. This will minimize trips to the store and the need to dine out for lack of options at home. Try to do most of your shopping through discount warehouse-type stores, which offer low prices for buying in bulk, or grocery stores that offer bulk purchases. If you live alone, don't be deterred—find a friend to share the large purchases with you.

Eating healthier, fresher, unprocessed, and more organic foods can seem to cost more. But it really doesn't when you factor in the more nutritious value you get and the long-term health benefits and reduced health problems.

Autos and Transportation

Cars can be major money pits. While you probably want a car that is safe and comfortable, you need to buy a car within your financial means. (For much more on the important topic of auto safety, please see Chapter 16, "Managing Risks Involves More Than Buying Insurance.")

When you buy a car, research what the car is worth. The dealer mark-up, especially on new cars, can be substantial. Numerous publications and services such as *Consumer Reports* provide this information. Before you purchase, also consider insurance costs of the different makes and models you're considering. Call auto insurers to shop for insurance quotes, as rates vary greatly and should factor into your decision.

Avoid taking an auto loan or lease. The seemingly reasonable monthly payment of loans and leases deludes people into spending more than they can really afford. In the long-term, paying with cash should be cheaper.

Also take a hard look at whether you need a car or as many cars as you think you need. Although living in a particular community may appear to save you money, it may not if it requires you to have a car because of the lack of public transit or the distance from work. Financial advisor Michael Terry tells me of a big city-based client who was offered a "great deal" on a car through work and was hot to buy it. After he showed her the cost of owning a car in the city (insurance, garage, etc.), she considered that she would only use the car on weekends and not every weekend. For what she was going to be paying, Terry figured she could rent a Mercedes every weekend and still have lots of money left over, so she decided not to buy the car.

Recreation and Entertainment

Often, spending money is equated with having fun. Many commercials and sales pitches (even game shows) imply this. Get rid of this mindset. Spending a lot of money isn't fun if it leads you into debt. Spending a lot of money that you don't have on an expensive vacation, for example, can lead to unrealistically high expectations and disappointment—especially when the credit card bill arrives.

Think of ways to substitute activities to reduce spending without reducing your enjoyment. Exchange invitations with friends to cook dinner at home rather than going out to restaurants. Find friends to visit when you travel. Attend a matinee movie instead of one during the high-priced evening hours.

Many of the most enjoyable things in life—time spent with family and friends, outdoor activities, etc., don't have to cost much or even any money at all. Be creative and take advantage of these.

Clothing

Avoid the temptation to buy new clothes for a new season, or to use shopping as a hobby. If you enjoy the visual stimulation, go window shopping and leave all checks and credit cards at home. (Carrying a small amount of cash is fine!) Avoid fashions that are trendy and that you will not wear after the trend moves on. Minimize clothing that requires dry cleaning, which is costly and exposes your body to unnecessary and unhealthy chemicals.

If you have old clothing that you absolutely refuse to wear anymore, make a donation to a charity such as Goodwill or the Salvation Army. Ask for a receipt and take a write-off on your tax return if you itemize. (See the section on taxes later in this chapter.)

Utility Bills

Check out opportunities to make your home more energy efficient. Adding insulation and weather-stripping, installing water-saving devices, and reducing use of electrical appliances can pay for themselves in short order. Many utility companies will even do a free energy review or audit of your home and suggest money-saving ideas.

Thanks to tax law changes, you may qualify for "Residential Energy Credits," which reduce your tax bill (see IRS Form 5695). Energy improvements that may be eligible for this new credit include things such as adding insulation, installing energy-efficient windows and doors, installing solar panels, and so on.

Insurance

Insurance fills a vital and useful role. You don't want to be in the position of absorbing a financial catastrophe. That's why, for example, you want adequate homeowner's and health insurance. If your home burns down or you have a major illness or accident, it could ruin you financially if you don't have proper insurance.

If you're dependent on your employment income, long-term disability protection is a necessity. Purchase term life insurance if others are financially dependent on your income. This is critical during your working years when you may have significant financial obligations, such as a mortgage and young children to raise.

On the other hand, there's no need to waste money on insurance. Many people overspend on insurance by carrying coverage that's unnecessary or that covers small potential losses. Coverage of small losses, such as $100 or $200, is not useful for most people since such a loss wouldn't be a financial catastrophe. Take high deductibles on your insurance policies—as much as you can afford in the event of a loss. If you are no longer dependent on your employment income and have sufficient financial resources to retire, there's no need to continue paying for disability insurance.

Also, be sure to shop around. Rates vary tremendously among insurers. Of course, an insurers' quality of service and financial stability are important as well. Ask insurers and agents selling policies to provide financial ratings for the company's policies you're considering. State departments of insurance—you can find links to their web sites at http://www.naic.org/state_web_map.htm—also compile complaints filed against insurers. (Please see Chapters 15 through 17 for more on smart insurance decisions.)

Kid-Related Expenses

Children don't come cheaply, but they also need not break the bank. Child care is often a major expense for parents of young kids. For some people, this is a necessity; for others, this is a choice. While there are certainly many reasons to work, check that your analysis of what you earn and what you spend on child care makes sense. How much of that extra income do you keep after factoring in taxes, commuting, and the other "costs" of that extra income?

Another challenge for parents is distinguishing between necessities and luxuries for the kids, who inevitably think everything they want is a necessity. More toys are not necessarily better. Share with your children the realities of your family's finances—this will help them to learn about financial responsibility and obligations and why you can't purchase every item advertised on TV. (For more on these issues, see Chapter 6, "Families and Money.")

Charitable Contributions

Many worthy charities and non-profits provide important and vital services that otherwise would not be available. Deciding how much and to which organizations you would like to contribute are personal decisions.

Your charitable contributions are part of your budget, and as such, should be reviewed. Did you know that Americans are among the most giving people on Earth? Can you afford the amount that you are contributing? Maybe you can afford more. Perhaps you're at a stage of life where you should give less. Again, the decision is yours—just give it some extra consideration!

Reducing Your Taxes

Federal, state, and local income taxes take a huge bite out of most peoples' income. So don't forget to consider taxes in the process of budgeting and planning your financial future.

Your taxes are not fixed. There's no reason that you can't utilize some of the simple and legal strategies to reduce your tax burden. First, it helps to know what your current tax rate is—most people don't. Taxes have a major impact on most major financial decisions such as investing, retirement planning, and real estate purchases. If you make these sorts of financial decisions without understanding and factoring in taxes, you're probably paying a lot more in taxes than you need to be. Understanding the tax implications might also cause you to take a different course of action.

You should know your tax rate for the simple reason that your tax rate should factor into many of your important personal financial decisions.

You pay income taxes on what's known as your "taxable income." This is simply the sum of your income, including from employment and investments, minus your allowable deductions.

If you pull out your tax return from last year or track your tax payments (check your paystubs and record of quarterly tax filings with the IRS), you can quickly figure the total taxes that you paid in a given year. Although it's enlightening to know the total income taxes you paid, this number alone won't help you make financial decisions.

A more useful tax number to know, which people are less likely to know, is their marginal income tax rate. This is the rate of income tax that you are paying on your last dollars of income. Many people don't realize that the income tax system is structured such that you pay a lower rate of tax on your first dollars of income. As your earnings increase, you pay higher rates of tax on your income but only on your income above certain threshold amounts. These brackets are transparent to you throughout the year since you pay tax at a steady rate based on your total expected income for the year.

Here are the tax brackets for the two most common filing categories: single people and married couples who file jointly.

2007 Federal Income Tax Brackets
Single Filers

Taxable Income			Tax Rate
$0	to	$7,825	10%
$7,825	to	$31,850	15%
$31,850	to	$77,100	25%
$77,100	to	$160,850	28%
$160,850	to	$349,700	33%
Over $349,700			35%

Married Filing Jointly

Taxable Income			Tax Rate
$0	to	$15,650	10%
$15,650	to	$63,700	15%
$63,700	to	$128,500	25%
$128,500	to	$195,850	28%
$195,850	to	$349,700	33%
Over $349,700			35%

In addition to federal taxes, most states have a state income tax. As you're considering your marginal income tax rate, count both federal and state income taxes. You can find your state income tax bracket in the booklet provided by your state containing the state tax forms. Alternatively, you can contact the state agency responsible for administering your state income tax—use the links at the web site www.taxsites.com/state.html or check the state government pages of your local phone directory or call toll-free information (800-555-1212).

Using Your Tax Rate

Knowing your marginal income tax rate allows you to assess the tax impact of various financial decisions. Suppose you're thinking about buying a home. You're concerned (or should be concerned!) about how owning a home will affect your monthly budget. In addition to your mortgage payment, you know that you'll owe property taxes, home-owner's insurance, as well as maintenance expenses.

With property in the United States, the cost of owning a home may seem much more expensive than renting if you total up your monthly housing expenses and compare these to the cost of renting. However, the tax benefits of home ownership change this comparison a great deal.

The mortgage interest and property taxes on your home are generally tax-deductible (on Schedule A as an "itemized deduction"). These home ownership tax breaks effectively lower the cost of home ownership.

How do you figure the potential tax savings of owning a home? A shortcut method is to take your marginal tax rate and multiply it by your expected tax deduction for mortgage interest and property taxes.

Suppose, for example, that you want to compare your current rent of $1,200 per month to the cost of owning a similar property and that your estimated ownership costs are as follows:

Mortgage	$1330
(assumes $200K mortgage @ 7 percent)	
+ Property Taxes	$250
+ Insurance	$90
+ Maintenance	$250
= Total Cost (pre-tax)	$1920
− Tax Savings	$500
= Total Cost (after-tax)	$1420

Note: This example assumes a combined marginal federal and state tax bracket of 33 percent. The comparison obviously depends on your tax situation, as well as the cost of purchasing versus renting the property in question. If you want to know more precisely how your taxes change with a home purchase or any other major financial decision, you may want to plug your assumed numbers into an actual tax form or use the tax planning module in a good software package such as TurboTax.

You can see in this example that the cost of buying a home for a quarter of a million dollars (compared to just $1,200 monthly rent) doesn't sound so bad on a monthly basis after factoring in tax savings ($1,420). With a fixed rate mortgage, most of your housing expense (mortgage) won't increase, but your rent will rise with inflation over the years. (See Chapter 10 for more on borrowing for home purchases.)

You pay taxes when you earn income from employment or from most investments held outside retirement accounts, and when you purchase many goods. The simplest and most powerful way to reduce the tax bite in your budget is to spend less (which saves you money on sales taxes) and invest what you save in a tax-advantaged way.

The single best way for all wage earners to reduce their taxable income is to contribute to retirement accounts, such as 401(k), 403(b), SEP-IRA, or Keogh accounts. Contributions to these accounts are generally free of federal and state tax. Thus, in the year of the contribution, you save on federal and state taxes. Taxes are owed when you withdraw the money, probably in retirement. Therefore, the prime advantage of these accounts is that, over many years, you get to hold onto and invest money that would otherwise go to taxes. You may also benefit if, like most people, you are in a lower income bracket in retirement. Even if your tax bracket doesn't decrease in your golden years, retirement accounts should still save you on taxes. (See the retirement planning section in Chapter 4, "Developing Your Personal Financial Action Plan.")

Two simple but important prerequisites prevent many people from taking advantage of this terrific tax break. First, you need to spend less than you earn so that you can "afford" to fund your account(s). You certainly don't want to contribute to retirement accounts if you are accumulating debt on a credit card, for example. Many people need to reduce their spending before being able to take advantage of a retirement savings plan.

The second obstacle to funding a retirement account is having access to one. Some employers don't offer retirement savings plans. If yours doesn't, lobby the benefits department and consider other employers who offer this valuable benefit. If you're self-employed, you may establish your own plan—typically a SEP-IRA or Keogh.

Married couples filing jointly who have adjusted gross incomes (AGIs) of less than $50,000 and single taxpayers with AGIs of less than $25,000 can qualify for a special tax credit for retirement account contributions. The credit can be for up to 50 percent of $2,000 contributed to a retirement account.

Whenever you invest money outside a retirement account, you should weigh the potential tax consequences. Income produced from your investments is exposed to taxation. In matters of financial health, remember that it matters not what you make but what you get to keep.

Suppose you are considering two investments. The first is a traditional bank savings account that is paying, say, 4 percent. Another alternative you are considering is a tax-free money market fund. Although this investment option pays less—3 percent—this return is federal and state tax-free. Which investment should you choose?

The answer depends on your tax bracket. The savings account pays 4 percent, but this interest is fully taxable. If, between federal and state income taxes, you pay 30 percent, then you don't get to keep the 4 percent interest. *After* paying taxes, you'll end up with just 2.8 percent.

Now compare this 2.8 percent after-tax rate of interest to the 3 percent tax-free money market fund yield. The tax-free money market fund provides you with more to keep. If you were in a low tax bracket, however, the savings account could be a better deal.

In addition to savings and money market accounts, bonds also come in tax-free and taxable interest versions. If you're in a higher tax bracket, tax-free bonds may be preferable.

Another issue to consider when investing non-retirement money is capital gains taxes. If you sell an investment held outside a retirement account at a higher price than what you purchased it for, you will owe tax on the profit, known as a capital gain. The tax rates for capital gains work a bit differently than on regular income.

Long-term capital gains—that is, for investments held for at least one year—are taxed at a maximum 15 percent by the IRS, even if you're in a higher income tax bracket. Losses from selling securities at a loss may be used to offset gains so long as the offsetting gains and losses are from investments for the long-term.

Short-term capital gains (which can be offset by short-term losses) on investments held less than one year are taxed at your ordinary income tax rates.

All things being equal, it's best to avoid investments and trading practices that produce much capital gains, especially short-term. Among mutual funds, for example, some funds, particularly those that engage in a lot of trading, have a tendency to produce greater capital gains.

In addition to reducing the amount of your taxable income, maximizing your deductions legally also trims your tax bill. Here are some good methods to consider:

➤ Check if you can itemize. If you haven't been itemizing deductions on "Schedule A" of your tax return, examine the deductions that you can claim to itemize. These include state and local income taxes, real estate mortgage interest and property taxes, charitable contributions (including out-of-pocket expenses and mileage costs), and job search and some other so-called miscellaneous expenses (discussed later in the chapter). The only way to know if you can take a larger deduction by itemizing is to tally them up and compare the total to the so-called standard deduction.

➤ Shifting and bunching deductions. If you have nearly enough deductions in a year, you might consider grouping together, or bunching, more of your deductions into one year. Suppose you expect to have more itemized deductions next year since interest rates are rising and you will be paying greater interest on your adjustable rate mortgage. So rather than contributing money to your favorite charities in December of this year, you might wait until January in order to qualify for itemizing in the next tax year.

➤ Convert consumer debt into tax-deductible debt. Interest on debt on credit cards and auto loans is not tax-deductible. Mortgage interest debt, on the other hand, is generally tax-deductible. If you have sufficient equity in your home, you may be able to borrow against that equity and gain a tax deduction to boot. Just be careful not to get into the habit of continually raiding your home's equity—remember, all that debt has to be paid back. Cut up those credit cards after paying off their balances with the home's equity.

➤ Own real estate. Mortgage interest on the first $1,000,000 of mortgage debt (and up to $100,000 of home equity loans) and property taxes are deductible expenses that you may claim on

Schedule A. These deductions serve to effectively lower the long-term cost of owning real estate.

➤ Learn about other legal deductions. A variety of other tax deductions may be claimed on your return, primarily on Schedule A. Most of these so-called miscellaneous deductions must total more than 2 percent of your adjusted gross income. For example, if you're searching for a new job within your chosen profession or field, you may claim job search expenses. Likewise, educational expenses that are required to maintain your current job or that improve your job skills may be tax deductible. So too are out-of-pocket expenses incurred relating to your job that aren't reimbursed by your employer. These may include subscriptions to professional journals and books, travel and entertainment expenses, and a home computer that is used for the convenience of your employer. Fees paid to a tax advisor and for financial publications are also deductible, as are fees paid for financial planning and investing advice.

➤ If you're self-employed, make sure to learn about completing Schedule C, "Profit or Loss from Business," and the many legal deductions you may take on that form.

Taxes and Children

You surely have enough challenges raising kids today without the headache of dealing with the IRS. The good news is that dealing with taxes for your children need not be complicated.

Your first tax encounter with the IRS as a family is securing a Social Security Number for your child. Your child must have a Social Security Number by one year of age for you to claim the child as a dependent on your tax return. Form SS-5, "Application for a Social Security Number," is available by calling the Social Security Administration at 800-772-1213 or by visiting its web site at www.irs.gov.

The IRS allows you a couple of different ways to defray child-care costs with tax breaks. First, through your employers' benefits plan, you may be able to set aside money on a pre-tax basis to pay for child-care expenses. Under current tax laws, you are allowed to set aside up to $5,000 per year on a "use it or lose it" basis. In other words, if the set-aside money is not used toward child-care expenses in the current tax year, you forfeit *all* of the unused money.

If you're not in a high tax bracket (e.g., the federal 15 percent bracket—that is, your taxable income is less than $31,850 for single filers and $63,700 for marrieds filing jointly), you may come ahead taking the "dependent care tax credit" instead. Each parent must work at least on a part-time basis in order to be eligible for the credit, and the children must be under the age of 13. (Exceptions are allowed if your child is physically or mentally handicapped.) Complete IRS Form 2441 to claim this credit.

Children have a unique system of taxation until they reach the age of 18. (After reaching the age of 18, all income your children earn is taxed as if it is their own and subject to the same IRS rules and tax brackets as adults' income.) Until age 18, kids get a bit of a tax break. The first $850 of income that children receive from investments is not taxed at all. The next $850 is taxed at the low federal rate of 15 percent. Everything above $1,700 is taxed at the same rate as the parents' tax rate.

Some parents and tax advisors are tempted to shift investments into the children's name to take advantage of this seeming tax break. Doing so may be a mistake, because of how the college financial aid system works. All things being equal, the more money that is in your child's name, the less financial aid she will qualify for. For more on planning a strategy for your children's educational costs, see the section on college cost planning in Chapter 4.

Quarterly Tax Filing Requirements

When you work for a company, your employer withholds money from your paycheck and sends estimated income tax payments to the IRS and your state. If you are self-employed or earn income in retirement or from other investments, you are responsible for paying estimated taxes to the IRS and your state on a quarterly basis.

You may contact the IRS (800-829-3676) and ask for Form 1040-ES, which comes with a worksheet that allows you to calculate your quarterly estimated payments or visit www.irs.gov.

If you run your own company, note that you are required to withhold and send in taxes from your employees' paychecks. This may include federal, state, and local taxes, including those for Social Security and unemployment insurance. IRS Forms 940 and 941 provide more details about these rules

---

10

Borrowing and Debt Management

"A pound of worry won't pay an ounce of debt."
—John Ray

"A man in debt is so far a slave."
—Ralph Waldo Emerson

People borrow money for many different reasons. Used wisely, debt can enhance your ability to accomplish your financial goals. When used for investment purposes, debt can increase your returns by allowing you to earn money not only from what you invest yourself, but also on the borrowed money.

Unfortunately, debt and credit can also be misused. When used for purposes of living beyond your means, debt can be a burden and hindrance to your ability to save money. (Perhaps that's why Emerson should have said, "A man in *consumer* debt is so far a slave.")

In this chapter, I explain how to assess when and how much debt makes sense for you to carry and how to manage your debt wisely and with as little cost as possible.

Ways to Borrow in Emergencies

Inevitably, unexpected expenses are going to pop up. So, what's the least costly way to handle these? The best way to "borrow" money in a pinch is to borrow from the First National Bank of You! Keep at least three months' worth of living expenses liquid as an emergency reserve. (See Chapter 14, "Your Investing Plan," for good places to invest this money.)

Beyond tapping into an emergency reserve, here are some additional ways to meet a short-term cash need:

➤ **Liquidate non-retirement investments.** Sometimes, people are reluctant to use their savings/investment money to pay for larger one-time expenses. Instead, you might be tempted to borrow money so as not to use or lose this money. Remember, however, that the growth of your financial wealth is driven by the difference between your financial assets and your financial liabilities. Odds are the high-interest rates you're paying on your consumer debt exceed your investment returns over the long-term.

➤ **Return recent purchases you can't afford.** If you're in a pinch and you realize that you can't afford some things you recently bought, return them. This would free up some cash to pay bills or meet other financial needs.

➤ **Slash non-essential spending.** Reduce or eliminate unnecessary expenditure such as for eating out, costly trips, memberships you're not really using, etc. See Chapter 9, "Your Spending Plan," for more ideas.

➤ **Borrow from family or friends.** Though easy to say and harder to do, borrowing from those who know and care about you may be a good bet. It's best to write up an agreement as to the terms, to ensure no misunderstandings. If you feel that there are strings attached, pursue other avenues.

➤ **Borrow from retirement accounts.** Some employers' retirement plans allow borrowing. The advantage is that this allows access to your funds without triggering a tax bill. Make sure that you can afford to repay the loan—otherwise, you will end up owing more tax. Remember that you saved the money in the first place for retirement, so avoid spending it now unless it truly is an emergency need.

➤ **Borrow through personal loans.** As a last resort, credit cards or other personal loans can be used. Be sure to shop around for the best rates.

Right Reasons to Borrow

Do you remember the first time in your life that you *borrowed* money? Perhaps you were in the school lunch line and realized you didn't have enough change to buy everything your little heart desired. So you asked a friend for a little assistance in your time of financial need. Odds were it was an interest-free loan that you soon repaid or reciprocated.

Why did you borrow the money? Ultimately, the reason we borrow money is to buy what we can't afford to pay for in cash today. Sometimes we may borrow money even when we have the cash because we have the money earmarked for some other purpose. When you purchase a home, for example, you may not use all of your available cash for a down payment. You should, in fact, keep some money reserved for emergency purposes.

Borrowing money, unless it is from a benevolent friend, costs you money in the form of interest. Thus, an important consideration is what the cost of borrowing is, versus the benefit you expect to gain. Some debt is worth incurring because it allows making a purchase that provides benefits in a way that exceeds the cost of the interest.

Consider the case of a high school student about to enter college. Most students need to take out a loan to help finance their college educational costs (unless the student is attending a low-cost institution or comes from an affluent family). A good college education costs a lot of money before the student has had much of a chance to earn any. The benefits of this education stretch out over many years after college, particularly considering the higher income college graduates generally earn compared to those without college degrees. Obtaining a college degree, then, is an investment in a student's future.

Borrowing money in order to invest and accrue future financial benefits is reasonable. For the following investment purchases, many people frequently consider financing part of the cost. All of these investments should be expected to increase in value over time:

➤ **Educational costs.** Quality education enhances your ability to earn greater future employment income.

➤ **Real estate.** Economic growth should increase the value of the property, and if the property is a rental, rental income should rise over the years.

➤ **Small business purchase.** If the company provides useful products and services and the company is well managed, the company's profits and value should increase over time.

The interest costs associated with borrowing for many of these investments is tax deductible. Compared with consumer credit, the cost of interest to borrow for these investments is also lower. With a home purchase, for example, home mortgage interest and property taxes are deductible (itemized on Schedule A of your Form 1040). With fixed rate mortgages now going for around 7 percent, the effective after-tax cost of borrowing money is just 4.7 percent for a moderate income earner who is paying approximately 33 percent between federal and state income taxes. With your own business, you may deduct the interest expenses on loans that you take out for business purposes. Interest incurred through borrowing against your security investments (through so-called margin loans) is deductible against your investment income for the year.

Borrowing for Home Purchases

If you hope to purchase a home, odds are you'll need to borrow money in order to swing it. Housing in most parts of the country is costly.

Financing a home can make financial sense for a couple of reasons. First, over long periods of time, real estate appreciates. As with the stock market, though, it's never a straight path higher. The health of your local real estate market goes through up and down periods that can't generally be anticipated or predicted in advance.

Second, once you own a home, the benefits of ownership and having a place to live "rent-free" last as long as you remain an owner. If you choose to someday sell, you'll have the equity to supplement your retirement income. (Or, you can stay put and live off of your home's equity through a reverse mortgage.)

As a renter, your cost is always increasing, and you build no equity. However, you may be able to save more of your income as a renter if you elect to live in an inexpensive rental. If you don't systematically save, however, you may not have much to show for the lower rent.

Owning a home certainly doesn't make sense for everybody or for every point in your adult life. Given all the costs of buying and later selling a home, it's usually a losing proposition to buy if you don't keep it for at least three to five years.

If you think you are ready to buy, the first and most important financial consideration is how much you can afford. When you borrow money for a home purchase, the loan is called a mortgage. The maximum size mortgage you may obtain from a mortgage lender is usually determined by a formula related to your income. Banks, the typical lender in mortgages, will add up your expected monthly housing costs:

➤ Mortgage (principal plus interest)

➤ Property taxes

➤ Insurance

(Be advised and be careful: Mortgage lenders ignore maintenance costs in their housing cost calculations, but you shouldn't in your budget!)

Most lenders will want your monthly housing costs to total no more than, say, 35% of your monthly gross income. So, for example, if you are earning $4,000 per month, your total monthly housing costs should not exceed approximately $1,400 per month.

Just because a lender is willing to allow you to borrow a certain amount of money to spend on housing doesn't mean that you should do so. Consider your other financial commitments and goals before you make the decision to buy a home or spend a particular amount. If, for example, you like to travel a lot and want to save a large percentage of your earnings so that you can retire early, you may not want to spend the maximum that a mortgage lender permits. Your home purchase should fit within your personal budget and your overall plans.

Your retirement planning goals are especially important to consider prior to purchasing a home. See the section on retirement planning in Chapter 4, "Developing Your Personal Financial Action Plan."

Choosing a Mortgage

Before you agree to purchase a home, you should give some thought to what type of mortgage you would like. Given all the different options and features available on a mortgage and all the various mortgage lenders, the number of combinations is mind boggling.

Before you get bogged down in these choices, let's start with the big picture. There are two major types of mortgages: fixed interest rate and adjustable interest rate mortgages.

Adjustable rate mortgages (also known as ARMs) have a fluctuating or variable interest rate and are more complex to understand. A formula that specifies an interest rate index determines the interest on an adjustable rate mortgage. For example, a particular adjustable mortgage's interest rate may be tied to the interest rate on one-year treasury bills plus 2.5 percent. Because the adjustable interest rate is linked to interest rate movements in general, an adjustable mortgage's interest rate (and your payment) will change over time. Because you, as the mortgage borrower, are accepting more risk, adjustables start at a lower interest rate than a comparable fixed rate loan.

As the name suggests, a fixed rate loan maintains a constant and level interest rate. The primary benefit of a fixed rate mortgage is that you know with complete certainty what your payment will be. Because the mortgage lender is locking in your rate for the entire 15- or 30-year term of the loan, you will generally pay a premium in the form of a higher interest rate.

Your first mortgage decision is whether you want a fixed or adjustable rate loan. To solve this quandary, weigh two important issues:

➤ **How long do you plan to stay?** Because adjustables start at a lower rate of interest and should remain lower unless interest rates rise, you would save interest charges and have lower payments in the early years of your mortgage with an adjustable. All other things being equal, the shorter the time period you expect to hold a property, the more beneficial an adjustable rate mortgage will be.

➤ **How much risk can you accept?** Because an adjustable rate mortgage can increase if interest rates rise in general, ask yourself if you can handle these higher payments. Make sure that your budget will allow you to accept the higher and highest possible payments allowed on your ARM. If you can't afford the higher payments or you can't deal with the psychological stress of volatile future mortgage payments, stick with a fixed rate loan.

Sometimes, prospective home buyers are steered into an adjustable rate loan because it allows them to stretch and buy a more expensive home. Be careful that you've taken the time before you close on a deal to fully understand what impact higher payments may have on your budget. You may be better off buying a less-expensive property if it allows you to better accomplish your other financial goals. Remember—you have to live with and be able to make the payments.

Beware that with some adjustable rate mortgages, while the underlying interest rate may change, say, monthly, the actual payment may adjust less frequently, such as once or twice per year. Therefore, if rates rise in between payment adjustments, your outstanding loan balance will increase (known as negative amortization) unless you make higher than required monthly payments. Avoid taking loans with this feature because you could end up with more mortgage debt than you figured you could afford.

After you make the fixed versus adjustable decision, you will sift among a number of other different mortgage options and features. Here are the most common ones you'll confront:

➤ **Points.** In addition to the interest charges that are the bulk of your monthly mortgage payment, mortgage lenders will also charge a one-time chunk of interest known as points. One point is equal to one percent of the loan amount. For example, if you're looking for a $200,000 mortgage and the lender quotes a loan that charges 1.5 points, that means that you will pay $3,000 up-front. While you may be tempted to think that fewer or lower points are better, it's not that simple. If you are willing to pay more points, the lender will lower your interest rate on the loan. On a fixed rate loan, for example, if you expect to stay in the property a long time, lowering the interest rate by paying more points may be to your advantage. Of course, your ability to pay the points with cash on hand is an important consideration.

➤ **Fees.** Lenders charge all sorts of other fees for items such as your credit report, appraisal of the property, and loan processing fees. Ask the lenders you're considering to itemize in writing the anticipated fees in your case. These fees, like points, are paid up-front. However, unlike points, they are not tax-deductible in the year of purchase.

➤ **Interest only.** In recent years, more lenders have been offering "interest-only" loans, which have some similarities to negative amortization loans. With an interest-only mortgage, all of the payments made in the initial years of the loan go toward interest cost—the principal amount does not decline as with a traditional mortgage. Then, when the loan does begin amortizing, the monthly payment amount jumps significantly, which can jolt your budget. I do not recommend these loans unless you completely understand the risks and downside.

➤ **Pre-payment penalties.** Some mortgage loans come with a provision that penalizes you for paying down or paying off your loan balance sooner than scheduled on the original loan agreement. Avoid loans with this provision unless you're certain you won't violate it.

➤ **Title insurance.** When you purchase a home, the mortgage lender will want you to buy title insurance to protect against the risk that the seller of the property may not hold legal title. This is in your best interest.

Refinancing

The two most common reasons people seek to refinance a mortgage (taking out a new mortgage to replace your current mortgage) are to save money and to opt for a larger mortgage. If interest rates decline, you may be able to refinance into a lower cost loan. Just because a loan offers a lower interest rate does not mean that it will save you money. To refinance a loan, remember that you will have to shell out money for title insurance, loan fees, and points all over again. With a lower interest rate and monthly payment on a refinanced loan, figure out how long it will take to recoup the cost of refinancing.

Be careful in calculating your refinance savings not to overlook the fact that you'll lose some of the tax benefits when your mortgage payment declines. You can't simply assume that the full amount of the mortgage payment decline is "savings." Use your marginal tax rate to calculate how much your taxes will increase if your mortgage payment declines.

Sometimes, home owners want to refinance in order to take out a larger mortgage. Perhaps you're considering remodeling, expanding your home, or need money to pay for educational costs. Borrowing more against your home can make good financial sense because mortgage interest is generally tax-deductible and the interest rate tends to be lower than on personal loans. Just be sure that you can "afford" the higher payments given your overall budget and financial goals.

A less-common reason to consider refinancing is to select a different type of mortgage. For example, if you're holding an adjustable rate loan and interest rates have plummeted, you may consider refinancing into a fixed rate loan. Be careful: It's difficult, if not impossible, to predict interest rate movements. A better reason to change the type of mortgage you hold is if your personal circumstances change or you've simply decided that you're more comfortable with a different type of mortgage.

Paying Off Debt Early

For debt that you incur to purchase a home, investment real estate, or a business, you may be in a position to pay off that debt more quickly than the loan requires. The question is, should you? The answer depends on several factors:

➤ What is the interest rate that you are paying?

➤ What else could you do with the money?

➤ How willing are you to take risk when investing your money?

A few examples will highlight how to think through the decision. Suppose that you have a loan outstanding that is costing you 11 percent, which is a relatively high interest rate. You've contributed fully into a tax-deductible retirement account and don't like taking a lot of risk with your investments. In this case, you should consider paying down the loan balance with excess cash that you have.

Take another case. Suppose that you owe money on a mortgage that is at an interest rate of 7 percent, a fairly low interest loan. You haven't fully funded your retirement accounts. You are young and willing to invest fairly aggressively. In this case, your best move is to simply keep up the regular payments on the mortgage rather than paying off the mortgage faster. You can slash your taxes by contributing more into your retirement account, whereas you gain no tax benefits from making larger than necessary mortgage payments.

Assessing Consumer Debt

List each of your loans/debt (not your first mortgage) separately. Not all items on this chart apply to all loans:

Loan Type	Debt Balance	Interest Rate	Monthly Payment	Month/Year of Final Payment
Home Equity	$ _____	_____ %	$ _____	___/___
Auto	$ _____	_____ %	$ _____	___/___
Tuition	$ _____	_____ %	$ _____	___/___
VISA/MC	$ _____	_____ %	N/A	N/A
_____	$ _____	_____ %	$ _____	___/___
_____	$ _____	_____ %	$ _____	___/___
_____	$ _____	_____ %	$ _____	___/___
_____	$ _____	_____ %	$ _____	___/___
Total	$ _____	_____ % (Avg.)	$ _____	

Strategies for Getting Out from Under High-Cost Consumer Debt

If you already have accumulated high-interest consumer debt through credit cards, auto loans, and the like, getting rid of it as soon as possible is vital to your long-term financial health. Many folks are in the same boat as you.

If you have accessible savings to pay down these debts, by all means use it. You're surely paying a greater interest rate on the debt than you're earning from your savings. The earnings on your savings are also taxable, while the interest on consumer debt offers no tax breaks. Just be sure that you have access to sufficient emergency money through family or through other channels. The only loans to consider going slow with repayment are those at attractive interest rates, such as lower-interest rate student loans. If you think you can consistently net a better after-tax return on your investments than you are paying on your loans, taking your time with repayment makes financial sense.

If you lack the savings to make your high-cost debts disappear, start by "refinancing" your high-cost credit card debt onto lower interest rate cards. Most credit cards allow you to transfer existing balances onto theirs. Then work at reducing your spending to free up cash to pay down these debts as quickly as possible.

Among banks with low interest rate cards are 5 Star Bank: 800-776-2265. Be careful with come-ons from cards offering low balance transfer interest rates. You will often find much higher rates apply if you make other charges on your card or if you miss or are late with monthly payments. Such fees are typically listed in the fine print.

If you've had a tendency to run up credit card balances, get rid of your credit cards and obtain a VISA or MasterCard debit card. Merchants accept these debit cards just the same as they do credit cards. Debit and credit cards look like and function the same way that credit cards do with one notable exception. As when you write a check that is cashed, debit cards are connected to your checking account. Thus, when you make a purchase with the debit card, the money is deducted within a day or two from your account. And, debit cards don't offer credit, so you can't spend what you don't have.

A final and "last resort" option for some people heavily into debt is to file personal bankruptcy, which can discharge certain debts such as those on credit cards, auto loans, and medical bills. If you found that your total consumer debts exceed 30 percent of your annual income, you may be a candidate for bankruptcy.

The drawback to bankruptcy is that it remains on your credit report for a minimum of seven years. If you already have derogatory information on your credit report, such as late payments or chargeoffs, however, the incremental damage in your filing bankruptcy is not that great.

A major bankruptcy bill passed Congress and was signed into law in 2005. Although this law makes it more challenging to go through the process of bankruptcy, it is still a viable option for people in over their heads with debt, particularly consumer debt. Please see my book, *Personal Finance For Dummies*, to learn more about your options and how to proceed.

> *"Credit buying is much like being drunk. The buzz happens immediately, and it gives you a lift... The hangover comes the day after."*
> —*Joyce Brothers*

Compulsive Spenders and Debtors

A wealth of recent research now shows that some people are compulsive spenders and shoppers. This concept is no great surprise to observers of human behavior, including psychologists, therapists, and financial counselors like me who've worked with people with spending problems. Academic researchers and mental health experts agree that for some people, spending money does for them what abusing food, drugs, or alcohol does for others. Compulsive spenders who invest a damaging amount of time and financial resources into shopping typically suffer from anxiety disorders, depression, and low self-esteem. Compulsive shoppers get a "high" from shopping and spending. These feelings of euphoria provide a distraction from and help bury (at least while they're shopping) negative feelings about themselves and their lives.

Compulsive shoppers tend to be female due in part to the fact that women do more of the shopping in households. Gender-related estimates state that as many as nine people in ten with this problem are women. Compulsive shoppers are typically lonely and bored and schedule their lives around shopping. When addicted shoppers hit the stores, they can't leave without making a purchase. They generally buy multiple items financed with credit cards, and in some cases, through repeated home equity loans.

Do You Have a Shopping Problem?

Compulsive spending can be a devastating behavior, but a misaligned mindset toward spending and shopping that doesn't reach that level can also severely affect your financial and personal well-being. Although there's no perfect diagnostic test to see whether you or someone you care about has a problem with shopping and spending, the following questions are a good starting point.

➤ Do you feel guilty about shopping?

➤ Do you argue with your spouse or partner about shopping? Do you hide purchases and/or receipts or lie about what you've bought?

➤ Does shopping reduce the time you spend with your kids, friends, or family? Do you use shopping as an escape from difficulties and unhappiness at home?

➤ Is your shopping causing financial trouble? (A certain level of affluence can rule out this particular result.)

➤ Is the shopping, spending, and accumulated debt leading to feelings of helplessness, anger, confusion, fear, or depression?

➤ Does the act of shopping and the accompanying interaction with salespeople give you a feeling of worth, importance, and control?

➤ Do you tend to accumulate items, including duplicates and triplicates of items that you never use?

➤ Are the costs associated with shopping, in terms of time and financial resources, negatively impacting your overall personal health and well being?

Debtor's Anonymous, an organization patterned after Alcoholics Anonymous, was formed in the mid-1970s by individuals who recognized that some consumers literally could not control their shopping, spending, and getting in debt habits. This organization has developed a series of questions to help identify whether a person is a compulsive spender. They say that most compulsive debtors will answer "yes" to at least 8 of the following 15 questions:

1. Are your debts making your home life unhappy?

2. Does the pressure of your debts distract you from your daily work?

3. Are your debts affecting your reputation?

4. Do your debts cause you to think less of yourself?

5. Have you ever given false information in order to obtain credit?

6. Have you ever made unrealistic promises to your creditors?

7. Does the pressure of your debts make you careless of the welfare of your family?

8. Do you ever fear that your employer, family, or friends will learn the extent of your total indebtedness?

9. When faced with a difficult financial situation, does the prospect of borrowing give you an inordinate feeling of relief?

10. Does the pressure of your debts cause you to have difficulty sleeping?

11. Has the pressure of your debts ever caused you to consider getting drunk?

12. Have you ever borrowed money without giving adequate consideration to the rate of interest you are required to pay?

13. Do you usually expect a negative response when you are subject to a credit investigation?

14. Have you ever developed a strict regimen for paying off your debts, only to break it under pressure?

15. Do you justify your debts by telling yourself that you are superior to the "other" people, and when you get your "break," you'll be out of debt overnight?

11

Investing for Bountiful Harvests

"Dollars do better if they are accompanied by sense."
—Earl Riney

An investment is something you put your money into, in the hopes of collecting or withdrawing more in the future. All money, therefore, is in some sort of investment, even what's put in "parking places" such as bank accounts or money market funds.

Sometimes people make the mistake of feeling as if their money is wasting away or not "invested" if it's in a parking place. They may rush to invest the money elsewhere with the hope of earning a higher return. Later, they may find that these seemingly more attractive investments were also riskier. The risk is that the investment can and sometimes does decline in value. Some investments are riskier—or more volatile—in value.

There's nothing wrong with taking risk. In fact, an investor needs to accept risk in order to have the potential for earning a higher return. However, some money you should try to protect and take little or no risk with it. For example, your "emergency reserve" money should not be in an investment subject to fluctuations in value. This money should be "parked" someplace secure and accessible.

There's also a risk in not taking enough risk. Take investing for retirement. In order to be able to retire, you'll need a certain amount of money saved. If the money you're accumulating is invested too conservatively and grows too slowly, you will need to work more years before you can afford retirement. So, in addition to understanding the different investments available, you also need to select those investments that meet your particular needs.

It is helpful to discuss the major dimensions on which investments differ from one another. First, investments may produce current income, typically in the form of interest or dividends (which are paid out profits to corporate stockholders). If, for example, you place your money in a bank certificate of deposit that matures in one year, the bank might pay, say, 4 percent interest. Likewise, if you invest in a treasury note issued by the federal government, which matures in two years, you may be paid, say, 5 percent interest.

Other types of investments, in contrast, may be more growth oriented and not pay much, if any, current income. A growth investment is one that has good potential to increase in value in the future.

Investments that are more growth oriented, such as real estate or stocks (investments in companies), allow you to share in the success of a specific company or local economy in general. The yield on a good stock from its dividend typically is well below the interest rate paid on a decent corporate bond, but some stocks do offer decent dividend yields.

Income-oriented investments, on the other hand, such as treasury bills, don't allow you to profit when the company or organization profits. When you lend your money to an organization, such as by purchasing bonds, the best that can happen is that the organization will repay your principal with interest.

Some other dimensions on which investments differ from one another include these:

➤ **Susceptibility to inflation.** Some investments are more resistant to increases in the cost of living. For example, the purchasing power of money invested in bonds that pay a fixed rate of interest can be eroded by a rise in inflation. By contrast, the value of investments, such as real estate, and precious metals, such as gold and silver, often benefit from higher inflation. Especially when investing for longer periods of time, it's important to diversify your investments to include those that are inflation resistant.

➤ **Taxability.** Apart from investments in tax-sheltered retirement accounts, the interest or dividends produced by investments are generally taxable. The profits (known as capital gains) from selling an investment at a higher price than it was purchased for are also taxable.

➤ **Sensitivity to currency and local economic issues.** Not all investments move in concert with the health and performance of the U.S. economy. Investments in overseas securities allow you to participate directly in economic growth internationally as well as diversify against the risk of economic problems in the U.S. International securities are susceptible, however, to currency value fluctuations relative to the U.S. dollar. Because foreign economies and currency values don't always move in tandem with ours, investing overseas helps to dampen the overall volatility of your portfolio. Investing in U.S. companies that operate worldwide serves a similar purpose.

Financial instruments such as options and futures, also known as derivatives, are not investments. Most derivatives represent short-term bets on the price movement of an underlying security, such as a stock, or a commodity (e.g., farm products, precious metals).

Individual investors should stay away from these instruments. Professional investors sometimes use derivatives as a way to speculate or leverage their potential returns. The downside: A derivative holder can lose all of her investment if she guesses wrong. Used properly, derivatives are also sometimes used by the pros as a way to hedge investment risk. Proper hedging requires financial sophistication and costs money—so it's best left to the pros. Don't put money in these vehicles unless you treat it as gambling money that you are willing to lose.

Proven Intelligent Investments

Investments are often chosen out of habit, convenience, or inertia. Investing should be a proactive process based on your needs and goals. Only after assessing your personal situation, your concerns, and your desires should you select your investments, which will help you forge your way.

If you read or listen to the financial news, you've probably heard lots of buzzwords and jargon: blue chips, junk bonds, equity-income, hedge funds, municipals, ETFs, and so on. Among all the major securities exchanges where you can purchase stocks and bonds, as well as investment companies that sell myriad investment products, there are literally tens of thousands of choices. So, if you are confused and/or overwhelmed, there's good reason.

Forget, for a moment, all the different investment names you have swimming around inside your head. Imagine a simpler world in which you have just two—count them, one, two—investment options. The two major choices are lending investments and ownership investments.

A lending investment, as the name suggests, is an investment where you are lending your money, typically to an organization. For example, when you place your money in a bank account, such as a savings account, you are essentially lending your money to a bank for an agreed-upon interest rate.

Bonds, which are IOUs issued by companies, are another common lending investment. If you purchase, say, a five-year bond issued by UPS at 7 percent, you are in essence lending your money to UPS for five years in exchange for 7 percent interest per year. If things go according to plan, you'll get your 7 percent interest annually and your principal (original investment) back when the bond matures in five years.

With ownership investments, by contrast, you own a piece (sometimes all) of an asset that has the ability to produce profits or earnings. Stocks, which are shares of ownership in a company, and real estate are ownership investments.

In a capitalistic economy, individual investors build wealth through being owners, not lenders. For example, if UPS doubles in size and profits over the next five years, as one of their bondholders, you won't share in the growth. As a stockholder, however, you should benefit from a stock price driven higher by greater profits.

Students at the top business schools now pay in excess of $100,000 for a mere 18 months of education. Armies of Ph.D.s and finance professors have spent decades researching the financial markets and returns of different assets and the risks of those assets. The biggest insight from all of this work is that risk and return go hand in hand. If you wanted "safe"—as defined by lack of volatility and low likelihood of the value of the investment declining—you would have to settle for relatively low returns. Those who desire more attractive returns and who seek to earn investment returns well ahead of the rate of inflation must seek out investments that provide an ownership stake.

Investors in ownership assets have earned far superior returns over the years and decades than lending investors. Over the past two centuries, U.S. stock market investors have earned an average of 10 percent per year, whereas bond investors have earned just 5 percent per year.

The three time-tested ways to build wealth with ownership investments are to invest in stocks, real estate, or small business. Let's deal with each of these in turn.

Stocks

Stocks, which are shares of ownership in companies, historically, have produced returns averaging about 9 to 10 percent per year. To some people, such returns seem like chump change because they expect to double, triple, or quadruple (or more) their money in short order. That's why financial-market and magazine reports that focus on high-flying stocks are so dangerously tempting. Why wait seven or eight years for your investment to double, which is how long it takes with a 9 to 10 percent annual return, when some stocks double or more in less than a year? ("The rule of 72" says that if you take 72 and divide it by your annual return, that will tell you about how many years it takes to double your money.) Well, the reason, quite simply, is that risky investment schemes often crash and burn. Consistently saving a portion of your income and moderate returns produces awesome long-term outcomes.

Although some people are able to start their own businesses or achieve high incomes from their work, the best chance for most of us to build the wealth that we desire to accomplish our personal and financial goals is through systematic saving and investing. Consider that through the miracle of compounding, for every $2,500 per year that you can invest in a tax-deferred account returning an average of 10 percent per year, you'll have about $220,000 in 20 years and $1.7 million in 40 years.

Investing in stocks is one of the most accessible ways for people to invest for long-term growth. When companies go "public," they issue shares of stock that people like you and I can purchase on the major stock exchanges, such as the New York Stock Exchange.

As the economy grows and companies grow with it and earn greater profits, stock prices generally follow suit. Stock prices don't move in lockstep with earnings, but over the years, the relationship is pretty close. In fact, the price-earnings ratio—which measures the level of stock prices relative to (or divided by) company earnings—of U.S. stocks has averaged approximately 15 during the past century. While the ratio has varied and been as high as 30+ and as low as 6, it tends to fluctuate around 15. (It has been slightly higher during periods of low inflation and low interest rates.)

You can choose to invest in stocks through making your own selection of individual stocks or through letting a mutual fund manager do it for you. Researching individual stocks can be more than a full-time job, and if you choose to take this path, remember that you'll be competing against the pros. (Please see the section later on investing in stocks via funds versus picking your own stocks.)

Efficiently managed mutual funds offer investors of both modest and substantial means low-cost access to high-quality money managers. Mutual funds span the spectrum of risk and potential returns from non-fluctuating money market funds (which are similar to savings accounts), to bond funds (which generally pay higher yields than money market funds but fluctuate with changes in interest rates), to stock funds (which offer the greatest potential for appreciation but also the greatest short-term volatility).

Even during a successful mountain climb, setbacks occur. And so it is with wealth-building investments such as stocks. The U.S. stock market, as measured by the Dow Jones Industrial Average, has fallen more than 20 percent about every six years. That's the bad news. The good news is that these declines lasted, on average, less than two years. So if you can withstand declines over a few years, the stock market is a terrific place to invest for long-term growth.

One of the biggest mistakes that novice investors make is in trying to time—in other words, jump in and out of—the stock market. Market timing is difficult if not impossible to do, even for the best professional investors. It is far more important and valuable to save regularly and invest than trying to earn a few extra percent per year with market timing.

Consider two hypothetical people, Ms. Saver and Mr. Timer, who are each good at one investing strategy. Ms. Saver, as her name suggests, is a consistent saver and is able to save $2,000 per year over the next decade. Mr. Timer, on the other hand, spends dozens of hours following the financial world and is convinced he can beat the markets. Mr. Timer saves just $2,000 in the first year. Ms. Saver stays invested in the stock market and earns an average 10 percent per year return. Mr. Timer studies and trades in and out of the market and is able to eke out an extra 2 percent per year return (earning 12 percent per year). At the end of the decade, Ms. Saver will have accumulated $31,875, whereas Mr. Timer will have just $6,212.

Please note that in reality, few market timers can beat the market average returns and many actually underperform a "buy and hold" approach. The reason for the underperformance is quite simple. The stock market can move up quickly, and if you're sitting on the sidelines during one of these upward movements, you miss out.

Over the past 15 years, if you had bought and held a diversified portfolio of stocks, you would have averaged annual returns of about 11.5

percent. If you had missed out on just the 10 best days when the stock market went up over this 15-year period, you would have only averaged annual returns of 8.1 percent. Missing the 30 best days would have slashed your annual average return to just 3.1 percent!

So, not only does excessive trading lead to your possibly being out of the market on the best days and reduce your returns, it can also increase your transaction costs and taxes.

A simple way to stack the stock market odds in your favor is to minimize fees and commissions when investing. All things being equal, lower commissions and fees paid to purchase and hold investments increase your investment returns. With mutual funds, for example, load funds, so named because they deduct a sales commission from your investment, perform worse on average than no-load funds. Mutual funds, which charge higher ongoing fees (operating expenses), also tend to perform worse on average than those that have lower fees.

Real Estate

Investing in real estate is another time-tested method for building wealth. Over the generations, real estate owners and investors have enjoyed rates of return comparable to the stock market.

> *"More money has been made in real estate than in all industrial investments combined."*
> —*Andrew Carnegie*
>
> *"The best investment on earth is earth."*
> —*Louis Glickman*

The best place to start with real estate ownership is to buy your own home. The equity (difference between the market value of the home and loan owed on it) in your home that builds over the years can become a significant part of your net worth. Among other things, this equity can be tapped to help accomplish other important financial goals such as retirement, college, and starting or buying a business.

Over your adult life, owning a home should be less expensive than renting a comparable home. The reason: As a renter, your housing costs are fully exposed to inflation (unless you're the beneficiary of a rent-controlled apartment). As a homeowner, the bulk of your housing costs—your monthly mortgage—is not exposed to inflation if you financed your home purchase with a fixed-rate mortgage. A homeowner's property taxes, insurance, and maintenance costs do generally grow with overall increases in the cost of living.

Real estate investment decisions are undoubtedly the toughest ones to make. With all those digits in the sticker price, buying a home is rightfully frightening. But it's not only about all that money; it's the actual and implied commitment to establish roots and stay put for a while. Selling a home is no picnic either, especially since most people buy another home after selling. That's two transactions—double the stress and headaches.

Given ever-present economic uncertainties and worries and other issues in life we face, people often ask me if they should buy a house instead of renting or if they already own a home, they ask if they should sell before prices drop. My short answer is that it depends upon your local real estate market and your personal situation.

One of my favorite analyses to determine whether buying or renting is advisable is to compare the monthly cost of renting a given home to the monthly (after-tax) cost of owning that same home (mortgage payment + property taxes + insurance + maintenance – tax benefits). You shouldn't be paying a large premium to buy and own. If the (after-tax) ownership costs greatly exceed the rental costs, renting is a better value and ultimately may attract enough prospective buyers to weaken housing prices.

If you're a renter who has been thinking about buying, you're in a market that's already weak, and you're motivated to buy, you can probably get a decent deal on purchasing a home, especially if the rental costs of a given property are close to the ownership costs. That's not to say that prices won't fall further after your purchase. But you should accept the fact that none of us has a crystal ball and realize that once it's clear that times are getting better, the market will likely have moved higher.

If your local real estate market is just beginning to show signs of weakness, renting is a good value, and you have some personal ambivalence about buying, you should probably wait. Perhaps your job is at risk due to your employer's financial situation or the industry you're in. Maybe you don't wish to stay in your current geographic area for much longer.

Purchasing and then ultimately selling a home is a costly proposition. You've got loan fees, real estate agent commissions, title costs, and other expenses that can easily gobble up 15 percent of the home's value between the two transactions. That's why I suggest that you plan on holding your home for at least three and preferably five years. Expecting 15 percent appreciation just to cover your transaction costs over shorter time frames is foolish.

With regards to selling, if you must sell because you have to move, price your house realistically. If a locally softening economy gets you depressed because your house doesn't net as much as you expected, remember that when you buy, you'll benefit from the lower prices unless you're "unlucky" to be moving from a depressed housing market into a strong one.

Don't consider opportunistic selling—selling now and expecting to buy back in after a big price drop. Real estate prices don't generally plunge in a recession. It's also impossible to call the bottom (and the top). And remember all those transaction costs. Over the decades of your adult life, owning a home should be a wise investment. You've just got to accept some down periods along the way. The fact that you can't easily trade or sell a house for little cost is actually a good thing. Unlike the ease of selling stocks, homeowners tend to hold for longer periods of time and profit because of the longer-term appreciation of the housing market. (When you do sell your home, know that you can shelter up to $250,000 in profits free of tax if you're single, and $500,000 for married couples filing jointly. Should you be so fortunate to have profits in excess of these large amounts, you would pay a maximum of 15 percent in long-term capital gains tax.)

In addition to building wealth through home ownership, you can also consider investing in real estate that you rent out, often referred to as investment property. If you don't desire to be a landlord—one of the biggest drawbacks of investment real estate—consider investing in real estate through real estate investment trusts (REITs). REITs are diversified real estate investment companies that purchase and manage rental real estate for investors. You can invest in REITs either through purchasing them directly on the major stock exchanges or through a real estate mutual fund that invests in numerous REITs.

If you wish to invest directly in real estate, residential housing—such as single-family homes or small multi-unit buildings—is a straightforward and attractive investment for most people. Before you venture into real estate investing, be sure that you have sufficient time to devote to it. Also be careful not to sacrifice contributions to tax-deductible retirement accounts in order to own investment real estate. In the early years of rental property ownership, many investors find that their property's expenses exceed its income. This "negative cash flow" can siphon off money that you could otherwise direct into your retirement accounts to earn tax benefits.

Novice real estate investors often make the mistake of not thoroughly researching the income and expense realities of particular properties before they buy them. Inexperienced landlords also make mistakes when trying to rent their properties and end up with more vacancies and headaches than they expected. Thus, the early years of rental property ownership can be filled with unexpected losses, which, in the worst cases, have bankrupted owners who already were stretched thin because of the initial purchase price.

When selecting real estate for investment purposes, remember that local economic growth is the fuel for demand for housing. In addition to a vibrant and diverse job base, a limited supply of both housing and land on which to build is another factor that you should take into consideration. When you identify potential properties in which you might invest, run the numbers to understand the cash demands of owning the property and the likely profitability.

Small Business

A third way many Americans have built substantial wealth is through small business. The most successful small business owners generally earn the highest investment returns. More of the world's wealthiest individuals have built their wealth through their stake in small businesses than through any other vehicle. Small business is the engine that drives much of our economic growth. Most new jobs created are created in smaller firms.

You can participate in small business in a variety of ways. You can start your own business, buy and operate an existing business, or simply invest in promising small businesses.

If you have the self-discipline and a product or service you can sell, starting your own business can be both profitable and fulfilling. Consider first what skills and expertise you possess that you can use in your business. You don't need a "eureka" type experience where a totally new idea comes to you. Millions of people operate successful businesses such as dry cleaners, restaurants, tax preparation firms, and so on that are hardly unique.

Start exploring your idea first by developing a written business plan. Such a plan should detail what your product or service will be, how you will market it, who your customers and competitors are, and what the economics of the business are, including the start-up costs.

If you don't have a specific product or service you desire to sell but are skilled at managing and improving the operations of a company, buying a small business might be for you. Finding and buying a good small business takes much time and patience, so be willing to devote at least several months to the search. You will also likely need to enlist the help of financial and legal advisors to help inspect the company and its financial statements and put a deal together.

> *"Success or failure in business is caused more by mental attitude even than by mental capacities."*
> *—Walter Scott, psychology professor and former President of American Psychological Association*

"Safe Money" Investments

Bonds and savings type vehicles like money market mutual funds certainly have a place in your portfolio. (I'll help with allocating money among different investments in Chapter 14, "Your Investing Plan.") For money that you expect to use within the next couple of years or for money that you need to earn a relatively high current income from, bonds and money funds can make great sense. Historically, such investments have produced returns close to the rate of inflation (3 percent) to a bit more (5 percent for bonds) than increases in the cost of living.

While stocks and real estate offer investors attractive long-term returns, they can and do suffer significant declines in value from time to time. Thus, these investments are not suitable for money that you think you may want or need to use within, say, the next five years.

Money market and bond investments are good places to keep money that you expect to use sooner. Everyone should have a reserve of money that they may access in an emergency. Keeping about three to six months' worth of living expenses in a money market fund is a good start. Shorter-term bonds or bond mutual funds can serve as a greater income-producing, additional, or secondary emergency cushion.

Bonds can also be useful for some longer-term investing for diversification purposes. For example, when investing for retirement, placing a portion of one's money in bonds helps to buffer stock market declines. When investing for longer-term goals, however, some younger investors may not be interested in a significant stake, or any stake at all, in boring old bonds.

Investing in Stocks or Funds

Over the years, increasing numbers of investors have turned to mutual funds for their stock market investing rather than picking and choosing individual stocks on their own. There's still tremendous debate about the merits of these two very different approaches, and there are many, many sources pushing investors to individual stocks. Various web sites, financial magazines, and television programs advocate for individual stocks. You will rarely see a panel on a major network discussing good mutual funds, but you will frequently see debates for which stocks to buy and sell now.

Numerous private money managers bash mutual funds since funds are often their competition. Financial newsletter writers and book authors mislead investors into thinking that picking their own stocks is the best approach to investing in the market.

The principle arguments that stock-picking advocates make for going that route are the following:

➤ You will make more money.
➤ Most mutual funds fail to beat the broad market averages, so why settle for mediocrity?
➤ You can control tax-related issues, such as when you buy and sell securities and recognize taxable gains or losses.

Let's go through each of these.

Stock pickers love to point out examples of stocks that, had you only bought them many years ago, would have made you a gazillionaire. Who among us wouldn't have loved to have bought stock in companies such as Amgen, Best Buy, Microsoft, and Wal-Mart, which increased in value 30-fold or much more in the years and decades since they went public?

	Initial Price*	Recent Price	$10,000 Invested Now Worth	Annualized Return
Amgen	$0.10 (Sept '84)	$55	$5,500,000	32% per year
Best Buy	$0.14 (Apr '85)	$55	$3,929,000	32% per year
Microsoft	$0.08 (Mar '86)	$27	$3,375,000	33% per year
Wal-Mart	$0.05 (Aug '72)	$50	$10,000,000	23% per year

* Initial prices are adjusted to reflect stock splits and dividends.

Imagine if you had invested $10,000 in each of these stocks in the first month they issued stock. As the table shows, your total of $40,000 invested in each of these stocks would have grown to more than $24 million! The only problem here is that this is investing with a rear view mirror—20/20 hindsight! Plenty of companies that issue stock see their stock prices actually go down—in some cases to nothing if the firm goes bankrupt. And among the stocks that do rise, most price increases are far, far less spectacular than those shown in the table.

Now, what if you simply had invested $10,000 on each of the four dates shown in the table and earned an average of 10 percent per year on your money (the historic, long-term average for all stocks)? You'd have about $500,000. A far cry from $24 million, but a handsome sum nonetheless on just $40,000 invested.

Over the years, I have NEVER, EVER met an individual investor who picked stocks on his own and could tell me his portfolio's return for each of the past five years! If the motivation to pick your own stocks is that you think you can earn higher returns than a money manager running a mutual fund, you should calculate what your actual returns, net of all trading fees and after taxes, have been each year over the past five years. Once you've done that, compare your returns with those of the relevant market averages and those earned by comparable mutual funds. If you can consistently beat the averages and the pros, you're not in the right profession, my friend—become a professional money manager!

Now, it is true that most mutual funds fail to beat the relevant market index. There is a simple reason for this—the expenses, which on plenty of funds are more than one percent—place a drag on returns. Most of the studies I have reviewed on this topic typically show that over the long-term (10+ years), about 7 out of 10 funds underperform the relevant market average. However, that's *not* an argument for picking your own stocks! There's a simple and powerful way to increase your mutual fund returns—shun costly funds (more on this later when I recommend funds you should consider in Chapter 14).

In addition to stock-picking advocates, over the years I've heard many investment club proponents who cite the supposed superior performance of investment clubs. The National Association of Investors Corporation, which published the book *Starting and Running a Profitable Investment Club*, claims that their book will teach you, "…a method so successful that 60% of investment clubs outperform the market."

If this statistic were true, it would mean that investment clubs perform better on average than professional mutual fund managers! Using trading records from a large discount brokerage firm, Professors Brad Barber and Terrance Odean conducted a thorough review of 166 investment club accounts over a six-year period. They found that the average club actually *underperformed* the broad stock market average by more than three percent per year. Furthermore, they found that the majority (60 percent to be exact) of the clubs analyzed underperformed the broad stock market index. Also of interest was the fact that they found that the average club turned over a whopping 65 percent of its portfolio annually, which increases trading costs and taxes. Investment clubs clearly aren't learning that the point of stock investing is for the long-term!

An investment club from Beardstown, Illinois, got a book deal (*The Beardstown Ladies' Common-Sense Investment Guide: How We Beat the Stock Market—And How You Can, Too*) because of its claimed returns averaging nearly 24 percent per year, far ahead of the stock market averages of that period. Not until years after the club penned a best-selling book that claimed to have a system for beating the system did it come out that they only really earned a 9 percent annualized return, which placed its returns far below the market averages! So egregious was this situation that the book's publisher, Hyperion, lost a class action lawsuit brought on behalf of defrauded book buyers.

The Truth About Mutual Fund Expenses

One of the ways that stock-picking advocates seek to damage the reputation of all mutual funds is by claiming that mutual fund fees are outrageously high. Indeed, some funds do have high fees, but avoiding them is a simple matter to do. (See Chapter 14 for how to pick the best mutual funds and for a short list of recommended funds.)

One private money manager I know well routinely bashes mutual funds. His firm's salespeople, whom I recently spoke with (without identifying who I was and what I do for a living), made the erroneous and incorrect claim that Vanguard, well known for its low-cost mutual funds, offers funds that in the aggregate cost customers in excess of two percent per year including so-called "hidden fees." (It's actually just 0.5 percent!) This same firm claims that the average global mutual fund costs investors nearly 3 percent per year annually when all fees are included, including "hidden fees." (It's actually under 2 percent, and I should note that most global funds have high fees and should be avoided for that reason—more in Chapter 14 on this important point.)

All mutual funds are required by Securities and Exchange Commission (SEC) regulations to clearly publish their annual expense ratio in their prospectus. What's missing from this number are the brokerage/transaction costs that fund companies incur when buying and selling stocks for their funds. I would like to see the SEC include these costs in the annual expense ratios that fund companies report, but that's a separate issue. A fund's brokerage costs can be found in the fund's "Statement of Additional Information."

Private money managers who criticize funds for not including brokerage costs in their expenses make factually incorrect arguments and assumptions about funds' brokerage costs. One private money manager said regarding a recent article I had written on hiring a private money manager versus using mutual funds, "I believe you omitted one important fee component of a mutual fund. That is, the cost mutual funds incur when trading their stocks. For example, the Vanguard Morgan Growth fund has an expense ratio of 0.41 percent. With an average trading cost of 1 percent per year, the cost of ownership is now 1.41 percent, in my example. In our firm, I would suggest that the average fee charged for one of our managed account programs (managed by our firm research staff) for an account over $500,000 is 1.2 percent. This includes all trading costs, management fees, etc. In this case, we are then less expensive than the Vanguard Morgan Growth fund."

My response to this note was as follows: "Of course there are brokerage costs. No way, no how are they anywhere near 1 percent, especially at Vanguard! I hadn't examined these costs in a while, so your note got me to look into this further for the fund you cited—Morgan. It does annoy me these brokerage expenses are not included in a fund's operating expense ratio and that you have to hunt for it in the Statement of Additional Information, which I did for Morgan Growth. For the past fiscal year, Morgan Growth paid a total of $7,553,000 in brokerage fees. During that fiscal year, that fund averaged about $4.3 billion in assets. If you do the math, the brokerage commissions come in at 0.18 percent, which brings the fund's total costs to 0.59 percent.

And actually your comparison of investor shares of Morgan Growth to fees charged on your firm's $500+K accounts isn't fair. An investor with that amount can use the Admiral shares of Morgan, which charge just 0.24 percent per year. Adding 0.18 percent to that brings you to 0.42 percent—a heck of a deal, don't you think! Your firm's all-inclusive fee of 1.2 percent is quite a bit higher than that...."

As for control, it's true that you can exercise control over when you decide to buy and sell individual stocks and other securities. This is easier said than done and requires a lot of ongoing vigilance, analysis, and tax expertise, which few people have, and is costly. This is an issue for non-retirement account investing, and there are good solutions with funds that can be chosen with tax considerations in mind. (There are tax-friendly funds.)

Investing in individual stocks requires extensive research and time, if you want to do it well. When taken to an extreme, the time and energy some folks expend watching their investments can negatively impact their emotional and mental well-being, their personal relationships, and, in the cruelest twist of all, the performance of that portfolio they're lavishing so much attention on.

Carl installed new software on his office computer that allows him to follow his stock portfolio minute by minute. This enables him to constantly monitor his stocks during the trading day, and when a supervisor or someone else is nearby whom he doesn't want to see what he's doing, he simply minimizes that part of his computer screen. When Carl is away on vacation, he carries a PDA with him so he can receive stock price updates and alerts. After promising his family that their vacation would be "work" free, he constantly invents scenarios to steal away and check the stock ticker. He lies to them at the hotel pool, for example, claiming that he needs to go back to the room to get his sunglasses when he simply wants to check on his stock's prices.

Paul is a marriage and family counselor by profession. "I got overconfident with my stock picking. Some of my stocks soared, and I met with success in a previous company where I was responsible for choosing investment funds, one of which returned 90 percent in a year," says Paul. During a major down period for the market, Paul was "psychologically devastated" as he lost about two-thirds of the money he'd saved over the prior ten years. Paul's challenge was that his early investment success in a strong stock market led him to believe that he had the magic investing touch, which caused him to trade excessively and take risks. When the market reversed course, losses came in droves to Paul's poorly diversified portfolio. "I realized that if I was going to be a stock trader, I had to work at it full-time and be prepared anxiety-wise to handle it. I thought that I really had it all figured out. Now, I know I don't," says Paul. He is typical of investors who fail to do adequate research and incorrectly chalk up their gains to their own genius (rather than simply being in the stock market while prices were rising), which can lead to investing in things that they don't really understand.

Steven has an MBA from a leading business school, but his stock picks in the late 1990s, despite a soaring market, were faring poorly. "I'm embarrassed to say that I was buying stocks solely on the basis of friend's tips or using products that I liked," says Steven. For example, Steven's Apple computer had a Global Village modem that he liked, so he bought stock in the company, which soon went bankrupt. "I didn't do my research," says Steven, adding, "I was busy with my work as the executive director of a non-profit. I was being greedy trying to select small companies in the hopes they'd be the next Microsoft so that I could realize big gains quickly. It was exciting investing in risky stocks."

When I interviewed Steven in 1999, he was just gushing about Dell. He'd even call me back and go on and on about how wonderful a company and stock it was. At the time, shares were around $50, but they eventually plunged below $20 during the bear market, taking Steven and many other latecomers with it. Dell stock has not recovered and now, more than eight years later, is still down by nearly 50 percent from its prior heights. (Interestingly, Steven has started up his own mutual fund and is struggling to make a go of it. He is a smart networker and got himself onto a major television investing show despite his lack of experience and success.)

If you're going to buy some individual stocks, be clear as to why you're doing so. Invest no more than, say, 20 percent of your stock holdings in total in individual stocks. You should be stock picking more so for the educational value than because you expect to earn market-beating returns. Be mindful of the common mistake individual stock-picking investors make with being overly optimistic about company's future earnings, which is the single most important stock price determinant in the long-term. When investors fall in love with a company and its stock, they tend to lose sight of the harsh realities of competition and economic downturns.

Veteran planner Harold Evensky gives clients who are eager to invest in individual stocks the following "test" when they come to him with their stock ideas:

➤ Who is the president of the company, and what is his/her tenure?

➤ What is the single largest product/service of the firm, what percentage of the firm's net profit does it contribute, and what share of that market does the firm control?

➤ Who is the major competitor in this area, and what has that firm's growth been over the last five years versus the firm you're interested in?

Evensky says, "If they can't answer these questions, I say, 'don't buy.' No one has ever passed. Almost all fail at 'Who is the president?'"

Another problem that some investors have is getting fixated on a particular price for an investment. Often, this point of stubborn fascination is the original price that they paid for an investment (or it could be the value of an investment when they inherited it). When investors fall into this trap, they can lose their ability to objectively assess the merits or shortcomings of an investment.

The price per share that a stock trades for, in and of itself, is completely and utterly meaningless unless you know the company's earnings per share and other important financial information. A surprising number of investors, however, leap to erroneous assumptions about the attractiveness, or lack thereof, of a company's stock on the basis of the price per share. Some investors shy away from stocks that trade at higher prices per share concerned that they may be overpriced.

Companies knowingly take advantage of this human tendency by using stock splits to entice investors to buy their stock. This was a major mechanism by which grossly overvalued technology and Internet stocks continued to attract more investors. The wildly popular Cisco Systems, for example, split five times alone in the latter half of the 1990s! These decisions enabled the company to keep the stock price well under $100 per share and attractive to far more investors. Had the splits not occurred, the stock would've been trading at nearly $1,500 per share. Investors who snapped up the stock in late 1999 and early 2000 were paying an outrageous price-earnings (PE) multiple of more than 200. (During "normal" times, the overall stock market sells at a PE of about 15 to 20, whereas fast-growing companies typically sell at about a PE of 30 to 50.) The very next year, 2001, the economy tanked, and Cisco's earnings took a huge hit—dropping by about half. Cisco's stock got hammered—plunging nearly 87 percent in just over a year.

Internet darlings Yahoo! and Amazon.com also managed their stock prices in similar fashion during frenzied buying of their shares in the late 1990s. At its peak in 2000, Yahoo! reached $125 per share, but it would've been about $1,500 in the absence of its numerous splits in the latter 1990s. At its peak, its PE was an astounding 521! Yahoo's stock plunged nearly 97 percent during the bear market. Amazon.com's stock price reached $113 in 1999, but in the absence of its stock splits, the price would've been $1,356 per share. Amazon's PE ratio was infinite because the company had no earnings! Its stock plunged 95 percent during the bear market.

Stock-Picking Resources

If you want to research and invest in stocks of your own choosing, leverage off of good resources. Be aware that you will have to pay for some of these, unless you frequent a public library that subscribes to them.

Common to all of these recommended resources is that the firm's producing the research don't have notable conflicts in terms of performing paid services for the companies they are evaluating. Many brokerage firms, for example, produce research reports on stocks of companies from which they derive highly lucrative investment banking business.

Among the more cost-effective and quality resources of use to individual investors are the following:

➤ **Morningstar.** This investment research company follows more than 2,000 stocks of mostly larger companies domiciled within the U.S. In addition to a lot of data, Morningstar's stock reports include analyst commentary as well as a summary of what those who like and don't like the stock think are its strengths and weaknesses. An annual subscription costs $145 per year (www.morningstar.com).

➤ **Schwab.** If you are a customer at Schwab, one of the nation's largest brokerage firms, you have free access to its independent research, which has a solid track record, as well as the research from other independent firms such as Argus Research and Standard & Poor's.

➤ **Value Line.** This firm has been one of the longest-running providers of stock research reports. Its reports pack an enormous amount of information on a single page, and its rating system has a pretty good long-term track record. The software or print version of its reports costs $598 per year ($75 for a three-month trial).

My biggest caution with all of these research report sources is to be careful to not blindly use their numeric or letter grades (or suggested prices for buying and selling or price targets). Read and understand the reports. To learn more about analyzing and researching stocks, please see my book *Investing For Dummies* (Wiley).

Of course, investors with an inflated sense of their abilities make mistakes investing in funds—in fact, when investors turn to mutual funds, they have a tendency to make the same types of investing errors that they do with individual stocks. Too often, investors put their money into actively managed funds (and sometimes narrowly focused industry "sector" funds) that are currently near the top of the short-term performance charts rather than choosing low-cost index funds that will outperform the highfliers in the long run.

Develop an overall allocation plan among various investments (more on this in Chapter 14). After you develop your allocation plan, stick with it. Don't make knee-jerk decisions to change it based upon the latest hot sectors. Keeping in mind that the goal of an asset allocation plan is to develop a mix of stock and bond holdings to accomplish your goals, I know of no better way to accomplish that, with relatively minimal effort, than to invest in diversified mutual funds. These funds allow you to forgo the difficult and stressful process of picking stocks and deciding how much to place in various industries. If you're investing partly for fun and you enjoy researching and tracking individual stocks, earmark a portion—perhaps no more than, say, 20 percent of your money—for individual stocks. By all means, do your homework to identify good companies to invest in, but after you've identified a dozen or so companies in different industries, buy 'em and hold 'em for the long haul.

As another component of your long-term mindset, if you're going to invest in individual stocks or market sectors, de-emphasize or avoid stocks and sectors at the top of the performance charts. Think back to the last time you went bargain shopping for a consumer item. You (should have) looked for value, not high prices. For example, if you took the time to research and identify value stocks in the late 1990s, you likely found some terrific buys as the herds were ignoring many solid offerings to chase after popular growth stocks.

12

Cultivating Good Investing Habits

"Nobody really knows what the stock market is going to do. There may be some people who have some inside information about individual stocks, but they sure as hell are not going to go on television and tell you."
—Dave Barry's Money Secrets: Like: Why Is There a Giant Eyeball on the Dollar?

Saving money may be a challenge, but investing wisely and side-stepping dangerous temptations and habits poses other major hurdles. The best investing habits can easily translate into hundreds of thousands, if not millions, more dollars for your future. Equally important is the peace of mind that comes from feeling in control and understanding how to properly direct investments.

The best investors have a simple plan, do their homework, and maintain a long-term perspective. They also understand the vital importance of keeping the fees and taxes that they pay to a minimum.

Investing is clearly more complicated than just setting your goals and choosing solid investments. In addition to considering your goals in a traditional sense before investing (when do you want to retire, how much of your kids' college costs do you desire to pay, and so on), you should also consider what you want and don't want to get from the process of investing. Is it a hobby or simply another of life's tasks, such as maintaining your home? Do you desire the intellectual challenge of picking your own stocks, or are you content entrusting some of those decisions to others? Deciding how you feel about these considerations will shape your approach to managing your investments. Don't just ponder these questions on your own. Discuss them with family members, too—after all, you're all going to have to live with the investment decisions and results.

This section covers simple, yet powerful, principles that can maximize your chances for the best investment returns and help you sidestep common mistakes that many other investors have suffered through. Misery may love company, but being on the front lines of the school of hard knocks hurts financially. Why not get your education now and make the most of the future investments that you make?

Understanding Fees

It stands to reason that if you're earning, say, 5 percent investing in a money market fund, 6 percent in a bond fund, or 9 to 10 percent per year in stocks, the fees that you pay can be a huge drain on your returns. I've seen managed accounts at hotshot investment companies where you can pay upwards of 3 percent to have your money managed by investment professionals wearing designer suits and working in mahogany paneled offices in prestigious locations. Funny thing is, though, your money doesn't care if the people who are managing it are located on New York City's Park Avenue, Flatbush Avenue in Brooklyn, or Omaha, Nebraska. It also doesn't care how well dressed the folks are who are managing it. But even if you earn, say, 9 percent per year in a predominantly stock managed portfolio, paying 3 percent per year in fees is giving away a whopping one-third of your total returns.

Unfortunately, taxes can gobble a large share of your returns as well. You may find your pre-tax return of 9 percent knocked down to just 6 percent after taxes. So, a 3 percent management fee is actually sucking away half of your take-home returns!

Even if you're only paying 1.5 percent, what if you could pay 0.5 percent instead?

If you think that saving one percent annually in fees doesn't matter, think again! With $10,000 invested over 25 years, you'd end up with $22,000 more, saving just one percent in annual fees. So, if you had $100,000 invested, that would add up to more than $220,000 more, and with one million invested, a whopping $2.2 million more! That's why when I get down to the brass tacks of recommending specific invest-ment approaches and vehicles in the next chapter, I steer you toward low-cost, high-quality options.

Often, high fees go hand-in-hand when you work with salespeople. Some investors assume knowledge, competence, and ethics on the part of hired advisors if the person has an important-sounding title such as vice-president, dresses the part, and occupies plush, high-cost office space. But the fact of the matter is that such accouterments can just as often be leading indicators of a salesperson earning unnecessarily big commissions and fees siphoned from investors' dollars.

Additionally, placing too much trust in an "expert" can lead to laziness when investors spend too little time monitoring their investments and making decisions without doing independent research. Figuring that Joe Financial Consultant is an expert, some investors blindly follow him straight into bad investments (for the investor, not the commissioned agent) without ever questioning recommendations or analyzing their investments' performance over time.

Mary, an older widow living on a modest fixed income, was drawn to a bank salesperson pitching an annuity with a high initial "teaser" interest rate. She developed anxiety symptoms and sleep problems because of buyer's remorse. She was too proud and ashamed to ask for help with getting out of the annuity, which she felt was a mistake to purchase. Mary didn't need the tax shelter (and the associated high fees) of an annuity, and she would not likely keep her money in the annuity long enough for any small tax benefits to make up for its relatively high fees.

Nick and Joyce had two young children and knew that they needed to buy some life insurance, but they never had gotten around to it. One day, a salesperson, who was a friend of Nick's, called the couple at home and pitched them some costly whole life policies (which combine life insurance with a low-return investment account). Without doing any research or comparison shopping, Nick and Joyce each bought a policy. Due to the high costs, they got far less insurance coverage than they really needed, and they paid nearly triple what they should have for the type of policy they bought because they failed to shop around.

Monitoring and Trading Your Investments

One surefire way to increase your fees, taxes, and stress levels is to closely monitor your investments and jump in and out of your holdings based on the current news and your mood. I've seen time and time again that investors who are the most anxious about their investments and most likely to make impulsive trading decisions are the ones who watch their holdings closely, especially those who monitor prices daily. The investment world seems so risky and fraught with pitfalls that some people believe that closely watching an investment can help alert them to impending danger. Investors who monitor their holdings closely trade more and, not surprisingly, earn worse returns.

When asked, such investors routinely tell me that they watch their investments daily because they believe that doing so maximizes their chances of making smart moves. Many people are overconfident in their own abilities and knowledge, especially relative to others.

In a survey conducted by Robert Shiller of Yale University, consider how individual investors answered the following multiple choice question:

> When trying to pick individual stocks, trying to predict, for example, if and when Ford Motor stock will go up or IBM stock will go up, is
>
> 1. A smart thing to try to do; I can reasonably expect to be a success at it.
> 2. Not a smart thing to try to do; I can't.
> 3. No opinion.

A whopping 40 percent of investors surveyed chose the first answer! Lots of folks believe they can time the markets and know when and what to buy and sell.

In a study entitled "Boys Will Be Boys: Gender, Overconfidence, and Common Stock Investment" (published in the *Quarterly Journal of Economics*), Brad Barber and Terrance Odean found that men tend to be more overconfident, trade more, and earn lower returns than women. Their analysis of tens of thousands of brokerage accounts demonstrated that, "...men trade 45 percent more than women and earn annual risk-adjusted net returns that are 1.4 percent less than those earned by women. These differences are more pronounced between single men and single women; single men trade 67 percent more than single women and earn annual risk-adjusted net returns that are 2.3 percent less than those earned by single women."

And, when overconfident investors/traders start losing money, their judgment actually gets even worse. In a landmark study by Dr. William Gehring and Dr. Adrian Willoughby of the University of Michigan, researchers analyzed what happens when people make risky choices in gambling games and lose. Subjects who suffer such losses experience heightened brain activity symptomatic of distress, which caused them to be more likely to make knee-jerk and irrational decisions to try and quickly win the money back. Unfortunately, the Internet has aggravated the problem by enabling the worst offenders to track stock prices and news releases by the minute.

To add insult to injury (and give you yet another good reason to trade less), researchers have found a clear link between daily tracking of investments and poor mental health. A study published in the *Journal of Social & Clinical Psychology* reported that those who follow the stock market closely generally had the worst problems with pessimism and depression. Researchers believe that these results are due to the fact that such investors are closely monitoring a situation that *they have no control over*, and when things go against them, they get demoralized.

Remember the saying, "Ignorance is bliss." I'm not advocating sticking your head in the sand and ignoring your investments, but if you follow every little up and down, the down times will inevitably wear on you. The stock market inevitably goes through some extended down periods, and closely following things during such periods can be especially distressing and depressing.

What these studies didn't highlight is the damage done beyond the investor's poor mental health. Most of us don't have much free time, and if so much time is being devoted to tracking investments, the investors' personal relationships, family members, and friends pay the price too. In my counseling work, I frequently heard about these broader problems. Typical is the following complaint one woman made to me: "Every day, my husband spends hours on the Internet following his individual stocks. He says we have been doing well, but we never go anywhere or do anything together. This type of investing worries me."

If you consider investing to be your hobby, ask your loved ones and friends to honestly tell you if your perceived hobby has grown into something more problematic. If you're afraid to raise the subject because of what you expect the answer to be, then you probably already have all the information you need to objectively answer your concerns.

And take this test to see if your investing habits are problematic for you or someone you care about. For a period of one week, keep track of how much total time you spend monitoring stocks, including time reading about stocks, looking at stock prices, watching the financial networks, and conversing with other investors, including online chat groups. Compare this total to the amount of time spent during these days socializing with friends. (Work time doesn't count.) If the first number comes close to or actually exceeds the second number, that's a red flag.

Now, I know people who view investing as a hobby. Some belong to investing clubs, other people simply enjoy reading about personal finance matters, and still others relish the time spent researching and tracking various investments. We all have hobbies. One of mine is researching and learning about personal health issues. I consider my time spent reading about nutrition, exercise, and other health-related concerns to be a hobby because I enjoy doing it and talking with others who share a similar interest. I have no doubt that I benefit from my hobby (and I have evidence to back it up).

I raise the example of one of my own hobbies to illustrate a broader concern about hobbies crossing a line and becoming obsessions. In my own case, what if I spent hours every day poring over medical journals and reports, worrying about the latest conflicting studies, and constantly tinkering with my personal health practices, and in the process, I was neglecting my family, friends, and professional commitments? In that case, most sensible people would consider my behavior to be problematic and indicative of an obsession or fixation that far surpasses the "hobby" level. So, it's not just about how much time you spend at something, but it's also the *consequences* of that time spent.

I've come to define a successful investor as someone who, with a minimal commitment of time, develops an investment plan to accomplish important financial and personal goals and earns returns comparable to the market averages.

I know well from my years as a financial planner, lecturer, and writer that there are some people who have control issues with their investments. These folks have great difficulty turning over their money to someone else to manage—which is what you're doing when you invest in a mutual fund. In my experience, such investors prefer investing in real estate and individual stocks of their own choosing.

The rise of the Internet and online trading has created the illusion of more control and involvement. Now investors can watch every little movement of their favorite stocks and jump in and out with a quick couple of clicks on their computer's mouse. The advent of the Internet and growth of online trading capabilities spawned a whole new generation of short-term (sometimes, even day) traders. Interestingly, in other parts of our lives, a lack of self-control is readily acknowledged as leading to problems (like overeating, overspending, or overworking). But most folks have a harder time seeing how the quick and easy access to our investment money, which is highly valued by some investors, can cause problems due to our lack of control and lead to overtrading.

Chasing Hot Sectors

Some investors, feeling strength and safety in numbers, are lured into buying hot stocks and sectors after major price increases. We find it reassuring to buy into something that's going up and gaining accolades. The danger in following such a path is that you're buying into investments that are selling at inflated and soon-to-be-deflated prices. Sometimes entire stock markets (e.g., Japan in the late 1980s) get overheated, while, at other moments, specific industries are driven to excess valuations (e.g., Internet and technology stocks in the late 1990s). A herd mentality can take over at such times, as well as performance envy. We hear about and know others who seem to be getting rich easily, and this is especially infuriating when some of these people aren't likable or all that bright!

> *"There are only two emotions in Wall Street: fear and greed."*
> —William Lefevre
>
> *"In Wall Street, the only thing that's hard to explain is next week."*
> —Louis Rukeyser, former host of PBS's Wall Street Week

In the late 1990s, Harry, who had never paid much attention to the stock market, loaded up on technology stocks. We were entering the Information Age, and the new economy and the companies that were driving it—like Dell, Cisco, JDS Uniphase, Amazon, eBay, American Online, Yahoo, and Lucent—were growing fast. For years, Harry had heard of more and more people seemingly making millions off this sure-win trend. The only problem was that Harry hadn't a clue about how to value a company and its stock, and he also didn't recognize the risk of recession. When technology stocks crashed in the early 2000s, Harry became so frightened that he no longer invested *any* money in stocks after losing so much. He retreated into cash but then became tempted to try his hand at real estate since that avenue provided what he felt was more direct control over his investment.

If you take a step back and examine these soaring stock and sector situations with an open mind, you can come to the conclusion that the higher prices rise, the greater the risk that the investment will soon fall. But typical investors don't think that way. Robert Shiller, professor of economics at Yale University, conducted a survey of Japanese investors and found that just 14 percent were expecting a major correction at that market's peak in 1989, when Japanese stocks were selling at outrageous price-earnings multiples (the level of stock prices relative to corporate profits). By the mid-1990s, after most of the correction had taken place, when the Japanese market was down more than 60 percent from its peak and selling at *less risky* levels (versus the inflated prices of the late 1980s), more than twice as many investors (32 percent) were expecting a crash.

Developing Better Investing Habits

Investors, and people in general, tend to place too much emphasis on recent events. Before September 11, 2001, most people went about their daily lives and didn't think about terrorism. Post September 11th, far more people think and worry about the risk of terrorists striking again. The same simplistic thinking occurs with investments. Stocks and sectors that are doing well are usually expected to continue to perform. Likewise, many investors flee falling investments. Investors tend to get more optimistic as prices rise and increasingly pessimistic as prices fall. More often than not, investors make simplistic extrapolations of the past and fail to research and do their homework. This is why many studies have found that the average investor has a tendency to buy high and sell low and actually ends up earning returns lower than the market averages.

That's why I especially like admittedly rare company investment plans, such as select 401(k)s, that limit people to trading only a few times a year. (Once per quarter is common.) Instituting a similar restriction for your own personal investment accounts can prevent you from making emotional, impulsive reactions to current bad (or good) news.

Difficult times and market declines will occur. So, be sure to invest new money on a regular basis, such as monthly or quarterly (known as dollar cost averaging), so that you'll benefit from buying during market downswings. Also, consider investing in highly diversified, less volatile mutual funds of mutual funds (such as Vanguard's LifeStrategy funds) that hold several funds investing in stocks worldwide as well as bonds. (You must be careful investing in funds of funds to avoid those with extra layers of high fees—those that I recommend in Chapter 14, "Your Investing Plan," don't suffer from that problem.)

If you're the type of investor who is unable to mentally and emotionally withstand the volatility of riskier growth-oriented investments such as stocks and hold on through market declines, you may be better off not investing in such vehicles. Recognize, though, the "risk" you're taking by placing all of your money in low-return investments like CDs: You'll have to work more years and save more money to reach your financial goals or accept a lower standard of living.

While some investors realize that they can't withstand losses and sell at the first signs of trouble, other investors find it so painful and unpleasant to sell a losing investment that they'll continue holding a poorly performing investment despite the investment's poor future prospects. The late Amos Tversky, a Stanford psychology professor, and Daniel Kahneman of Princeton documented how people find accepting a given loss more than twice as painful when compared with the positive emotion associated with a gain of equal magnitude.

Because most investors find losses more painful to accept compared with the pleasure they get from gains, they often take on more risk holding onto a clear loser to avoid having to actually take a loss. Most investors also prefer to lock in a small gain rather than risk losing it while waiting for a larger gain. These tendencies can cause investors to hold onto their losers and to sell their winners far too early because they don't want the pain that comes with realizing a loss. University of California professor Terrance Odean conducted a study of brokerage accounts and found that the winning stocks that people sell greatly outperformed the losers that they hold onto.

According to investment manager Ken Fisher, when investments fall, some people hold on, thinking it's too late; then, when the market comes back, they have an overwhelming desire to get out at the point where they break even. "Even though there can be tax benefits, investors like to avoid having to recognize a loss and the humiliation that comes with it," says Fisher. When you sell and actually realize a loss, it's seen as admitting to your poor investment decision, an act that can be personally humbling. Other folks, including your tax preparer and spouse, may see what you did as well. (One way to "save face" is to say that you sold to harvest your losses for the tax benefits.)

As you research and follow your investments, restrict your diet of financial information and advice. Quality is far more important than quantity. If you invest in diversified mutual funds, you really don't need to examine your fund's performance more than once *per year*. This recommendation may surprise you, especially if you're an Internet-tracking junkie suffering from investment-information overload, but I assure you that I'm serious. An ideal time to review your funds is when you receive their annual reports. Although many investors track their funds on a daily or weekly basis, far fewer bother to read the funds' annual reports.

Doing so will help you keep a long-term perspective and gain some understanding as to why your funds are performing as they are and how they're doing in comparison to major market averages.

When you invest in stocks and bonds, you must accept the fact that there will be short-term declines, sometimes substantial drops, in your investments' values. This is never enjoyable. For inexperienced or nervous investors, bailing out when it appears that an investment isn't going to be profitable and enjoyable can be tempting. Some investors run to dump falling investments precisely at the times when they should be doing the reverse—buying more. For example, in 2002 and early 2003, the U.S. stock market endured several periods of heavy selling. After peaking in 2000, the market had already sustained a significant decline and then plunged further in the first week that it was open following the September 11, 2001 terrorist attacks. The events of September 2001 helped drag down the economy, corporate profits plummeted, and then the war in Iraq started. So, plenty of negative news was floating around, and it was too much for many investors who bailed out of falling stocks. Investors, though, who sold at the lows of 2002–2003, missed out on a 50 percent rally within the next year (and much more in the following years).

I can usually tell when a stock market decline is close to running its course. I'll see a peak in calls and e-mails coming in from investors worried whether they should sell before it gets worse. The worries almost always stem from things they've heard on the news: on the radio, television, online articles, you name it. Most of what the general news media reports on—murders, major accidents, bankruptcies, etc.—is negative and frankly depressing. And the financial media often follow the same prescription—sensational reports "sell." A steady diet of that is enough to turn you off to investing (and perhaps life in general) during difficult times.

I recently interviewed Bernard Goldberg, former veteran CBS reporter and producer. "A very high percentage of business stories are negative," said Goldberg, who is the author of *Bias: A CBS Insider Exposes How the Media Distort the News* (Harper) and *Crazies to the Left of Me, Wimps to the Right: How One Side Lost its Mind and the Other Lost its Nerve* (Harper). "Even when they've reported the stock market hitting new all-time highs in recent months, there's always a 'but' about all the negative things," he adds.

The Journal of the American Medical Association conducted a survey of the impact of the 9/11 events and feelings of post-traumatic stress. The study found that the people who were the most distressed, not surprisingly, were those who watched the most television. This confirms my experience as a financial counselor that the people most upset by stock market declines and the negative happenings surrounding such falls were those who listened to the most media reports.

A simple solution is to not track your investment values closely. Examine your returns over longer periods (months and years, not days and weeks) to help keep the proper perspective. During difficult times, minimize your exposure to financial news coverage. Tuning into the financial cable networks and listening to commentators dwell on the carnage around them on the trading floor won't encourage you to hold onto or add to your investments.

The key to effectively dealing with events that negatively impact your investment portfolio is not to panic. Slow down and pull back from stressful situations and news before making future decisions. As with everything in life, recognize what you can and cannot control. Don't waste your time or energy by closely following things that you have no control over.

> *"Grant me the serenity to accept the things I cannot change; courage to change the things I can; and wisdom to know the difference."*
> —The Serenity Prayer

13

Pundits, Predictions, and Confronting Your Fears

"Like the cosmetics industry, the securities business is engaged in selling illusions."
—Paul Samuelson

"Never make forecasts, especially about the future."
—Samuel Goldwyn

Too many people, in my experience, believe that they need some self-styled (and often self-serving) expert to predict what will happen with the economy, foreign trade, interest rates, the value of specific investments—you name it—in the minutes, days, weeks, months, and year ahead. You'll notice how short I kept the time frames here, and that's a big part of the problem. CNBC has done segments where in the middle of the afternoon, it asks floor traders on the New York Stock Exchange to pontificate how the market will behave through the close of business that day! The vast majority of the segments on television, especially where gurus proffer predictions, are generally confined to what is expected to happen within the next year.

With all these predictions floating around, too many look to these pundits to tell them not only what to buy, but also when to buy and sell it. Some investors accumulate personal portfolios that provide a history of all the pundits they've ever looked to for predictions! An even more significant problem are people who jump into and out of the financial markets based upon broad brush predictions for the economy, the stock market, terror alert levels, and so on.

Jim Cramer: Stock Market Maven or Uncalibrated Opinions?

Many pundits appeal to our fears and greed. We'd like to make more money by knowing and buying what's about to rise and dumping what's about to fall. That's largely the basis of the "successful" program *Mad Money* with Jim Cramer. By successful, I mean for the network CNBC and its host Jim Cramer, not for the viewers. Anyone who has done some channel flipping can't help but notice Cramer's flailing arms, loud voice, and crazed-looking expressions. I have watched his show on numerous occasions and had followed his career for years prior to his arrival on cable television.

SmartMoney magazine did a big article on Cramer in the 1990s, which purported to show what a great stock picker he was with the hedge fund that he ran at the time. The piece stated Cramer's supposedly high hedge fund returns. However, when I inquired, I learned that those returns were self-reported by Cramer. I tried on several occasions to contact his company and get more details and documentation, and my calls were never returned.

I have long counseled that you should never believe a claimed return unless it has been independently audited (the way that all mutual fund returns are). To date, I have never seen an independent audit of Cramer's claimed hedge fund returns, but I have found several sources that track his public stock-picking recommendations.

"A couple of years ago, they asked us if we wanted to be on the distribution list for their Action Alerts Plus online newsletter and they sent us emails for about six weeks and then stopped. Mark Hulbert sent them a reminder six months ago and they still haven't sent it," said John Kimble, Senior Analyst with the *Hulbert Financial Digest*, when asked about Cramer's online newsletter. *Hulbert Financial Digest* is the only independent organization that tracks the recommendations of newsletter writers.

There is a web site (www.yourmoneywatch.com) that (unbelievably) tracks all of the stock recommendations on Cramer's television show. The web site is operated by Michael McGown, who has been tracking Cramer's television show picks since July, 2005. Over that time period, Cramer's picks are up just 9 percent, which is far worse than the broad market averages. (Over this same period, the Dow, S&P 500, and Russell 3000 indexes are all up more than 20 percent.) His overall average with simply picking stocks that go up is pretty dismal. The most recent tally shows that out of 1,189 stock recommendations, a whopping 412 (35 percent of the total) have gone down! This statistic is all the more amazing when you consider that during this period, stocks in general were trending higher at a healthy rate.

Despite the fact that the stock market was rising strongly throughout this period, 106 of Cramer's stock picks dropped by more than 20 percent!

And 25 of them plunged by more than 40 percent, as follows:

LAB (LABRANCHE & CO IN)	−40.74
FDC (FIRST DATA CP)	−41.82
DXCM (DEXCOM)	−43.26
COLY (COLEY PHARMACEUTI)	−43.98
FDG (FORDING CDN COAL)	−44.53
VPHM (VIROPHARMA INC)	−45.32
PPCO (PENWEST PHARM CO)	−45.45
FLDR (FLANDERS CORP)	−46.13
TOMO (TOM ONLINE INC.)	−48.29
MRH (MONTPELIER RE HLD)	−48.40
WLT (WALTER INDS INC)	−48.58
ACV (ALBERTO-CULVER CO)	−49.59
TMY (TRANSMERIDIAN EXP)	−49.63
RMBS (RAMBUS INC)	−50.67
CHS (CHICO'S F A S INC)	−52.63
NTMD (NITROMED)	−52.68
XMSR (XM SATELLITE RADI)	−53.52
GEMS (GLENAYRE TECHS)	−54.67
OPWV (OPENWAVE SYS)	−57.70
HITK (HI-TECH PHARMACAL)	−61.69
BMD (BIRCH MTN RES LTD)	−62.08
CTHR (CHARLES & COLVARD)	−64.79
LEND (ACCREDITED HOME L)	−73.01
NBIX (NEUROCRINE BIOSCI)	−82.29
CPST (CAPSTONE TURBINE)	−83.61

CXO Advisory Group tracks the performance of many gurus' recommendations, including those of Cramer. They evaluated Cramer's regular column in *New York Metro* because, "…of its lengthy archive and manageable pace. We selected from that commentary all articles which address the future direction of the overall stock market, plus articles focusing on high-profile stocks and sectors." CXO then tracked the future performance of Cramer's recommendations.

CXO found that Cramer's picks (monitored from 2000 onward) were worse than average and even worse than simply flipping a coin. Cramer's picks fared better than the market averages only 46 percent of the time. Regarding Cramer's predictions, CXO comments that, "His predictions sometimes swing dramatically from optimistic to pessimistic, and back again, over short periods. It is difficult to infer his guiding valuation theory, if he has one. We wonder whether he tends to be swayed by the arguments of forceful advocates with whom he most recently interacted...He seems more a stream of uncalibrated opinion than a stock market maven."

When I documented Cramer's mediocre returns in my syndicated column in 2006, along with the fact that Cramer's organization, TheStreet.com, failed to return my phone calls seeking audited performance numbers to prove his boastful claims for his now-closed hedge fund, Cramer sent me a nasty e-mail and copied the top brass at CNBC on the missive as well. In it he said:

> "Your hilariously scatological take on me and my performance is only outdone by your colossal slothfulness and lack of intellectual capacity. I make all numbers available, in an audited fashion, to EVERY news entity that contacts me, in fact to every person that contacts me. Alas, though, you have to contact me, to get them. You can't pull them out of the ether."

I responded to Cramer's e-mail and copied the same people he had on his original e-mail message to me. I said in my message that I had contacted the media relations person at TheStreet.com twice and received no return call. And, I waited an entire week before running the column. I also pointed out that I had made a similar contact and request back in the 1990s and was also ignored. (At that time, I contacted his hedge fund numerous times after the *SmartMoney* article ran.) I noted that the *SmartMoney* article "performance numbers" had apparently not been audited, which I found troubling.

Regarding Cramer's claim that he provided audited numbers to every news organization that requests them, I said, "...since I now have your attention, I am hereby requesting them....Also, since I have never seen your 'audited' numbers published anywhere in the news media, could you please also cite those places where those audited numbers have been published?"

I never got the numbers, or any further response for that matter.

So, buyer beware of prognosticators claiming market-beating returns who have no proof of their supposed superior performance. Ignore predictions—unless you know the maker's track record and it's worthy of your respect!

Unfortunately, the news media has no shortage of nicely dressed, articulate lads and ladies willing to spout off and make predictions. That's how Cramer got his regular gig—he used to be a guest on CNBC and never was shy about his stock-picking opinions. The public fascination with talking heads is what gets the talking heads on the air, and it gets enough viewers to stay tuned in. (Rex Sinquefield of DFA refers to this as "financial pornography.") But in the months and years down the road, few will remember who predicted what. There's little, if any, accountability, and that's the beauty of the game for the market gurus—especially when they can falsely claim excellent returns.

> *"If all the economists were laid end to end, they would not reach a conclusion."*
> —George Bernard Shaw
>
> *"The economist can, of course, give us the facts. That is his job. He is a good cartographer, but a bad pilot."*
> —Vincent Massey
>
> *"In economics, the majority is always wrong."*
> —John Kenneth Galbraith

How Predictions Affect Investors

While it's a problem when people blindly follow predictions, an entirely different but significant problem is the paralysis and confusion some investors feel from all the talking heads and scribes. Carole was typical of clients who came to me in this situation. She was spending way too much time and energy consulting many different predictive sources, which reinforced her belief that she didn't know what she was doing. When Carole came to see me for financial advice, she was a medical professional earning about $60,000 annually. Single and in her late thirties, she rented a modest apartment and had a $100,000 sum from her own savings and some inheritance. Eager to learn more about money, she read financial publications and attended seminars, but she still confided in me that she felt as if she never really understood "what's going on with money." I learned that her father had made her major financial decisions over the years but died a few years earlier, leaving her alone and with even more money to manage.

As Carole described her work, she spoke confidently and without hesitation. When our conversation turned to money, however, her self-assured aura cracked as she nervously fidgeted in her chair. While she desired to cut back on full-time work by her fifties, she disliked "risky investments." Making choices froze her, and she kept her money invested in a bank account and some bonds that a broker sold to her and she didn't understand. Her lack of knowledge was further highlighted by the fact that the bonds were being called (paid off early— before the planned maturity); she had no idea that such a thing could happen and wasn't even clear what it meant.

Like so many of the people who came to me for financial counseling, Carole knew the importance of living within her means, making wise investments, and securing proper insurance. However, a number of barriers hampered her attempts to make sound financial decisions. The greatest obstacle was that Carole was convinced that managing her money was beyond her capabilities. When she wrote down all the reasons why she couldn't make sound investing decisions, it became clear that many of her statements, and the beliefs that they reflected, came from what her father had told her over the years.

I put her on a financial news diet, an approach I often advise folks to take when they're on investment-information overload. We reviewed everything that she was reading and listening to and pared down the list by about three-quarters. Instead of plugging into the financial-news free-for-all, Carole enrolled in the personal financial management course that I used to teach at the University of California. In addition to reading quality investing books, she also performed various investment exercises (you'll do this as well in Chapter 14, "Your Investing Plan") that steadily built her confidence and financial acumen while helping to deprogram the self-doubts she had accumulated through her father's influence. Carole began investing a small portion of her money in highly diversified funds that included bonds and stocks to get her feet wet and gain confidence with slightly riskier investments than she was used to that would allow her money to grow.

Stock Market Predictions of People in High Places

Whenever someone rich and powerful predicts what the stock market will do, such calls tend to get a lot of attention and more weight than they deserve from individual investors. Consider these predictions and comments about the stock market at the very top of the market as the Great Depression and stock market crash were beginning:

> *"Stock prices have reached what looks like a permanently high plateau."*
> *—Irving Fisher*

> *"Believing that fundamental conditions of the country are sound…my son and I have for some days been purchasing sound common stocks."*
> *—John D. Rockefeller*

> *"Those who voluntarily sell stocks at current prices are extremely foolish."*
> *—Owen Young*

Clearly, these men were wrong—very wrong! In less than three years, the U.S. stock market dropped by more than 80 percent.

And then there was President Richard Nixon's call in 1970, "Frankly, if I had any money, I'd be buying stocks right now." More than a decade later, U.S. stocks had treaded water and were at the same level.

Addressing Investing Fears

While different people follow pundit's predictions for differing reasons, many people do so because they not only would like to get rich and get rich quicker, but also because they are fearful and would like to believe that prognosticators will save them from bad things.

Helping people overcome their stock investing fears and worries, whether they were the product of a lack of experience or bad experience, was one of my challenges as a financial advisor. When we're young, we learn (sometimes the hard way) not to touch a hot stove or to lean back in our chair. Self-inflicted pain from easily avoidable behavior is a powerful teacher.

After a major market slide like the one we had in the early 2000s (U.S. stocks slid about 50 percent over three years), it's understandable on one level why some people decided that they don't want to have anything to do with stocks. In the years leading up to the market peak in the spring of 2000, investors snapped up stocks and shunned bonds. (Some believed that the Internet had created a new paradigm where profits and price-earnings ratios didn't matter and that stocks could continue soaring.) Three years later, many investors were doing just the opposite—dumping their beaten-down stocks and buying more highly priced bonds. Opening up our investment statements personalized the pain we'd already experienced listening to the daily news reports of falling stock prices.

It takes courage (some might call it foolishness and stupidity) to buy stocks in the face of war, terror alerts, talk of smallpox, sagging retail sales, and more corporate layoffs and profit disappointments. Few investors had the constitution to buy stocks after such a brutal bear market. Those who buy after such a significant drop are rewarded— and often without having to wait for long.

That's why I say that if you're uncomfortable with investing and you're watching and listening to excessive amounts of negative, hyped news, the first thing you need to do is change your media diet. To be a successful long-term stock market investor, you must be reasonably optimistic. Much of what's in the news is bad news, and the more of that you subject yourself to and dwell upon, the more fearful and unwilling you're going to be to invest. Successful investors see the glass as half full rather than half empty.

My favorite stock market strategy for skittish investors is to buy the most conservative stock funds you can find that will join in any future appreciation but not get clobbered if more tough times lay ahead. Participate in the upside, but limit your downside. Among the safer stock mutual funds, buy value-oriented funds from the more conservative fund management companies. Value stock funds, such as Fidelity Value, Masters Select Value, Fairholme, and Vanguard's various value index funds, invest in shares that are selling at a low price relative to the intrinsic value of the company. See Chapter 14 for more ideas.

Buy good balanced funds, such as Dodge & Cox Balanced, Fidelity's Freedom funds, T. Rowe Price Balanced, and Vanguard's LifeStrategy funds, instead of holding stocks and bonds separately. Such funds offer the feeling of a smoother ride as stocks and bonds diversify and soften the ups and downs in a portfolio. Interestingly, and not surprisingly, studies show investors stick with less volatile funds longer.

Some people are not comfortable with investing on their own, and you may still not be at ease enough to pick from the short list of funds that I've provided. If you lack the confidence to invest on your own, and you're attracted to the idea of hiring someone to help you (more on this in Chapter 19, "Hiring Financial Help"), first work at gaining a basic investing education. How can you possibly assess the competence and discern the agenda of someone that you're considering hiring if you don't at least have a working knowledge of the topic yourself? Learn the jargon and how to evaluate investments by reading up on the topic. I'm a fan of good books, which are free from the inevitable conflicts of interest that come from advertising. (I recommend ones that fit the bill and that I like in Chapter 18, "Information and Edutainment Resources.") Also, seek independent second opinions before acting on an advisor's recommendations. Any financial advisor upset with you for seeking a second opinion isn't someone you should be working with.

14

Your Investing Plan

"The man who makes no mistakes
does not usually make anything."
—Edward Phelps

Before you jump into investing in this mutual fund or that certificate of deposit, you should consider some important personal and financial issues. If you don't, you're putting the cart before the horse. For example, don't begin with planning your investments if you have consumer debt and haven't dealt with that or if you haven't developed an overall financial plan. Other parts of this book can help you with these tasks.

A critical issue to weigh before investing is the length of time you have in mind. Most of the better investments are relatively liquid—that's not the concern. The potential problem is that if you invest your money into a risky investment and it drops in value just before you need to sell, you could be forced to take a loss. Thus, you should be concerned about matching the risk or volatility of your investments with the time frame that you have in mind.

Suppose that you have some money that you'd like to invest because you plan to use it for a down payment on a home in a few years. With a short time frame in mind, investments such as stocks or real estate would not be appropriate since they can fluctuate a great deal in value from year to year. These more growth-oriented (and volatile) investments, on the other hand, can be useful in working toward longer-term goals such as retirement that may be a decade or more away.

In addition to the time frame, your need to take risk should also be factored into your investment decisions. If the money that you're investing for retirement, for example, grows too slowly, you may not be able to retire when you want or with the lifestyle you desire. To reach your retirement goal, you may need to take more risk.

While your goals may require you to take more risk, that doesn't mean that you necessarily should do so. If you're going to become a nervous wreck and follow the stock market's every move, it may not be worth it for you to take as much risk, and you should consider rethinking your goals. Also, if you're in the fortunate position of not needing to take much risk because you're well on your way toward your savings goal, taking more risk than necessary might cause you to lose what you have.

A final consideration about investing your money is your tax situation. If you invest without paying attention to taxes, you may be overlooking simple ways to maximize your returns.

Two simple yet powerful moves will help you to invest in a tax-wise way. First, you should make sure to contribute to your retirement accounts (see Chapter 4, "Developing Your Personal Financial Action Plan") so that less of your money is taxed in the first place. This will reduce your taxes both in the years you make your contributions as well as each year your money is invested.

Second, with money that you invest outside retirement accounts, choose investments that match your tax situation. If you're in a high tax bracket, you should avoid investments that produce significant highly taxed distributions. Thus, you should avoid taxable bonds, certificates of deposit, and other investments that pay taxable interest income and that tend to distribute short-term capital gains (which are taxed at the same high tax rates as ordinary income).

If you are in a high tax bracket and would like to invest in bonds outside a retirement account, you should consider municipal bonds that pay federally tax-free interest. (It's free of state taxes where the bond was issued, unless it is the state you live in.) Also consider growth-oriented investments, such as stocks, real estate, or investments in yours or someone else's small business.

Assessing Your Current Portfolio

Before we leap into how to invest your current money, let's cover what to do with your current investments. While I advocate doing your homework so that you can buy and hold solid investments for the long haul, there are times when selling is appropriate. In fact, if you've been holding investments that seem to be doing poorly over an extended period, closely examine the situation. Try to determine why they've done so poorly. If a given investment is down because similar ones are also in decline, and the long-term perspective still holds, perhaps so should you.

However, if there's something inherently wrong with the investment in question, such as high fees or poor management, take the loss, and make doing so more palatable by remembering two things. First, if it's a non-retirement account investment, losses help reduce your income taxes. Second, consider the "opportunity cost" of continuing to keep your money in a lousy investment—what future return could that money be providing if you switched into a better investment?

A useful way to evaluate your portfolio once a year or every few years is to imagine that everything that you currently own is sold. Ask yourself whether you'd choose to go out and buy the same investments today that you were holding. This is an especially good question to ask yourself if you own lots of stock in the company you work for. Are your reasons still valid for holding your investments?

Be careful when assessing your current holdings that you don't dump a particular investment just because it's in what will turn out to be a temporary slump. Even the best investment managers have periods as long as a year or two during which they underperform. (Sometimes this happens when the manager's style of investing is out of favor for the time being.) But remember, my definition of temporary is one to two years, not months or days.

Just as we get attached to people, places, and things, some investors' judgment may be clouded due to attachment to an investment. Even if an investor makes the decision to sell an investment based on a sound and practical assessment, his attachment to it can derail the process, causing him to refuse to part with it at the current fair market value. Attachment can be especially problematic and paralyzing with inherited assets. Over the years, I've worked with many clients (and family members) who had great difficulty being objective with and letting go of inherited investments.

Inertia is also a problem for some people. It wasn't unusual for me to work with clients who had accumulated tens or hundreds of thousands of dollars in checking accounts. One client even came to me with $1.5 million in his *checking account*! Clients, including the fellow with $1.5 million in cash, who amassed their savings from work income, were often fearful of selecting an investment that might fall in value. These people knew how long and hard they had to work for their money, and they didn't want to lose it.

Last but not least, remember to keep bigger picture issues in mind. When I first started my work as a financial planner/counselor, I was surprised at how often I'd meet with clients who had excess cash in a low-interest money market fund or savings account while they carried high-cost debt like auto loans and credit-card balances. I was able to convince many of these people to pay down the high-cost debt after I showed them how much they could save or make by doing so. Likewise, I found that investors who preferred individual stocks would fret when one of their holdings fell, and they wouldn't examine their overall portfolio's performance. Too frequently, such investors would dump a stock currently in the hole because they'd dwell on that stock's large decline and overlook how little impact this one holding had on their overall portfolio.

When purchasing a new investment, many people fail to consider their overall asset allocation. Typically, they read an article somewhere or get a tip from a colleague and then wind up buying a recommended investment. In addition to not having done sufficient homework, investing in this fashion leads to a hodgepodge of a portfolio that's often not properly diversified. Failure to make an overall plan usually leads to a plan for failure, not success.

Wanting to be a loyal, team player, other folks fail to consider the big picture and overinvest in employer stock. This strategy is particularly dangerous because a company that falls on hard times can not only lead to the loss of a job, but also the loss of retirement assets when the stock takes a permanent nosedive. (Investing more than 10 percent of your financial assets in your employer's stock may be too risky.)

Asset Allocation

When you're just investing money for the short-term—for example, for emergency purposes—you simply choose a good money market fund or savings account, and you're on your way (more on the details later in this section). However, when you're investing for longer-term financial goals such as retirement, you'll end up investing in an array of different investments. Those investments may include such things as stock mutual funds, both U.S. and international, bonds and, perhaps, real estate.

How you divide up your money among these different types of investments is known as asset allocation. Don't be intimidated by this term or the prospect of making such a weighty decision. Asset allocation need not be complicated.

The subject of asset allocation is most often considered for money invested for the longer-term—that is, over 5 years and preferably 10 or more years. Before you begin the process, make sure that you have an emergency reserve of three to six months living expenses tucked away. Estimate even more if your income and job are unstable and you don't have family or friends you could reliably call on financially. Three months is sufficient if your income is safe and stable and/or you have other resources you can easily tap.

Other investments that you hold outside of retirement accounts, such as stocks, bonds, and mutual funds that invest in stocks and bonds, can quickly be converted into cash. The problem with considering these investments for emergencies is that since they fluctuate in value, the selling price may be much less than what you paid originally.

While real estate is not a good reserve since it takes time and significant expense to sell, taking out a home equity line against your home can offer convenient, reasonably low-cost access to money. Just be sure to set one up when you're financially healthy. If you wait until you are in a financial pinch to seek out an equity loan, you may have difficulty getting one. The easiest time to get a loan from a banker is when you really don't need one!

Worksheet—Asset Allocation for Retirement

The following worksheet should be used as a starting point for deciding on your asset allocation for retirement savings. Please read the following descriptions carefully, as they address a number of possibly conflicting factors. For example, in addition to addressing your tolerance for risk, they also raise the issue of how much growth you may need to accomplish specific goals. If you haven't yet done so, complete the retirement planning process in Chapter 4 so that you have a good sense of where you stand in terms of working toward your goals.

1. Start with your age: _____

2. Subtract the following:

   ➤ 20 points if you are comfortable investing for growth; can tolerate wide short-term price swings (remember: stocks can drop 10 percent, 20 percent, or more over relatively short periods of time); need to earn at least 9 to 10 percent per year on your investments to reach your retirement goal; or are comfortable accepting the risks inherent with growth investments.

➤ 10 points if you are willing to take some risk for growth but want more of a balance and less volatility in your investments; want/need to earn returns of about 8 percent per year.

➤ 0 points if you can't stomach wide price swings that inevitably occur when investing in things such as stocks; you're well on your way to achieving your savings goal and are more concerned about losing what you have because you can achieve your goal by earning 7% or less return per year.

(If you fall in between one of the two descriptions above, choose a point total in between the two descriptions.) _____

3. Difference (subtract line 2 from line 1) equals approximate percentage of your investments that you should consider placing in fixed income vehicles (e.g., bonds and bond funds). _____

4. Subtract the result above (line 3) from 100, and that's the percentage of your investments to consider placing in growth-oriented instruments such as stocks and real estate. _____

Mutual funds are an ideal investment vehicle to help you carry out your asset allocation. The advantages of the best mutual funds are many:

➤ **Diversification.** Mutual funds typically invest in dozens of securities. For example, if you want to invest in stocks, you should hold stocks in different industries and different stocks within an industry. This is what a good stock mutual fund does for you (The same logic works for bond funds too.)

➤ **Professional money management.** Unless you have lots of money and free time on your hands, researching investments will at best be a part-time hobby for you. A mutual fund manager and her team of analysts are devoted full-time to selecting investments and monitoring them on an ongoing basis.

➤ **Cost effective.** Good money managers don't come cheaply. However, because mutual funds buy and sell large blocks of securities and typically manage hundreds of millions or billions of dollars, the cost of their services is spread out.

In short, good mutual funds offer you a low cost, professionally managed way to diversify your investment dollars.

Several different types of mutual funds exist. Which ones work for you depends on the level of risk you desire and are able to accept. With regard to the volatility of your invested principal, **money market funds** are the "safest" types of mutual funds. Money funds maintain a fixed price of $1 per share. As with a bank savings account, you make your money from the dividends (just like the bank account's interest). The main difference and advantage that the best money funds have over bank savings' accounts are that the better ones generate a higher yield. Because there is little if any risk of bankruptcy, money funds are not insured the way bank accounts are.

Bond funds are nothing more than diversified portfolios of bonds. The attraction of bond funds is that they pay higher dividends than do money market funds. For investors, such as retirees, who want more current income on which to live, bond funds can make sense. The drawback or risk of bonds is that they fluctuate in value with changes in interest rates. If the overall level of interest rates rises, the market value of existing bonds will decrease. Why? With new bonds being issued at higher interest rates, the price of existing bonds must decrease enough so that the resulting yield or interest rate is comparable to that offered on new bonds. Longer-term bonds are more volatile with changes in interest rates since your principal is being repaid more years down the road

Stock funds invest in shares of stock issued by a group of companies. Funds typically focus on U.S. or international companies. Stock funds are the most volatile of mutual funds, but they also hold the promise of higher potential returns. On average, stocks have returned investors about 10 percent per year over the decades. Over short time periods, however, stocks can drop significantly in value. Drops of more than 10 or 20 percent are not uncommon and should be expected. Thus, you should not commit money to stock funds that you expect to need or use within the next five years. Although they are completely liquid on a day's notice, you don't want to be forced to sell a stock fund during a down period and possibly lose money.

Here are some examples of how different people could allocate their retirement money among mutual funds:

> Nina is single and 25 years old. She wants to be serious about saving for retirement. She is new to the investment world and wants to ease into things so as not to make a major mistake. Beyond her emergency reserve of six months' living expenses, she'd like to allocate her money in her 401(k) plan among the four options that it offers: a money market fund, bond fund, and a U.S. and international stock fund. See Figure 14.1.

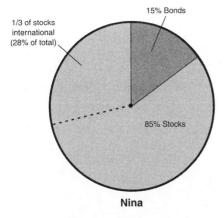

15% Bonds

1/3 of stocks
international
(28% of total)

85% Stocks

Nina

Figure 14.1
85% in stock funds with a third of that overseas and the remainder in bonds.

Ethan and Ellen are both in their mid-40s and are on track to achieving their retirement goals. They want their money invested for growth in order to have a secure retirement as well as help their children with college costs. Having traveled extensively abroad, they believe that there are tremendous growth opportunities overseas and want to be aggressive investing there as well. See Figure 14.2.

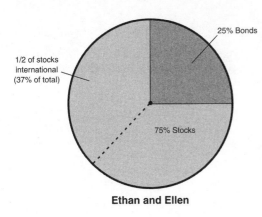

25% Bonds

1/2 of stocks
international
(37% of total)

75% Stocks

Ethan and Ellen

Figure 14.2
75% in stocks (half internationally) with the remainder in bonds.

Pat and Chris are both 50 years old and are concerned about preserving their capital—they have sufficient assets and want to protect them. Growth is a secondary concern. They have a year's worth of expenses in a money market fund as they are nearing retirement. See Figure 14.3.

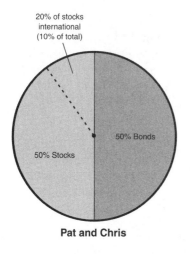

Figure 14.3
50% in stocks (20% of which is overseas) with 50% in bonds.

Pat and Chris

Pauline is single and 75 years old. Her Social Security and small pension cover her living expenses. She lives a modest lifestyle. While she doesn't need much income from her investments, she doesn't like the risk and volatility of the stock market. See Figure 14.4.

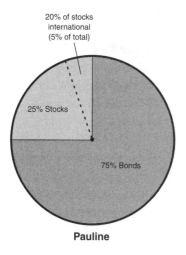

Figure 14.4
25% in stocks (20% of which is overseas) and 75% in bonds.

Pauline

Protecting Yourself from Corporate Losses

You've surely heard tales of companies engaged in layoffs, simultaneously experiencing earnings declines and plummeting stock prices. In the worst cases, employees who've invested significant chunks of money in their firm's stock end up losing their jobs and holding deflated retirement plans. Although you can't completely eliminate your anxieties about job losses and stock price plunges, you can take action to minimize the fallout from future corporate disasters.

When considering a job offer, thoroughly review the company's benefit's package, especially its retirement-plan investments. Be wary of plans that require you to hold too much company stock for too long. I don't have a problem with investing some money—say 10 or 20 percent of your 401(k) account—in your employer's equity. But, unless you can truly withstand the risk, I'd stay away from plans and employers that require more significant amounts than that to be held in company stock. This isn't about showing your loyalty and faith in the company; it's about avoiding a foolish and dangerous lack of diversification. No one in the executive suite is going to shed a tear about your losing your job and retirement dreams. And, even if they did share your sorrow, it's not going to bring your job and investment money back. Protect yourself and diversify. Here are some additional, sensible steps you can take:

➤ Seek out independent reviews of the investment choices in the company's retirement plan. Give preference to broadly diversified mutual funds and shun individual stocks and sector (or industry) funds.

➤ Try evaluating the company culture, its value system, and the management team's ethics. It's natural to avoid asking tougher questions when you're trying to get a job offer, so save the more difficult queries for after you secure an offer.

➤ Take the time to speak with numerous people at your prospective employer. Ask them what they like and don't like about the company and what kinds of people fit in best and what types don't. Also, inquire about the ethical standards, expectations, and behaviors of senior management.

> ➤ Take off your rose-colored glasses and be open to the possibility that the company isn't the right place for you, even though you've gotten what appears to be an attractive job offer. The more informed and careful you are before signing on, the better positioned you should be to deal with inevitable setbacks.

Allocations for Shorter-Term Goals

Not all of your investments will be made for longer-term purposes. Perhaps you're saving money for a home down payment or for your children's educational expenses. In these cases, traditional asset allocation does not work because the time horizon is short. Here are some guidelines to consider:

Time Frame for Money Need	Investing Guidelines
Within the next year or two	Money market funds, savings accounts, and treasury bills and CDs with a matched maturity.
3 to 5 years (e.g., home down payment)	Shorter-term bond funds and treasury bills and CDs with a matched maturity.
5 to 10 years	Balanced portfolio of stocks and bonds—perhaps no more than 50% to 60% in stocks.
10 to 20 years	Balanced portfolio of stocks and bonds—more skewed toward stocks the longer the time frame and the greater the need to accept risk to make the money grow.

Before you begin making any of these investments, be sure that your overall finances are in order and read the next section.

Next Steps

Before you start to invest, make sure that your financial foundation is stable. Have you:

➤ Paid off your high-interest consumer debt, such as on credit cards and auto loans?

➤ Established your emergency cash reserve?

➤ Funded your available retirement accounts?

➤ Learned about the different types of investments, risks, and potential returns?

➤ Taken the time to understand your current financial status and how much you need to save and what returns you need to earn in order to achieve your financial goals?

Selecting the Best Mutual Funds

Although there are potential rewards from investing in the stock and bond markets, there can also be significant risks. You can minimize some of those risks by investing in the best professionally managed mutual funds. I seek to maximize your potential investment returns while minimizing risk by screening and selecting "best mutual funds," using the following criteria:

➤ **Efficiency (low operating expenses and load fees).** Within a given sector of mutual funds (for example, short-term bonds), funds without loads (sales commissions) and with low annual management fees have a greater probability of producing higher total returns. I recommend those funds that maintain low operating expenses and no-load (sales charges) fees.

➤ **Historic rate of return versus risk.** Funds that assume higher risk should produce higher rates of return. Thus, in order for a fund to be recommended, it must consistently deliver a favorable rate of return given its risk.

➤ **Track record** of the fund manager and the mutual fund company within the fund sector (for example, international stocks, domestic growth stocks, bonds, etc.).

➤ **Overall performance and track record of mutual fund family company (for example, Vanguard, Fidelity, etc.).** Does the fund company consistently look out for shareholder's interests? Has the company been involved in scandals?

How Much Low Expenses Really Do Matter

If you analyze the returns of mutual funds, you will quickly see that lower expenses translate into higher long-term returns. Conversely, higher expense funds tend to produce inferior long-term results. The following analysis grouped stock funds by their annual expense ratios. Those funds with expenses among the lowest 25 percent were placed into quartile 1, the next lowest in quartile 2, and so on. As you can see for all fund types, the funds with the best returns (over a decade-long period) were the funds with the lowest expenses.

Please also note that the highest expense funds had returns even lower than expected given the difference in their expense ratios. This can be explained by additional negative attributes common to higher cost funds. First is the troubling pattern of higher cost funds taking greater risks, which often don't work out, to produce better returns—ironically due to the higher costs dragging down returns! Second is the fact that fund companies with the highest costs tend to be the least concerned with doing what's in their shareholder's best long-term interests.

Mutual Funds Ranked by Expense Ratio and Market Capitalization

Quartile	Large-Cap Median Expense Ratio	Median Return	Mid-Cap Median Expense Ratio	Median Return	Small-Cap Median Expense Ratio	Median Return
1	0.78%	8.08%	0.91%	11.40%	0.95%	11.00%
2	1.05%	6.97%	1.20%	9.98%	1.23%	10.75%
3	1.39%	6.67%	1.49%	8.01%	1.48%	9.84%
4	1.94%	5.94%	2.08%	7.61%	2.14%	6.62%

Vanguard has been the lowest cost provider of mutual funds. The following table shows the percentage of Vanguard funds that outperformed the average return of their competitive peer groups over various periods. As you can see, expenses matter greatly for all types of funds but especially with more conservative funds such as money market and funds holding bonds.

	1 Year	3 Years	5 Years	10 Years
Stock funds	83%	86%	81%	69%
Balanced funds	58%	64%	86%	100%
Bond funds	84%	78%	89%	96%
Money market funds	100%	100%	100%	100%
All Vanguard funds	82%	83%	85%	85%

Sources: Lipper Inc. and Vanguard.

Selecting the most appropriate funds for you also requires an understanding of your investment goals and your needs and desire to accept risk. If you do not understand what you are investing in and the risks that are entailed, then you should not invest. This is one of the reasons people make mistakes and poor investments when working with stock brokers and other commissioned-based investment salespeople. Financial salespeople rarely take the time during their sales pitch to understand your needs and overall financial situation and goals. They might also obscure the risks and drawbacks of what they sell.

Selecting funds simply on the basis of the past rate of return is a common mistake made by novice investors. As all mutual funds state, "past performance is no guarantee of future results." Analysis of historic mutual fund performance proves that many of yesterday's top performers turn into tomorrow's losers. Many of today's high return funds achieve their results through taking on high risk. High-risk funds usually decline in price faster in a changing economic environment and during major market declines.

For investments outside of tax-sheltered retirement accounts, you may want to check with a fund to determine when capital gains are distributed. Doing so will allow you to avoid making an investment in a fund that is about to make a capital gains distribution (typically in December), as this will increase your current year tax liability. Low-cost exchange-traded funds (ETFs), discussed later in this chapter, can help minimize taxable distributions too.

Selecting the Right Money Fund

One simple way to boost your returns without taking additional risks is to replace your current non- or low-interest bearing bank checking or savings account with a money market mutual fund (which also happen to come in tax-free flavors if you're in a higher tax bracket). Some of these accounts even come with unlimited check-writing privileges so you could even ditch your bank checking account altogether if you so choose.

There are hundreds of money market funds that invest about one trillion dollars of individuals' money. These funds are heavily regulated by the Securities & Exchange Commission: Money market funds' investments may only be in the highest credit quality securities and must have an average maturity of less than 90 days. Money market funds maintain a constant $1.00 per share price. In the highly unlikely event that an investment in a money market's fund portfolio goes sour, a large money market fund would certainly cover the loss.

State tax exempt money market funds invest in high credit quality short-term debt issued by state and local governments. The interest from these funds is exempt from both federal and state taxes if the fund invests in your state's securities.

General-purpose money market funds invest in super safe short-term bank certificates of deposit, corporate commercial paper (short-term debt) that is issued by the largest and most credit-worthy companies, and U.S. government securities. Although these funds are not insured through FDIC insurance programs, to date, no major money market mutual fund has ever lost investor's principal investment.

The securities that these funds buy are extremely safe; many are guaranteed or backed by a federal government agency. The risk difference versus a bank account is negligible. The 1980s highlighted how poorly much of the savings and loan industry was run and the fact that banks are not perfectly safe either. The FDIC insurance system is just that—an insurance system. If there was such an economic disaster in the U.S. that money market funds' investments declined in value, the whole U.S. banking system would be in jeopardy, and the FDIC insurance system could collapse.

If you want the peace of mind that a bank account's insurance offers, you can select a money market fund that invests exclusively in U.S. government securities, which are virtually risk free, as they are backed by the full faith and credit of the federal government (as is the FDIC insurance system). These types of accounts typically pay less interest, usually one-quarter to one-half percent less.

Here's how to decide which type of fund is the best fit for your tax situation and will likely provide you with the greatest return. What I'm doing here is comparing the past year's yield on Vanguard's taxable money market fund—Prime Money Market. You can get the most recent numbers from its web site or by calling Vanguard. I will walk you through the analysis using calendar year 2006 returns—you can do this with updated data for the most recent year:

	Example
1. Vanguard's Prime Money Market past year total return:	4.88%
2. Obtain your federal income tax bracket by using Chapter 9. Suppose it is:	28%
3. Amount lost to taxes (multiply line 1 by line 2):	−1.37%
4. Subtract line 3 from line 1:	= 3.51%

Now, over this same one-year period, Vanguard's Tax Exempt Money Market fund, which pays dividends free of federal tax, produced a total return of 3.37%. So, for the investor above in the 28% tax bracket, he have netted more in the taxable (Prime) fund than in the tax.

If you're from a larger state for which there are some decent state-specific money funds (e.g., such as CA, NJ, NY, OH, or PA), you can go through the same analysis and factor in state as well as federal income taxes.

Investing in Stock and Bond Funds

In earlier sections in this chapter, I walk through how to develop an allocation among different types of funds (see the sections, "Worksheet—Asset Allocation for Retirement" and "Allocations for Shorter-Term Goals"). Having a plan for what percentages to put into different types of investments is a crucial but not final step in the process. Now, we're going to pick some specific funds.

The first step in this process is deciding between actively versus passively managed funds. Most mutual funds are managed by portfolio managers who continually research and trade in an attempt to hold those securities with the best future prospects. Funds that are managed in such a fashion are known as actively managed funds. Some funds' managers trade little, perhaps changing over about 10 percent of their portfolio yearly, whereas others trade heavily, turning over their entire holdings two to three times each year.

In contrast, passively managed funds, also known as index funds, invest in a relatively fixed basket of securities that track a broad market index. For example, the Standard & Poor's 500 Index tracks the performance of 500 larger company stocks in the U.S. You can invest in mutual funds that mimic the S&P 500 Index.

The advantages of these index funds are several. First, index funds can be operated at far lower cost since you don't need a portfolio management team researching and monitoring securities. Lower fund expenses translate into higher returns for index fund shareholders. Second, the majority of actively managed funds lag behind the market rate of return, largely due to their higher fees. Finally, an index fund should be error-free because it mirrors the market and won't perform worse than the market.

If you're considering investing in an actively managed mutual fund, be sure to compare its performance to an appropriate index. Don't be quick to accept the fund's choice of comparison. In an effort to make themselves look better than they really are, many funds will compare themselves to others that aren't truly comparable.

A fund's performance should always be compared to a market index that tracks the rate of return of similar securities. For example, a fund that focuses upon investing in larger company U.S. stocks would be compared to the S&P 500 index. When investing outside of retirement accounts, you should also be sure to compare the after-tax returns on a given fund to its relevant index. Over longer investing periods such as a decade, studies have shown that approximately three-quarters of the actively managed funds underperform the comparable market index.

Here are three options to consider for using active versus index funds when investing in stock and bond funds:

➤ **Use only index funds.** If you wish to place all of your stock and bond market money in index funds, you will do fine over the long-term and not be at a disadvantage.

➤ **Use a mix of index and actively managed funds.** Jack Bogle, founder of low cost and index fund pioneer Vanguard, uses a mix of actively managed and index funds. I do too. Index funds can form the core of a portfolio, and you can choose the best actively managed funds to complement the index funds.

➤ **Use only active managed funds.** This is a riskier approach, but advocates would argue it offers more upside potential if you select and manage your portfolio of funds well.

For the portion of your portfolio that you're going to index, here are three funds I recommend:

➤ Vanguard Total Bond Market Index

➤ Vanguard Total Stock Market Index

➤ Vanguard Total International Stock Index

Each of these funds has a $3,000 minimum initial investment (except for an education savings account, where the minimum is $2,000). Also, you will pay a $10 annual account fee for each fund with a balance less than $10,000. If you're starting out or have much less than $50,000 to invest, consider using Vanguard's exchange-traded funds (ETFs) or a fund of funds. The first batch of these funds has an estimated retirement date (e.g., T. Rowe Price Retirement 2040 would be the fund for a person expected to retire around the year 2040) attached to it with the logic being that as that date approaches, the fund managers gradually scale back on the risk of the fund (by moving money from stock funds into bond funds). Among the better such fund of funds out there are the following:

➤ **Fidelity Freedom funds.** Fidelity's target retirement funds' entries by far use the most different funds—typically around two dozen. Their annual operating expense ratios range from 0.6 to 0.8 percent, and they are among the most aggressive.

➤ **T. Rowe Price Retirement funds.** These typically invest in about 6 to 10 funds at T. Rowe Price, most of which are actively managed. The annual operating expense ratios range from about 0.6 to 0.75 percent.

➤ **Vanguard Target Retirement funds.** These low-cost funds (operating expense ratios of just 0.2 percent) invest almost entirely in about six index funds.

If you would rather keep more of a fixed mix of stock and bond funds over time, you could instead use one or two of the Vanguard Life Strategy funds. Each of these funds of funds uses a handful of index funds along with Vanguard's Asset Allocation, which does vary its allocation somewhat over time between stocks and bonds (hence the small range of allocations possible for each fund:

Vanguard LifeStrategy Income Fund	20–30% stocks; 70–80% bonds
Vanguard LifeStrategy Conservative Growth Fund	40–50% stocks; 50–60% bonds
Vanguard LifeStrategy Moderate Growth Fund	60–70% stocks; 30–40% bonds
Vanguard LifeStrategy Growth Fund	80–90% stocks; 10–20% bonds

Since these are funds of funds (minimum investment is $3,000), you can comfortably use them for one-stop shopping. Their management fees are low—in the neighborhood of 0.25%. If you seek an asset allocation that is in between two of these funds, simply divide your money between the two closest funds.

Worksheet for Actively Managed Funds

Once you've decided on your overall asset allocation and what portion you wish to place in index funds versus actively managed funds, then you can begin to decide which actively managed funds you wish to utilize.

What follows are actively managed funds that I recommend in various categories that can help you fill out your asset allocation:

Percent in Category		Percent in Fund
_____	Bond Funds	
	Dodge & Cox Income	_____
	Vanguard Bond funds (all)	_____
_____	Balanced Funds (Stocks and Bonds)	
	Vanguard Wellesley Income	_____
	Vanguard Wellington	_____
_____	U.S.-Focused Stock Funds	
	Fairholme Fund (FAIRX)	_____
	Fidelity Disciplined Equity, Equity-Income, Low-Priced Stock	_____
	Masters Select Equity, Small Company, and Value	_____
	T. Rowe Price Equity-Income	_____
	Vanguard Strategic Equity	_____
_____	International Funds	
	Dodge & Cox International Stock (DODFX)	_____
	Fidelity Diversified International	_____
	Masters Select International	_____
	Oakmark International (OAKIX)	_____
_____	Global Funds (Invest in Stocks Worldwide)	
	Oakmark Global (OAKGX)	_____
	T. Rowe Price Spectrum Growth (PRSGX)	_____
	Tweedy Browne Global Value (TBGVX)	_____
	Vanguard Global Equity (VHGEX)	_____

Hedge Funds

In recent years, increasing numbers of high net worth individuals have been hearing about and investing some of their money in hedge funds. These managed investment portfolios are like small mutual funds that have fewer regulations placed on them. For sure, there's a certain snob appeal and exclusivity accompanying hedge funds. It's kind of like belonging to a very exclusive (and very expensive) country club.

The Securities and Exchange Commission (SEC) requires hedge funds to verify that an investor meets certain criteria. To be an "accredited investor," an individual must have an annual income of at least $200K ($300K if married) for each of the past two years and a minimum of $1 million dollars (this does not include your home) in financial assets. Some hedge funds use a higher definition—that of a "qualified investor." This requires having at least $5 million in financial assets.

Not only do hedge fund investors need to have big investment account balances, but they also need to be willing to pay hefty fees. Hedge fund fees are made up of two parts—a management fee and a performance fee. The management fee typically is between one and two percent per year. This alone exceeds the total operating fees charged on most mutual funds. But hedge funds also have a so-called performance fee that is generally a whopping 20 percent of the hedge fund's return. The following example demonstrates how the fees on a mutual fund compare to a hedge fund during a relatively good year for the stock market:

	Mutual Fund	Hedge Fund
One-Year Return (before expenses)	16%	20%
Management/Operating Fee	1%	1.5%
Performance Fee (20% of return)		4%
Total Fees	1%	5.5%
Net Return to Investor	15%	14.5%

So, even though the hedge fund had a better year before fees, the high fees caused it to produce lower net returns to the investor. If the hedge fund had equaled the mutual fund's returns before fees (16%), after expenses it would have netted just 11.3%, far behind the mutual fund's 15%.

Numerous sources publish hedge fund returns, and I review the returns of various classes of hedge funds and compare them to mutual funds. Overall, the average hedge fund underperforms mutual funds, and the reason is pretty simple—those high hedge fund fees.

With the benefit of 20/20 hindsight, you can see which hedge funds have done the best. Predicting which ones will do the best in the future is darn hard.

Hedge funds defend their high fees by stating that they have an incentive because of the performance fee to produce high returns for their investors. There's some truth to that; however, many mutual funds include a modest performance fee in their operating fee structure that provides similar incentives at far lower cost. Also, mutual funds that perform poorly will see shareholders vote with their feet and dollars.

Because the hedge fund performance fee can be such a huge prize for the hedge fund managers, it causes many managers to take great risks. That means that when things don't work out the way they had hoped or expected, the damage and losses can be magnified. A number of previously successful hedge funds have crashed and burned when their aggressive risks backfired.

15

Insurance

---

*"There are worse things in life than death.
Have you ever spent an evening with
an insurance salesman?"*
—Woody Allen

Although some people worry more than others, most people take some precautions, buy insurance, or take other actions to reduce risk. Even the most brazen among us don't walk around high-crime urban neighborhoods counting wads of cash after dark. But some people do pretty dumb things—like driving a car without wearing a seatbelt or allowing their kids to do the same. One woman I know who never wears a seatbelt thinks they are uncomfortable and aren't really going to save her "…if she's meant to go" (her words). But, she refuses to get on an airplane after the September 11th terrorist attacks. Statistically, of course, this makes no sense at all. Every month, about 3,000 people die in auto accidents on U.S. roads—about the same number of folks killed in the 9/11 attacks. And, this happens month after month after month. (She didn't know this fact.)

Of course, human behavior is emotionally driven. The horrible images of the 9/11 attacks made an impression on many people and altered behaviors. Few auto accidents are shown repeatedly on national television, and seeing the real time events unfold, as we were exposed to on 9/11, rarely happens.

Life is filled with risks. We can't eliminate them all, and most of us realize that reducing or eliminating certain risks takes time, money, and vigilance. Some people hardly ever leave their homes because they worry so much about the bad things that can happen to them in the world. Of course, bad things can happen at home too—including developing health problems that are exacerbated by inactivity.

Some risks have major financial consequences, and for those, the purchase of the right kind of insurance can eliminate the financial downside. That's the subject of this chapter. Plenty of risks can be greatly reduced without buying any insurance at all. Chapter 16, "Managing Risks Involves More Than Buying Insurance," will cover those topics. And Chapter 17, "Your Insurance Plan," will assist you with putting together an action plan to secure the best insurance for your situation at the best prices.

Don't Sweat (Insurance for) the Small Stuff

Plenty of companies and people will try to sell you insurance for "small stuff." Consider the following appliance service plan pitch. (I've deleted the exact name of the plan as that's not relevant.)

> Purchasing a Service Plan is one of the smartest consumer decisions you'll ever make. Protect yourself from the future cost of repairing your new product by purchasing a Service Plan!
>
> DESCRIPTION OF SERVICE PLAN AND HOW IT WORKS
>
> ➤ This warranty extension goes into effect after your original warranty expires.
>
> ➤ It gives you one year of parts and labor coverage on any appliance below $100.
>
> ➤ Your appliance warranty completely mirrors the manufacturer's warranty, and will be either carry-in or in-home service.
>
> ➤ Upon purchasing this extension, we will mail you a registration card, which you must fill out and send back via mail or online.
>
> ➤ YOU MUST REGISTER YOUR PRODUCT WITHIN 10 DAYS OF RECEIVING YOUR REGISTRATION CARD.
>
> WHY BUY A SERVICE PLAN?
>
> Q. What is a Service Plan?
>
> A. It is an economical way to extend the terms of your product's manufacturer's parts and labor warranty.
>
> Q. Why should I buy a Service Plan?
>
> A. Even the best products can eventually malfunction, and minor repairs can cost hundreds of dollars. By purchasing a Service Plan, you won't have to hassle with unexpected repair bills.

The pitch goes on to say that the normal price for this service plan is supposedly $30 but is yours today for only $20.

Could the appliance break after the manufacturer's warranty period ends? Of course it could! In fact, no appliance lasts forever, and you're guaranteed to someday have a problem or two. Please note, however, that this service plan "…gives you one year of parts and labor." Just one measly year! Suppose that you buy a blender for $79 on January 10, 2008 and the manufacturer's warranty is good for one year. This extended warranty that you could buy will cover your blender from January 10, 2009 until January 10, 2010.

Now, consider the cost. You're paying $20 to insure a blender that's worth only $79 (brand new)! How absurd is that! Note that in the sales pitch for the service plan, the company has the audacity to say, "Even the best products can eventually malfunction, and minor repairs can cost hundreds of dollars." This is incredibly dishonest given that this extended warranty plan is for appliances costing less than $100! And, what about the hassle and time involved for you to enroll in the extended warranty plan?

If you can afford to buy a $79 blender, you can afford to get it repaired. Even better, do your homework before buying the blender (or any consumer product for that matter) and make sure you get something that has a good track record. Problems do occur, and remember that the manufacturer's warranty may cover those. Reputable manufacturers stand behind their products. Take a few minutes to read the manual that comes with the product so you know how to properly use and care for it.

Alright, now consider a radio ad I recently heard for a new technology-based product that says it will keep hungry deer from chewing up your landscaping. While I enjoy deer and other wildlife, it does annoy me to see some plantings gobbled up and ruined, so I called. In addition to an installation fee of $1,000 or more, there was a monthly maintenance fee of $79 (because the company claims that it regularly needs to come out and adjust the devices that ward off the deer so that they don't become habituated to the way things are). I quickly figured that the damage done by the deer doesn't amount to that much money over time and that buying this company's products was similar to buying insurance for something that wasn't all that valuable. Yes, all the landscaping around a property would cost a lot to replace, but unless deer learn how to clear cut trees and take out entire lawns, the damage they can do is limited to particular shrubs, flowers, and bushes. So, I resolved to replacing future damaged plantings with things that aren't attractive to the deer and enjoying their company!

What is a small loss for you, me, or the person down the block all differ. Suppose for a moment that you're a billionaire like Bill Gates and you just bought a new $50,000 car. It probably doesn't make sense to pay for and carry collision insurance on your auto policy. If your car were totaled, $50,000 is a lot to lose, but not if you're Bill Gates and worth like $50 billion! That $50,000 amounts to just one-ten thousandth of one percent of his net worth of $50 billion!

What if you don't have Bill Gates-like wealth and you own an older car that's worth, say, $5,000? If your assets total, say, $25,000 or are non-existent, carrying collision makes good financial sense. Should you carry collision insurance on it if you have $1,000,000 in financial assets? That $5,000 car amounts to just ½ of one percent of your assets. You could go either way—I would probably lean toward dropping collision coverage in such a situation, but part of this decision making is one of personal comfort. By all means, examine the financial angle as I'm suggesting, but in the end, you have to decide where you'll draw the line—what losses you'd be willing to accept and which you'd rather not and therefore buy insurance to cover.

And, there's the rub. Insurance costs money—the more insurance you buy, the more money you will spend. I don't like wasting money on unnecessary insurance. Buy insurance for the big potential stuff, not the small stuff. And, remember, if you do insure for the smaller things, you've got to jump through plenty of hoops to collect.

Insurance Not to Buy

There are plenty of types of insurance to not waste your money on because such policies ultimately cover small potential losses or cover only certain losses that could be covered through a broader coverage policy.

An example is credit life insurance. This pays off some debt (mortgage or other loan) if you die. The American Council of Life Insurers only tracks such policies that pay off loans due within the next 10 years. About one-quarter of a trillion dollars worth of this type of insurance was sold in the late 1980s and early 1990s…the amount sold is now less than $200 billion per year, but that's still a lot of wasted money on unnecessary coverage. (If you need life insurance, buy a term policy that will cover these loans—see the life insurance section later in this chapter.)

Narrow healthcare plans are another type of insurance to avoid. This would include policies, for example, that pay a modest amount per day of hospitalization or that only pay for certain illnesses such as cancer. Another one to bypass is dental insurance if the cost is coming out of your pocket for the coverage. Dental plans aren't going to cover the really big expenditures, especially if there's a medical need (covered under health insurance) to do corrective work on your mouth, and you certainly don't need to waste money on insurance to pay for periodic teeth cleanings.

When you ship a package through the mail, unless you're sending something really valuable, don't waste money buying insurance. Although the U.S. Postal Service (USPS) does lose or damage things, consider that it will cost you $2.30 on top of the shipping cost to insure sending a gift worth $60. The Postal Service would have to lose such a package one out of every 25 times for senders to come out ahead buying such coverage! (If it stresses you to ship items without any insurance protection, then use UPS, which includes $100 of protection when you ship with it. Its shipping rates are often lower and its services faster than the government-run postal service.)

Home warranty plans are another example of wasted insurance dollars on small potential losses. You generally have to pay some of the cost of a service call anyway under these plans, and the costs covered are pretty limited. If someone else—a realtor or house seller—offers to pay for the cost of such a plan, I suppose you could take it. Alternatively, they could credit you the cost of the plan for you to use toward something for your home.

Buying Your Way out of the Costliest Risks

Smart mountain climbers take along gear to make their trip safe and comfortable. What would you do during an extended climbing trip, for example, if temperatures plunged and it started snowing with severe winds? How about if you or one of your hiking companions fell and broke a leg or got sick? What about exposure to an exotic disease like malaria?

Insurance is like appropriate hiking gear and preparation for your outdoor adventure. You hope you won't need it, but if you do, you're glad it's there to protect you against adverse or emergency conditions. On your hiking trip, your "insurance" might include clothing for inclement weather, a first aid kit, appropriate drugs and advance shots (such as for malaria), ropes for steep inclines, and so on.

You should purchase sufficient insurance to prevent a financial catastrophe. On the other hand, as I discussed earlier in this chapter, some small losses aren't worth the money and bother of your time to insure. That's why for all types of insurance that you purchase, you should take the highest deductible you can comfortably accept. The deductible represents the amount of money that you must pay out of your own pocket if you have a claimed loss. A high deductible helps keep down the cost of your coverage and also eliminates the hassles of filing small claims.

For each of the following types of policies, I explain who needs it and why. Chapter 17 explains how to get the proper coverage at a competitive price.

Long-Term Disability Insurance

During your working years, your future income earning ability is likely your most valuable "asset"—far more valuable than a car or even your home. Your ability to produce income should be protected or insured.

Even if you don't have dependents, you probably need disability coverage. Are you dependent upon your income? Long-term disability (LTD) insurance replaces a portion of your lost income in the event a disability prevents you from working.

Nearly everyone should carry LTD during their working years. One exception: You're already financially independent/wealthy and no longer need to work for the income but do so anyway.

Except for people working for the largest employers with comprehensive benefit plans, many people lack LTD insurance. According to a recent survey conducted by the U.S. Department of Labor, only 30 percent of all workers are even offered access to a long-term disability plan; those who work in blue collar and service jobs fare even worse—only 23 percent and 12 percent of those groups, respectively, have access to an LTD policy. Just 19 percent of those working for smaller employers (under 100 employees) have access to an LTD plan. Part-time workers are also particularly vulnerable, with just 6 percent of such workers having access to LTD insurance.

Even among those in the minority who have access to an LTD, many people don't enroll. One common reason many folks bypass coverage is that they believe the chances of disability are rare. Another perception is that only old people become disabled. Neither of these assumptions is true. According to the Centers for Disease Control and Prevention, National Center for Health Statistics, about 12 percent (one in eight) of Americans suffer from a limitation of activity caused by a chronic condition. Poorer people tend to be hardest hit:

Group	Percentage Suffering Activity Limitation Due to Chronic Condition
Age 18–24	4.1
Age 25–44	6.6
Age 45–54	13.0
Age 55–64	21.1
Poor*	23.1
Near poor*	17.0
Non-poor*	9.2

* Poor persons are defined as those people having an income below the poverty threshold. (The 2007 poverty threshold was about $20,650 for a family of four.) Near poor persons have incomes at least equal to the poverty threshold to up to twice the poverty threshold. Non-poor persons are those with incomes above twice the poverty threshold.

You generally can't predict when and what type of disability you may suffer. That's because many disabilities are caused by medical problems (e.g., arthritis, cerebral palsy, diabetes, glaucoma, multiple sclerosis, muscular dystrophy, stroke, etc.) and accidents (e.g., head injuries, spinal injury, loss of limb or amputation, etc.).

Consider my friend, David. In his early 40s, he was cleaning mildew off the side of his home one fine weekend Fall day. Standing on a ladder about 10 feet above the driveway, he was spraying a bleach mixture on his home's shingles when a bat came flying out straight at his face. He lost his balance and fell straight back. He was "lucky" to only have two broken arms and a badly bruised tailbone. Among the worst-case scenarios would be that he could have been disabled, perhaps permanently.

Life Insurance

If you have dependents, you may also need life insurance. Ask yourself and your family how they would fare if you died and they no longer had your income. If your family is dependent upon your income and you would want them to maintain their current standard of living in your absence and they would not be able to do so with your passing, you need life insurance.

Term life insurance, like most other forms of insurance, is pure insurance protection and the best way to go for the vast majority of people.

The other major type of life insurance is cash value coverage, which includes a life insurance death benefit (as with a term policy) and a savings and investment feature. You can't generally combine insurance with investing when you buy an auto, disability, or homeowner's policy, so why can you with life insurance? Thanks to an exemption in the tax code.

Those in the insurance business—insurance companies and agents who sell their products and earn commissions—have a bias in favor of cash value life insurance. The reasons (show me the money) are pretty simple. Cash value life insurance costs a lot more and provides far, far greater profits for insurance companies and commissions to the agents who sell it.

Even supposed non-profit organizations (such as the Life and Health Insurance Foundation for Education, which has the clever acronym LIFE, "…dedicated to addressing the public's growing need for information and education about life [and other types of] insurance") don't present a fair and accurate presentation of the alternatives and how to make an informed choice. LIFE says that term insurance is for people who need coverage for less than 10 years or for those on a "very limited budget."

Both of these arguments are ludicrous and inaccurate. (By the way, even though it's a non-profit, a little digging on my part uncovered the fact that LIFE does disclose that it was formed, "…by seven insurance groups, representing 160,000 agents.")

Let's start with the time frame over which a person desires insurance. Term life insurance is often called "temporary" life insurance, while cash value life insurance has been pushed as "permanent" life insurance. This extreme distinction highlights how bogus an argument this is since no one lives forever! Rather than saying it's permanent insurance, it might better be called life insurance for as long as you live! People who buy term insurance generally hold it as long as they have people financially dependent upon them. The classic situation would be where a worker is providing for his or her family. Eventually, kids grow up and move out (we hope), and we someday retire or have sufficient financial assets to provide for us into our old age.

The cost of life insurance increases with age for the simple reason that the odds of dying increase the older we get. That's why term insurance costs increase. With some cash value policies, insurers and agents create the illusion that the cost doesn't increase—what really happens is that the increasing cost of coverage is quietly being deducted from a cash balance resulting from such high payments in the early years of the policy.

The other argument that term insurance is for those on a tight budget is also silly. The converse to this is that cash value life insurance is better for the more financially flush. What's fascinating is that the average policy size for term is $166,000, whereas it's just $74,000 for cash value policies. The main reason for this is that cash value policies are so much more expensive for the level of coverage they provide, which is why most people can't afford to buy enough cash value coverage to properly protect their loved ones.

Consider that the amount of life insurance you should buy should be determined based upon how many years' worth of your income you seek to replace. For example, if you have young children and desire to replace your income over the next 20 years, you would multiply your after-tax annual income by about 15. So, if your after-tax income is $40,000 yearly, you should buy a $600,000 term life policy. So what good is $74,000 worth of cash value life coverage? Not much—that would be about the appropriate size policy for someone wanting to replace just $5,000 in yearly after-tax income over 15 years!

Cash value life insurance should only be considered by folks with a high enough net worth that they anticipate having an estate planning "problem." When you buy a cash value policy and place it in an irrevocable life insurance trust, the death benefits can pass to your heirs free of federal estate taxes.

Under current tax law, you can leave up to $2 million free of federal estate taxes to your heirs. (This amount increases to $3.5 million in 2009.) If you're married, you can pass on double these amounts through the use of a bypass trust. So, most people don't have an estate planning "problem." Therefore, one might think that the vast majority of people buy term insurance, not cash value policy. Surprisingly, 51 percent of all life insurance policies sold are cash value, and only 49 percent are term policies. Given the needs and level of affluence of the broad insurance-buying public, 95+ percent of the policies sold should be term! Few people need and would most benefit from cash value policies. The fact that many people are being sold the wrong type of policy is again highlighted in the fact that the average cash value policy sold is for only $74,000 in coverage. Clearly, these policies aren't being bought by wealthy folks but instead are being peddled to many middle class people.

> *"For almost 70 years the life insurance industry has been a smug sacred cow feeding the public a steady line of sacred bull."*
> —*Consumer Advocate Ralph Nader*

Health Insurance

In addition to evaluating your need for disability and life insurance, everyone should have a comprehensive health insurance policy. Even if you're in good health, you never know when an accident or illness can happen. Health care is expensive, and when you buy health insurance, you're protecting yourself from getting stuck with large medical bills and having to deplete your savings or going into hock for many years to pay them off.

Those who avoid dealing with money issues, especially those who are young, may think that they don't need health insurance as long as they're healthy. The problem is none of us knows when life will throw a medical curve ball. To keep the cost to a more reasonable level, buy a health insurance policy with high deductibles (the initial expenses you are required to pay out of your own pocket). You can save on taxes by saving in a tax-advantaged account, such as a flexible spending account or health savings account for out-of-pocket medical expenses (see Chapter 17 for more on these).

Another form of insurance that some people consider is long-term care (LTC) coverage. The desire to obtain such coverage springs from the concern that an extended nursing home stay or need for extended care in the home has limited coverage under Medicare, our government-provided health plan for those over age 65. Under current rules, Medicare pays for much of the first 100 days of a nursing home stay.

LTC insurance makes the most sense for those folks who fear depleting their assets with an extended illness or incapacity and who would not be satisfied with facilities accepting Medicaid, the state-provided health coverage for those who are financially needy. If you do consider LTC coverage, be sure to get a quality policy that provides truly long-term benefits. Keep the waiting period, which is the policy's deductible, as long as you can tolerate (at least 3 to 6 months) since this will help reduce the cost of the coverage.

Insurance on Your Assets

You work hard to earn and save money and buy a home, a car, and other things. These assets are valuable and would be quite costly to replace. Also, these assets could be attached in a lawsuit arising from those assets. Insurance can protect you from these potential problems.

For example, you should have comprehensive insurance on your home and car(s). If your home were burned to the ground, a comprehensive homeowner's insurance should pay for the cost of rebuilding the home.

Likewise, if your car were totaled in an accident, auto insurance will pay to replace the car.

In addition to protecting the potential cost to replace damage to your valuable assets, you can and should also secure adequate liability insurance for those assets. Both homeowner's and auto insurance come with liability protection. Make sure you carry liability coverage for at least twice the value of your net worth (assets minus liabilities).

In addition to the liability protection that comes with auto and homeowner's insurance, you can purchase a supplemental liability insurance policy known as an umbrella or excess liability policy. Purchased in increments of $1,000,000, this coverage provides greater liability protection on your car(s) and home(s) and can protect people with a larger net worth. Note that this coverage does not protect against lawsuits arising from your work.

As with other types of insurance that you purchase, take the highest deductible you can comfortably live with. The deductible represents the amount of money that you must pay out of your own pocket if you have a loss for which you file a claim. A high deductible helps keep down the cost of your coverage and eliminates the hassles of filing small claims.

16

Managing Risks
Involves More Than
Buying Insurance

*"The first step in the risk management
process is to acknowledge the reality of risk.
Denial is a common tactic that substitutes
deliberate ignorance for thoughtful planning."*
—Charles Tremper

W hile securing insurance is crucial to protecting your financial security, you can and should do more to manage risks than simply throwing money at insurance policies. Plenty of sensible non-insurance steps are free or low cost to take, can reduce your insurance costs, and improve the quality of your life. That's what this chapter is about.

Buy a Home at Low Risk for Natural Disasters

You live in your home and spend a lot of time there. You can buy insurance to cover the risks of flooding, hurricanes, earthquakes, and landslides, but do you really want to live through your home being totaled and possibly putting your life at risk?

An excellent warning sign for high-risk property is if you have difficulty in finding insurance and finding only highly expensive coverage from one or two companies.

The first item to investigate when considering a given home is the risk of flooding. You can start that process at The National Flood Insurance Program's (NFIP) web site at www.floodsmart.gov. Among the more sobering statistics from NFIP about floods is that, "Your home has a 26% chance of being damaged by a flood during the course of a 30-year mortgage, compared to a 9% chance of fire." The site's insurance center can help you with learning more about and securing flood insurance quotes.

Hurricanes are another disaster to prepare for, especially if you live in the South and/or along coastal areas. "We're eventually going to get a strong enough storm in a densely populated area to have a major disaster," says former National Hurricane Center Director Max Mayfield, adding "I know people don't want to hear this, and I'm generally a very positive person, but we're setting ourselves up for this major disaster." Mayfield warns that there could be 10 times as many deaths as from Hurricane Katrina and hundreds of thousands and perhaps millions homeless, particularly in the Southeast where Mayfield sees too many homes being built in storm zones. Mayfield argues that two main tactics can mitigate the impact of a devastating hurricane:

➤ **Improved building codes.** Housing and other buildings can be constructed to tolerate hurricane-force winds and storm surges. Don't buy and live in properties that don't meet hurricane-proof building codes.

➤ **Evacuation and preparedness plan.** Earthquakes are another disaster risk you must be smart about. The United States Geologic Survey (USGS) map clearly highlights the regions of the country at greatest risk. In addition to buying earthquake coverage if you live in a higher risk area, also be sure to make your house safer through the following measures:

➤ Anchor/bolt your home to the foundation.

➤ Strengthen cripple walls and pier-and-post foundations.

➤ Retrofit masonry foundations and unreinforced masonry walls.

➤ Locate gas and water shutoffs and have a wrench handy.

➤ Secure a water heater by strapping it to the wall studs and bolting it to the floor.

➤ Fasten shelves securely to walls.

➤ Place large or heavy objects on lower shelves.

➤ Store breakables (e.g., bottled foods, china) in low, closed cabinets with latches.

➤ Hang heavy items, such as pictures and mirrors, away from beds and couches.

➤ Brace overhead light fixtures.

➤ Repair fire risks, such as defective electrical wiring and leaky gas connections.

➤ Repair deep cracks in ceilings or foundations. Get expert advice if there are signs of structural defects.

➤ Store pesticides and flammable products in closed cabinets with latches and on bottom shelves.

➤ Identify safe places indoors and out (e.g., under a heavy desk or table); against an inside wall; away from windows, mirrors, pictures, or where heavy bookcases or other heavy furniture could fall over; or in the open, away from buildings, trees, telephone and electrical lines, overpasses, or elevated expressways.

For more information on earthquake risk assessment and preparation, consult the California Commission on Seismic Safety web site (www.seismic.ca.gov) and the Federal Emergency Management Agency's web site (www.fema.gov).

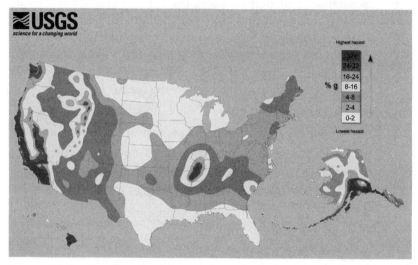

Figure 16.1 *Earthquake risk map from the United States Geologic Survey (USGS)*

Prospective real estate buyers can research environmental hazards and issues of a specific property they may buy. Environmental Data Resources produces an EDR Neighborhood Environmental Report, which costs about $100. You can order a report through an "EDR certified" home inspector, but you need not order a home inspection from that inspector. Call 800-624-0470 or visit EDR's web site at www.edrnet.com.

Maximize Your Personal Health

Whipping your finances into shape and saving and investing toward your future goals is pointless if you neglect your health, yourself, and your relationships. In the worst scenarios, you might not even be around to enjoy your retirement account balances.

I was inspired to run by a number of factors, including reading James Fixx's best-selling book, *The Complete Book of Running*, as a high school student. I ran track in high school and have continued running recreationally since. Fixx died of a heart attack while enjoying a summer New England run. Although Fixx understood the cardiovascular and other health benefits of running, he did not understand other personal health issues well. For example, he had smoked for many years well into his 30s and was significantly overweight. Although he quit smoking and lost weight, in his book he bragged about how much food like cheeseburgers, French fries, and milkshakes he could consume.

After his death, more facts emerged about Fixx's health. His cholesterol levels were apparently high, and an autopsy revealed significant blockage in his coronary arteries. A friend also disclosed that he had declined doing a recommended cardiac stress test.

While the world was made a better place by Fixx and his work as a writer, his case also highlights the holistic nature of personal health.

Buy a Safe Car and Reduce Your Driving Risks

Without a doubt, the most dangerous thing that you probably do is get behind the wheel of a car or travel as a passenger in someone else's vehicle. Yet, many people give insufficient thought to taking sensible measures to reduce their risk in cars.

For starters, we minimize and trivialize the risk. We say things to ourselves such as, "I drive short distances," or "My large SUV will protect me."

Car buyers often do little if any research on the safety records of cars they ultimately buy. In a survey conducted by *Consumer Reports*, only 12 percent (less than one in eight) of prospective new car buyers said that safety features were the most important consideration in their planned purchases.

Two excellent resources for auto safety information are the following:

➤ *Consumer Reports* (www.consumerreports.org)
➤ Insurance Institute for Highway Safety (www.iihs.org)

Compounding the fact that many people don't research and buy the safest cars, we overestimate how good our driving skills are. Consider how drivers responded to the following multiple choice options in a survey conducted by the Insurance Institute for Highway Safety:

My driving skills are much better or better than average 74%

My driving skills are average 25%

My driving skills are below average 1%

74 times as many people said their driving skills were above average than said they were below average! And, 99 percent of all respondents rated their skills as average or above! Clearly, that can't possibly be the case in the real world.

Those in the insurance and highway safety realms are well aware of when, why, and how auto accidents tend to happen. That's why the following tips compiled from the AAA Foundation for Safety, Liberty Mutual Insurance Group, and the National Highway Traffic Safety Administration (NHTSA) are so powerful:

➤ Don't tailgate.

➤ Signal early. Turn on your signals 5+ seconds before you turn or change lanes.

➤ Adjust and lock adjustable headrests to reduce head or neck injury in accidents.

➤ Know how to use your antilock brakes. In an emergency, stomp hard and keep your foot firmly on the brake—don't pump antilock brakes. Stay calm and ease off the gas while carefully steering in the direction of a skid.

➤ Green does mean GO...but first make sure the intersection is clear! Many side-impact accidents occur as a result of people not stopping for red lights.

➤ Adjust your mirrors to reduce blind spots.

➤ Focus. Distractions (such as adjusting music controls, passengers in the car, construction, and aggressive drivers) are factors in half of vehicle crashes.

➤ Avoid using your cell phone while driving. If you must make a call while driving, use a hands-free device (which is the law in many states).

➤ Avoid solar glare. At sunrise and sunset, you may encounter intense solar glare. Have sunglasses handy so that you are always prepared.

➤ Turn on your headlights when you use your wipers. It will help increase your visibility and will help other drivers see you. In many states, it's the law!

➤ Keep your car windows clear. Sun or headlights reflecting off a dirty windshield can prevent you from seeing what's in front of you. Clear snow and ice off your car so that it doesn't slide onto your windshield or fly onto someone else's.

➤ Don't use cruise control when the roads are wet. An activated cruise control system continually applies power and keeps your wheels spinning.

➤ Buckle up every time. Every 11 seconds, someone is injured, and every 12 minutes, someone is killed in a car crash. Seat belts reduce injuries and fatalities.

➤ Avoid sudden lane changes and excess speed, and be careful on curves with sport utility vehicles (SUVs) because of their higher center of gravity and roll-overs.

➤ Don't force large trucks to brake or swerve suddenly. Large trucks have many blind spots, so don't linger alongside them. If you can't see the driver in the truck's mirror, he can't see you. When passing a truck, don't pull back in front of it until you see the entire truck in your inside rearview mirror.

➤ Watch your speed. Speeding is one of the most prevalent factors contributing to traffic crashes, according to the NHTSA.

➤ Buy a tire gauge and check tire pressure monthly. For suggested tire pressure levels, check the placard located on the inside of your driver's side door. To check tread wear, insert a penny upside down in the groove of the tread on each tire. Look at the distance between the top of Lincoln's image and the edge of the penny. If you can see the top of Lincoln's head, it's time to purchase new tires.

➤ Select a designated driver before you and your companions start drinking. Don't wait until you arrive at your destination to decide who will drive home.

➤ Watch out for road rage. Be courteous and don't engage in aggressive actions—tailgating, blocking the passing lane, beeping the horn excessively, or using high beams to "punish" other drivers—that could provoke road rage.

Here are some additional tips for driving in the weather extremes of the winter and summer:

- ➤ Make sure you have enough coolant in your vehicle and that it's designed to withstand the winter temperatures you might experience in your area.

- ➤ Fill your vehicle's washer reservoir before the first snow hits. Use high-quality, "no-freeze" fluid. Keep extra on hand in your vehicle.

- ➤ Make sure your windshield wipers work, and replace worn blades. If you live in an area that gets a lot of snow and ice, consider heavy-duty winter wipers.

- ➤ Drive slowly. Increase your following distance to have plenty of time to stop.

- ➤ Stock your vehicle to handle common winter driving tasks (e.g., cleaning off your windshield) as well as supplies you might need in an emergency. Consider the following: snow shovel, broom, ice scraper, abrasive material (sand or kitty litter) in case your vehicle gets stuck in snow, jumper cables, flashlight and warning devices (flares and markers), blankets for cold protection, cell phone, water, food, and any necessary medicine for longer trips.

- ➤ Check your fluid levels—oil, brake, transmission, power steering, coolant, and windshield.

- ➤ Ensure all the lights on your vehicle are in working order. Check your headlights, brake lights, turn signals, emergency flashers, and interior lights. Check trailer lights, too—the failure of which is a serious safety hazard.

- ➤ Never leave children or pets unattended in parked vehicles—especially during warm weather.

Conquer and Avoid Addictions

Having worked at giving financial advice for nearly two decades, I have observed that addictions are a major impediment to accomplishing money goals. People with addictions have great difficulty changing their behavior and habits. This section highlights problems with gambling, drinking, smoking, and substance abuse. Plus, the ability to quickly and easily trade investments, especially through the Internet, has created a whole new set of problematic, addictive behavior. All of these issues have associated costs and are closely aligned with common financial problems. This section covers the major addictions that have touched virtually every family.

Millions of people have successfully conquered costly and deadly addictions. Doing so isn't easy or quick. "Addiction is a chronic disease, like diabetes, asthma, or hypertension. Just like these diseases, one course of treatment is unlikely to result in a complete cure. Ongoing treatment may be required before an addict achieves the final stage of recovery," says the Institute for Research, Education, and Training in Addictions.

Consider the following hurdles standing in the way of individuals with addictions getting the treatment that they need:

➤ **Denial.** Many people with addictions aren't willing or able to admit their problem and the damage it's causing to themselves and their loved ones. Others may understand some of the problems, but they aren't ready to give up their coveted substances and behaviors.

➤ **Shame.** The enormous humiliation that many people who suffer addictions feel often prevents them from seeking help. To help substance-abuse sufferers combat these feelings, many 12-step programs, such as Alcoholics Anonymous, provide a high level of confidentiality.

➤ **Uncertainty surrounding their options.** Even when people are motivated to finally get help, sorting through treatment options can be time confusing and intimidating. A general lack of knowledge about and reluctance to offer unsolicited referrals for substance-abuse treatment on the part of many primary care physicians exacerbates this problem. According to a survey conducted by The National Center on Addiction and Substance Abuse (CASA) at Columbia University, when presented with an adult patient with the early symptoms of alcohol abuse, a whopping 94 percent of primary care doctors failed to include substance abuse among the five possible diagnoses that they offered. Among the reasons, according to the report, explaining why physicians are missing or misdiagnosing patients' substance abuse are lack of adequate medical school training; skepticism about treatment effectiveness; patient resistance; discomfort discussing substance abuse; time constraints; and fear of losing patients.

➤ **Cost.** While I've discussed how costly many addictions are, the cost of treatment is perceived to be much higher because its cost is incurred over short periods. Insurance, sadly, often doesn't cover many treatments. "The best treatment programs for you depend upon how much money you have. Insurance won't generally pay for 28-day inpatient-stay programs," says Dr. John Morgenstern, VP Health and Treatment at CASA. Plus, consumers who understand the insurance business are justifiably worried that disclosing an addiction will be a black mark against them in terms of future insurance availability and cost.

➤ **Time constraints.** Even if someone locates good treatment options and determines how to pay for the needed help, carving out the necessary time is another significant hurdle. Treatment is time consuming, and work and family demands can stand in the way.

Gambling

The legalized gambling industry, euphemistically called the *gaming business*, now rakes in more than $80 billion annually, which is greater than the amount that Americans spend on tickets to sporting events, movies, theme parks, plays, concerts and live performances, and music combined!

Legalized gambling got off to a slow start in the twentieth century. The first casino opened in Nevada in 1931, and it wasn't until 45 years later (1976) that the first casino opened in another state, this time in Atlantic City, New Jersey. Today, more than 1,300 casinos operate in 36 states. Members of about one-third of American households visit a casino annually, and they average approximately six casino trips per year. Even closer to home, and much more accessible, are state lotteries. New Hampshire was the first state to have a lottery, but today, more than three-quarters of states run lotteries. Add in horse racing, dog racing, off-track betting, jai alai, Internet gambling, and video poker machines, and you can quickly realize that Americans have a plethora of opportunities to gamble away their money. In fact, 48 states now offer some form of legalized gambling. (Only Hawaii and Utah are left free of gaming.)

Accompanying this surge in available gambling options is an increase in the percentage of Americans with a serious gambling problem, a fact confirmed by studies by the Harvard Medical School Division on Addictions and Marc Potenza, director of Yale's Problem Gambling

Clinic. The introduction of a major gambling establishment approximately doubles the number of problem gamblers within a 50-mile radius, according to an analysis done by the National Opinion Research Center. For problem gamblers, gambling interferes with work, family life, friendships, and personal money management.

Casinos know the problem, and yet take steps to exploit it. They're well known for developing and utilizing mailing lists targeting compulsive gamblers—their best customers. These establishments inundate their biggest-spending customers with solicitations inviting these profligate gamblers to make free use of their hotel rooms, check out a sporting event on the house, and attend private cocktail parties, among other amenities. Who better to drop a lot of dough in the casino than a tipsy, addicted gambler?

In the end, that's what problem gamblers do—lose a lot of money. Then, they typically rack up more debt to feed their money-losing ways by borrowing on credit cards, through casino credit lines, and acquaintances until they end up in bankruptcy. In a study published in the *American Journal of Psychiatry*, 85 percent of callers to a problem-gambling help line reported financial problems due to their gambling. However, the financial strains induced by gambling are only one component of the problem.

Problem gamblers are four times more likely to abuse alcohol than the average person, eight times more likely to struggle with drug-abuse issues, and have a much greater incidence of divorce, child abuse, and domestic violence within the family. Gamblers also suffer from extremely high rates of psychological problems: 90 percent experience high rates of anxiety, and 80 percent suffer from depression caused by their gambling. These rates are nearly the same as those attributed to habitual cocaine users.

Dr. Hans Breiter, a psychiatry professor at Harvard Medical School, has published research documenting that both gambling and cocaine stimulate the same region of the brain that produces dopamine. "We cannot distinguish any difference between the brain pattern of someone gambling and someone ingesting cocaine," says Breiter.

Gambler's Anonymous Twenty Questions for Determining Compulsive Gambling

According to Gambler's Anonymous, a person who has a compulsive gambling problem will answer "yes" to 7 or more of these 20 questions.

1. Did you ever lose time from work or school due to gambling?
2. Has gambling ever made your home life unhappy?
3. Did gambling affect your reputation?
4. Have you ever felt remorse after gambling?
5. Did you ever gamble to get money with which to pay debts or otherwise solve financial difficulties?
6. Did gambling cause a decrease in your ambition or efficiency?
7. After losing, did you feel you must return as soon as possible and win back your losses?
8. After a win, did you have a strong urge to return and win more?
9. Did you often gamble until your last dollar was gone?
10. Did you ever borrow to finance your gambling?
11. Have you ever sold anything to finance gambling?
12. Were you reluctant to use "gambling money" for normal expenditures?
13. Did gambling make you careless of the welfare of yourself or your family?
14. Did you ever gamble longer than you had planned?
15. Have you ever gambled to escape worry or trouble?
16. Have you ever committed, or considered committing, an illegal act to finance gambling?
17. Did gambling cause you to have difficulty in sleeping?
18. Do arguments, disappointments, or frustrations create within you an urge to gamble?
19. Did you ever have an urge to celebrate any good fortune by a few hours of gambling?
20. Have you ever considered self destruction or suicide as a result of your gambling?

The American Psychiatric Association recognized gambling as a disease, and numerous insurers now cover some therapy and treatment for people with gambling problems. Some gamblers have found success in conquering their addiction by enlisting the support of their spouse or partner or friend and turning the family finances over to their spouse. If you or someone you love has a need for gambling-related treatment programs and resources, consider the following resources:

➤ The web site of the National Council on Problem Gambling has an excellent resource section (www.ncpgambling.org/resources) containing a compendium of online and print resources for gamblers seeking help and a directory of treatment programs and counselors. You will also find a useful list of issues to consider and questions to ask when evaluating various treatment programs. The organization also offers a 24/7 helpline at 800-522-4700, through which you can obtain a confidential referral to a counselor.

➤ Gamblers Anonymous (www.gamblersanonymous.org; 213-386-8789) is a 12-step organization that began in 1957. The organization's web site details the 12-step approach to conquering a gambling addiction and lists meeting locations organized by country (and by state within the U.S.). The sister organization, Gam-Anon, also offers a useful web site (www.gam-anon.org) tailored to the needs and concerns of family and friends of those suffering from a gambling addiction.

➤ The more comprehensive treatment centers, such as Hazelden and Sierra Tucson, discussed in the next section, handle gambling problems and associated mental disorders.

Substance Abuse: Drugs and Alcohol

Addiction to illegal and legal drugs is a massive problem in America. Various studies estimate that upwards of 20 million people currently use illegal drugs. Millions more wrestle with addiction problems involving tranquilizers, stimulants, and the non-medical use of various prescription painkillers, such as Vicodin, Percodan, Lorcet, Hydrocodone, and OxyContin.

Government Should Get Out of the Gambling Business

Addicted citizens, bankruptcy, abuse, and divorce aside, some people have been duped into believing that state lotteries are actually useful. The argument is that they supposedly help lower taxes and fund education.

Consider what happened recently in Pennsylvania where gambling regulators granted approval for Philadelphia to become the nation's largest city with a casino. An AP article cited Governor Ed Rendell who, "…rejuvenated a 25-year drive to legalize casino-style gambling in Pennsylvania by promising that slots revenue would help reduce property taxes and revive the state's declining horse-racing industry."

The truth is that states actually take in little revenue from lotteries—only about one-third of the money generated through ticket sales. (The rest goes to prizes and administration.) That percentage compares unfavorably with track records of charities, which are able to deliver about 80 percent of the money they bring in to the actual cause.

On average, states with lotteries have higher, not lower, taxes and spend less on education than states without lotteries. But lotteries are viewed by many lawmakers and constituents as "free" money. State governments are addicted to gambling revenue, especially when they're running deficits. Unlike cutting spending or increasing taxes, few people are motivated and mobilized to protest state promotion of gambling, as the true costs are often hidden within individual families.

Alcohol abuse is an even bigger problem. More than 50 million Americans are classified as binge drinkers (imbibing five or more drinks at a single occasion at least once per month). Nearly 20 million of these people can be considered chronic heavy drinkers, as they have at least five drinking binges monthly.

To the outside world, Rachel was an intelligent, warm, caring mother of two who lived in a beautiful home in California with her husband Bruce, to whom outsiders would have attributed the same qualities. Inside their home, however, Rachel struggled to keep her family together through Bruce's drinking problems and repeated marital separations.

Bruce's addiction to alcohol ultimately destroyed his marriage, caused his death at the age of 48, and wreaked havoc with the family's finances. "After the final separation and subsequent divorce, Bruce wasn't attending to his business, which required a lot of customer service... When he died, I lost my alimony and child support," says Rachel, "...95 percent of my financial difficulties were due to the alcoholism."

Because alcoholics are so adept at concealing their problems and family members and friends aren't often able to pinpoint the problem or overcome their denial, the disease of alcoholism can go on for years. Substance abusers of all types ultimately cause enormous damage to their household's finances and often don't get the help they need until those around them understand the problem and how to deal with it.

Alcoholism and substance-abuse problems, which often go hand in hand, are widespread and costly to both individual families and society as a whole. "When the effects on the families of abusers and people close to those injured or killed by intoxicated drivers are considered, such abuse affects untold millions more," says the American Psychiatric Association (APA). More than 41 percent of the nation's 42,000 annual traffic fatalities and more than one million injuries occur annually in alcohol-related traffic crashes according to the National Highway Traffic Safety Administration. Approximately two in every five Americans will be involved in an alcohol-related crash at some time in their lives. Traffic crashes, about half of which are alcohol related, are the single greatest cause of death for everyone between the ages of 5 and 27.

As a society, we have a warped perception of who alcoholics are. Many of us think of the visible alcoholics and drug abusers who we see wandering the streets. "Only about 3 percent of alcoholics are the problem on the street...the other 97 percent cuts across the population," says Michael Webb, a mental health professional who works with companies through employee assistance programs (EAP). Alcoholism has brought many famous people into treatment. The list includes former first lady Betty Ford; Kitty Dukakis, wife of presidential candidate Michael Dukakis; former NBA basketball player Chris Mullin; and Mary Tyler Moore, and it has led to the early death of others, including William Holden, Mickey Mantle, Elvis Presley, and comedian Chris Farley. However, most alcoholics and substance abusers aren't famous from their work nor are they down and out street people. To the rest of us, they appear to be ordinary people with strengths and weaknesses.

In fact, like Bruce, alcoholics can be great employees, be well educated, have top-paying professional jobs, and be good providers for their families. Family members, however, see more of the dark side. According to Rachel, "Bruce entertained clients and drank, and drank with other family members. He often didn't come home until late and became belligerent and argumentative. Everyone on the outside thought we had it made. We had a nice home, he drove a Mercedes, and we had two healthy kids. But, Bruce was so unhappy."

Bruce was successful and making money, but he wasn't good at managing it. Bruce didn't come from a financially stable home, and he loved having a lot of money in his pocket and spending it. "He was reckless with his money and liked to spend it on status items to show the world he had arrived and fit into the mold of his peers. He was terrible at saving money and spent a lot on alcohol and eating out," says Rachel.

Problems dealing with money can be an indicator of possible substance abuse problems and provide a clue to family, friends, and counselors that further investigation is necessary. Financial signs can include those that seem to result from carelessness but become chronic, such as late or unpaid bills, overdrawn checking accounts, maxing out sources of credit, and forgetting to tell a spouse or partner about purchases. Gambling problems and workplace difficulties often correlate with chemical addiction. "In the workplace, other possible indicators of such addictions include wage garnishments for debts, problems with expense accounts such as getting way behind in reports or paying back cash advances, and a bankruptcy filing," adds Webb.

Even with financial warning flags and other concerns, such as drunk-driving incidents, frequent arguments in the home, and accompanying medical ailments that often come with substance abuse, even immediate family members often can't identify the exact problem (or they're in denial about it). Rachel illustrates this challenge: "Bruce was really good at keeping his addiction a secret...but it got harder over time as he started drinking in the morning. Part of me was in denial. It wasn't until one of Bruce's office assistants said that she thought he was an alcoholic did I really begin to consider the possibility. I was an enabler. Bruce had always been attracted to people who could take care of him and cover for him."

In psychology circles, enablers like Rachel are referred to as a "codependent." In an interview aired on CBS' *60 Minutes*, former president Gerald Ford admitted to his own codependent behavior that created an accepting environment for his wife Betty's drinking: "I was a bad enabler. I made all kinds of excuses, made all kinds of alibis [for Betty]. That's a typical spouse's reaction." As is often the case, according to psychologists and substance abuse experts, the reach of codependency extends to children of alcoholics, as well as spouses, and sometimes to friends and coworkers. Betty Ford's adult children, for example, used to water down her drinks at functions where alcohol was served.

Betty Ford finally got the help she needed when confronted by family members in an intervention. "They went from one to another saying how I had let them down, how I disappointed them...I was so hurt. I felt I had spent my whole life devoted to them, and they were telling me I was failing them," said Betty Ford. But, this tough love approach worked. "The intervention was the only thing that saved Betty's life," claimed Gerald Ford in the *60 Minutes* interview. Within a week of the intervention, Betty Ford entered and successfully completed an inpatient alcohol treatment program at the Long Beach Naval Hospital's Alcohol and Drug Rehabilitation Unit and has been sober since. In fact, Betty Ford has been a champion of alcohol treatment. She founded and has maintained an active involvement in the Betty Ford Treatment Center, which has been in operation for more than two decades and has treated over 60,000 patients.

Getting addicted people into needed treatment is often difficult and may feel impossible given all of the obstacles discussed earlier in this chapter—time, costs, shame, denial, and not knowing where to turn for help. Interventions can help overcome these problems.

In a typical intervention, a paid professional (the interventionist) brings together family and friends to "confront" the person with the addiction. This is how Betty Ford's family got her into alcohol treatment. Relatives often turn to an intervention when they've exhausted other avenues for help or don't know how to proceed. To learn more about interventions, please consult the following books:

➤ *Intervention: How to Help Someone Who Doesn't Want Help* by Vernon E. Johnson

➤ *Love First: A New Approach to Intervention for Alcoholism and Drug Addiction* by Jeff Jay and Debra Jay

➤ *The Betty Ford Center Book of Answers* by James W. West

The alcoholic not only needs to quit drinking but also needs to address the underlying psychological issues accompanying the behavior. Those close to the alcoholic should also address such issues, as they're at high risk (especially children of alcoholics) for becoming alcoholics themselves. "People who come to me because a spouse or a child has a drinking problem often are reluctant to go into psychological counseling—some really hate looking at themselves," says Webb. Recovered alcoholics will tell you that doing so is difficult but well worth the effort.

A simple yet powerful diagnostic tool for screening for alcoholism within the medical community is the CAGE questionnaire, which was originally discussed by Allen, Eckardt, and Wallen in the journal *Public Health Reports* in 1988. CAGE is composed of just four questions:

1. Have you felt the need to Cut down on your drinking?
2. Do you feel Annoyed by people complaining about your drinking?
3. Do you ever feel Guilty about your drinking?
4. Do you ever drink an Eye-opener in the morning to relieve the shakes?

The study found that those individuals who are "problem drinkers" will answer "yes" to at least two of these questions.

Alcoholics Anonymous, a treatment program discussed later in this section, has twelve questions that you can also ask yourself. (Note the similarities with some of the CAGE questions.)

1. Have you ever decided to stop drinking for a week or so but only lasted for a couple of days?
2. Do you wish people would mind their own business about your drinking and stop telling you what to do?
3. Have you ever switched from one kind of drink to another in the hope that this would keep you from getting drunk?
4. Have you had to have an eye-opener upon awakening during the past year?
5. Do you envy people who can drink without getting into trouble?
6. Have you had problems connected with drinking during the past year?
7. Has your drinking caused trouble at home?
8. Do you ever try to get "extra" drinks at a party because you do not get enough?
9. Do you tell yourself you can stop drinking any time you want to, even though you keep getting drunk when you don't mean to?
10. Have you missed days of work or school because of drinking?

11. Do you have "blackouts"?

12. Have you ever felt that your life would be better if you did not drink?

AA says that if you answered "yes" at least four times, you are likely in trouble with your alcohol usage.

Among the best resources for alcoholics and those who care about them are the following:

➤ The National Council on Alcoholism and Drug Dependence (www.ncadd.org; 212-269-7797). This non-profit, which seeks to educate and advocate prevention, intervention, and treatment through its national affiliate network, was founded in 1944 by Marty Mann, the first female "graduate" of Alcoholics Anonymous.

➤ The United States Department of Health and Human Services Substance Abuse and Mental Health Services Administration web site (www.samhsa.gov) offers a user-friendly Substance Abuse Treatment Facility Locator online, or you can call their Referral Helpline at 800-662-4357.

➤ Alcoholics Anonymous (www.aa.org; 212-870-3400) is a self-help 12-step group program for alcoholics. Al-Anon (www.alanon.org; 888-425-2666) is a self-help 12-step group program for friends and family of alcoholics. The web sites from both organizations can provide you with local contact information (or you can check your phone directory for local chapters).

➤ The Boston University School of Public Health offers a web site (www.alcoholscreening.org) that includes educational materials, a searchable database of treatment resources, and links to various support groups.

➤ The Betty Ford Center (www.bettyfordcenter.org; 800-854-9211) is a non-profit alcohol and drug treatment program co-founded by former first lady Betty Ford after her own successful alcohol treatment. The center offers inpatient services for those suffering from addictions and their family members.

➤ Hazelden (www.hazelden.org; 800-257-7810) offers treatment programs in Minnesota, Oregon, Illinois, and New York. Hazelden takes patient education seriously, as is evidenced by the extensive list of quality publications that the organization produces and sells. Their web site also contains much free information.

- ➤ The Caron Foundation (www.caron.org; 800-678-2332) is a Pennsylvania-based, non-profit drug and alcohol treatment program that also has centers in New York and Florida.

- ➤ Columbia Presbyterian (212-305-6001) offers a couple of different treatment venues—McKeen and The Retreat—that are known for handling the more complex cases of substance abuse that also involve medical and psychiatric problems.

- ➤ Sierra Tucson (www.sierratucson.com; 800-842-4487) provides inpatient treatment for a variety of problems, including substance abuse, gambling, eating disorders, and associated mental health disorders.

Smoking

More than 70 million Americans engage in this costly and life-threatening habit. Approximately half a million Americans die each year due to smoking, which makes it the number-one preventable cause of death in the United States. The indictments against smoking are staggering, but just consider a few more statistics: 20 percent of all heart-disease fatalities, 30 percent of all cancer deaths, and 25 percent of all residential fire casualties are attributable to smoking.

Despite the clear and urgent health warnings about smoking that have been sounded for more than four decades, three in ten adults still smoke. The 1964 "Surgeon General's Report on Smoking and Health," prepared under Dr. Luther L. Terry, was the first compilation of the ills caused by tobacco usage. Thanks to this report and thousands of subsequent medical studies, there's irrefutable proof of how and why a half million Americans die annually from smoking. Tobacco contains countless poisonous chemicals including the highly addictive nicotine, carbon monoxide, ammonia, aldehydes, and tars. The regular inhalation of this toxic brew causes heart disease, stroke, emphysema (and other chronic obstructive pulmonary diseases), lung cancer, and numerous other cancers including those of the esophagus, mouth, kidney, and bladder. So-called secondhand smoke has also been proven to cause heart and respiratory problems, including lung cancer, in spouses and others frequently around smokers.

> **Motivation to Quit Smoking**
>
> Within 20 minutes after you smoke that last cigarette, your body begins a series of changes that continue for years.
>
> 20 minutes after quitting: Your heart rate drops.
>
> 12 hours after quitting: Carbon monoxide levels in your blood drop to normal.
>
> 2 weeks to 3 months after quitting: Your heart attack risk begins to drop. Your lung function begins to improve.
>
> 1 to 9 months after quitting: Your coughing and shortness of breath decrease.
>
> 1 year after quitting: Your added risk of coronary heart disease is half that of a smoker's.
>
> 5 to 15 years after quitting: Your stroke risk is reduced to that of a nonsmoker's.
>
> 10 years after quitting: Your lung cancer death rate is about half that of a smoker's. Your risk of cancers of the mouth, throat, esophagus, bladder, kidney, and pancreas decreases.
>
> 15 years after quitting: Your risk of coronary heart disease is back to that of a nonsmoker's.
>
> Source: U.S. Department for Health and Human Services, Centers for Disease Control and Prevention.

As people die due to continued usage, the tobacco industry must, of course, recruit its next generation of customers and victims. Smoking campaigns are targeted at young adults, with great success: Four in ten adults between the ages of 18 and 25 smoke. In addition, one in eight kids between the ages of 12 and 17 smokes despite the fact that it's illegal for minors to buy tobacco.

Smokers know the unhealthy and often fatal effects of smoking. They also know that, at $4 per pack, cigarette smoking is expensive. But let me crunch some numbers for you and provide a new financial perspective. Take a smoker who goes through just one pack per day. In addition to the health damage, consider the opportunity cost of having spent that money on smoking rather than investing it. If you took that $4 per day and invested in a diversified portfolio of stocks in a tax-advantaged retirement account, over 20 years, you'd have about $128,000, and in 40 years, you'd have amassed approximately $1,000,000. *At just one pack per day, cigarette smoking is a million-dollar habit! Those who smoke more than one pack a day have a multi-million dollar habit.*

In recent years, public education has made some progress in getting Americans to light up less and quit altogether. However, change has been slow, and far too many people still smoke way too much. The following are among the more useful smoking cessation resources and programs. When compared to seeking help for alcohol and drug addictions, your search for smoking cessation programs will yield many lower-cost alternatives.

➤ The Public Health Service convened a panel of smoking cessation experts to compile a summary of treatment protocols that have proven effective. Although the document, which you will find at www.surgeongeneral.gov/tobacco/tobaqrg.htm, is targeted to physicians, it contains a treasure trove of useful information on quitting smoking.

➤ QuitNet grew out of research done at the Boston University School of Public Health and now operates as a private company, partly owned by B.U. To access the web site (www.quitnet.com), you must register. One of its basic premises is that social support is important to stopping smoking. Basic services, such as a guide to quitting smoking and access to support forums, are free. The premium membership, which costs $40 for three months and $100 for one year, includes one-on-one counseling, online group counseling, printed materials featuring expert advice, medication advice, and discounts on smoking-cessation medication.

➤ Nicotine Anonymous (www.nicotine-anonymous.org; 415-750-0328) is another 12-step program, albeit with fewer meeting locations than the other 12-step programs recommended in this chapter.

➤ Hazelden Foundation (www.hazelden.org; 800-257-7800) offers an inpatient smoking cessation program in Minnesota.

➤ Champaign-Urbana Public Health District has two excellent booklets to convince you to quit smoking and to help you quit smoking. Visit www.mckinley.uiuc.edu/Wellness/AlcoholandDrugs/stepbystep/stepbystep.htm.

Protecting Teens and Kids

Companies and individuals who profit from addictions are always seeking to attract and retain long-term customers and will target teenagers (and in some cases, younger kids), who are the easiest converts due to their susceptibility to peer-group pressure and undeveloped decision-making skills. Parents must protect their children, who are so vulnerable and easily swayed to take risky and dangerous actions. Consider these statistics: The average age of first-time alcohol use is 12 years and 2 months, followed by 12 years and 6 months for cigarettes, and 13 years and 11 months for marijuana (the most popular illegal drug among adolescents).

How high are the stakes? "A child who reaches age 21 without smoking, abusing alcohol, or using drugs is virtually certain never to do so," says Joseph A. Califano, Jr., chairman and president of The National Center on Addiction and Substance Abuse (CASA) at Columbia University and a former secretary of the U.S. Department of Health, Education, and Welfare.

The risk that teens will smoke, drink, get drunk, and use illegal drugs increases sharply if they are highly stressed, frequently bored, or have substantial amounts of spending money, according to the "National Survey of American Attitudes on Substance Abuse VIII: Teens and Parents," a survey conducted by CASA:

➤ High-stress teens are twice as likely as low-stress teens to smoke, drink, get drunk, and use illegal drugs.

➤ Often-bored teens are 50 percent likelier than not-often-bored teens to smoke, drink, get drunk, and use illegal drugs.

➤ Teens with $25 or more a week in spending money are nearly twice as likely as teens with less to smoke, drink, and use illegal drugs, and more than twice as likely to get drunk.

➤ Teens exhibiting two or three of these characteristics are at more than three times the risk of substance abuse as those exhibiting none of these characteristics.

"High stress, frequent boredom, and too much spending money are a catastrophic combination for many American teens," said CASA chairman and president and Joseph A. Califano, Jr. "But it is a catastrophe that can be avoided through parental engagement. Parents must be sensitive to the stress in their children's lives, understand why they are bored, and limit their spending money."

The CASA survey also found that parents are more likely than teens to view teen drug use as a fait accompli. More than four out of ten parents said teens are "very likely" or "somewhat likely" to try drugs, compared to only one of ten teens who agreed with those statements. Teens whose parents believe that future drug use is "very likely" are more than three times more likely to become substance abusers than teens whose parents say future drug use is "not likely at all."

"Many parents think they have little power over their teens' substance use, and a disturbing number view drugs in schools as a fact of life they are powerless to stop," notes Califano. "How parents act, how much pressure they put on school administrators to get drugs out of their teens' schools, their attitudes about drugs, and how engaged they are in their children's lives will have enormous influence over their teens' substance use. Parent Power is the most underutilized weapon in efforts to curb teen substance abuse."

CASA recommends five ways that parents can reduce the risk of their teens engaging in smoking, drinking, or other substance abuse:

➤ Be sensitive to the stress in your children's lives, and help them cope. Kids today face all sorts of peer pressure in school to fit in socially. Academic pressures are problematic as well, particularly in high school and when children are preparing to apply to colleges. I can tell you as an alumni interviewer for my alma mater (Yale) that many of the kids I speak with today are leading the lives of overscheduled little adults. A 12-hour day isn't unusual for high school kids: After a 7-hour school day, most of these kids spend several hours on extracurricular activities and several more on homework.

➤ Understand when and why your children are bored, and help relieve their boredom. Children don't need non-stop entertainment, and you certainly won't be doing the best by your kids if you constantly plan out their days, activities, and social calendar. However, at key times, you can play a vital role in helping them to recognize opportunities and keep them from likely trouble.

➤ Limit the amount of money your children have to spend, and monitor how that money is spent. A simple way to track kids' spending is to have them use a VISA debit card that limits what they can spend because it's connected to a checking account that you monitor.

➤ Know who your children's friends are. Spend time speaking with their parents. Never assume—ask questions.

➤ Be engaged in your children's lives. Discuss their homework with them, attend their sporting events, participate in activities together, and talk to them about drugs.

17

Your Insurance Plan

---

*"Needing insurance is like needing a parachute.
If it isn't there the first time, chances are
you won't be needing it again."*
—Old saying

In this chapter, I will walk you through the process of reviewing your current insurance policies as well as providing specific suggestions for getting the insurance you need at the best prices. Although insurance is a dreadful and uninteresting topic for most people, I urge you to stick with me through this. You likely are paying too much for some insurance, missing some desirable coverage, and probably are wasting money on insurance you don't really need.

While you should periodically review your insurance coverage and needs (every one to two years), you should also do so when or before a major life change occurs. Those changes would include the birth of a child, move, divorce, death of a family member, retirement, and so on.

Retirement is an especially good time to review coverage. If you're able to retire, that should mean that you (and your family) are no longer dependent upon your earning income. Thus, you can likely discontinue your long-term disability and life insurance policies.

For each of your insurance policies, please locate a copy of the most recent information. You need information on the types and amounts of coverage you have, as well as accompanying descriptive material/pamphlets for the following:

➤ Employee benefits manuals (especially retirement savings plans and pensions, insurance—life, disability)

➤ Life insurance policies (purchased for any family member)

➤ All other insurance policies you have purchased on your own (e.g., health, disability, etc.)

Health Insurance

Let's start with your health insurance. Many people get coverage through their employers in a group plan, and, if you do, request documentation for your plans' benefits and costs. If you're self-employed or otherwise responsible for securing your own health insurance, contact your insurer or agent if you don't have your policy details handy.

For each plan, detail the insurer, your cost per month, and the family members covered:

	You	Spouse
Insurer	_____	_____
Your cost/month	$ _____ / month	$ _____ / month
Employer provided	yes ___ no ___	yes ___ no ___
Family members covered	_____	_____
	_____	_____
	_____	_____

With families with more than one plan, sometimes there is duplicate coverage. Unless your employers are paying the full cost of your plans and you couldn't use those benefit dollars in some other way, eliminate overlapping insurance.

As with other financial services and products including all types of insurance, be sure to shop for coverage that provides value—a good package of benefits at a competitive price. You don't always get what you pay for with health insurance. I have seen plenty of examples of expensive policies with mediocre benefits from insurers with lousy customer service.

In addition to shopping around for coverage, the single most important action you can take to dramatically cut your health insurance expenses is to enroll in a high deductible plan. Not only will this enable you to lower your premiums, but you can also sock money away into a Health Savings Account (HSA) and get a substantial tax break (see the sidebar on HSAs).

In addition to ensuring that a plan offers comprehensive major medical benefits (coverage of hospital, doctor, lab work, x-rays, etc.), see what wellness and preventative issues a plan covers. Also, how extensive and good is the list of medical providers? Does it include doctors and hospitals you have used or would like to use?

Given the high cost of medical care, choose a plan with high ($5 million+) lifetime maximum benefits.

As you shop among health insurance plans, give preference to those offered by the biggest and longest-standing insurers in the health insurance arena, such as Aetna, Anthem, Assurant, Blue Cross, Blue Shield, Cigna, Golden Rule, Health Net, Kaiser, United Healthcare, and WellPoint.

An insurance agent who specializes in health insurance may be of assistance to you, but beware that agents derive a commission based upon the amount of your premiums, so this presents agents with a conflict of interest not to advocate lower-cost plans and plan options.

Health Savings Account—Yet Another Tax Saver

Health savings accounts (HSAs), which are in their infancy, hold promise for people to be able to put money away on a tax-advantaged basis to pay for health care-related expenses. Money contributed to an HSA is tax-deductible; any investment earnings compound without tax and aren't taxed upon withdrawal so long as funds are used to pay for eligible health care costs.

The list of eligible expenses is generally quite broad— surprisingly so, in fact. You can use HSA money to pay for out-of-pocket medical costs not covered by insurance, prescription drugs, dental care (including braces), vision care, vitamins, psychologist fees, and smoking cessation programs, among other expenses. IRS Publication 502 details permissible expenses.

Most insurance premiums aren't eligible for being paid with HSA money, but some are. According to the IRS, you may "...treat premiums for long-term care coverage, health care coverage while you receive unemployment benefits, or health care continuation coverage required under any federal law as qualified medical expenses for HSAs."

To be eligible to contribute to an HSA, you must participate in a high deductible health plan that has a deductible of at least $1,100 for individuals, $2,200 for families. The plan must have a maximum out-of-pocket limit of no more than $5,500 for individuals and $11,000 for families. Ask health insurers which policies they offer that are "HSA compatible."

The maximum amount that you may contribute to an HSA is $2,850 for singles and $5,650 for families. (All of these dollar limits and amounts increase annually with the rate of medical inflation.)

If you work for an employer that offers an HSA and you wish to contribute to the account from your paycheck on a pre-tax basis, you must use the employer's provided HSA. Alternatively, you may find an HSA on your own and contribute after-tax dollars and then get your tax deduction when you file your tax return by filing Form 8889. Anyone (so long as you aren't covered by Medicare) who has an HSA-compatible policy may have an HSA.

Most HSAs require that some amount of money (e.g., $1,000) be invested in a safe option like a money fund or savings account, which is accessed with a debit card or checks that enable you to pay for medical expenses. Many HSAs offer a menu of investments—typically mutual funds. So, when comparing HSAs, you should compare the quality of those offerings.

Also be sure to examine fees, which can really add up on some HSAs. In addition to the fees of the offered funds, beware of load fees and maintenance fees of about $5 per month (which may be waived for regular automatic investments or once you meet a certain minimum).

So far, mostly banks and brokerages linked with banks are offering HSAs. Over time, I do expect the major investment providers such as the leading mutual fund companies to offer HSAs.

Among the HSAs that I've examined, one worth considering is offered by HSA Administrators (www.hsaadministrators.com; 888-354-0697).

Disability Insurance

As I discussed in Chapter 15, "Insurance," disability insurance is critical coverage to protect your income in the event a disability prevents you from earning income. You have a one in three chance of becoming disabled for more than 90 days between the ages of 35 and 60. At age 40, you are four times more likely to become disabled than to die.

For each disability insurance plan, detail the insurer and your cost per month:

	You	Spouse
Insurer	_____	_____
Your cost/month	$ _____ / month	$ _____ / month
Monthly benefit	$ _____ / month	$ _____ / month
Cost of living rider	_____ %/year	_____ %/year
Waiting period	_____ days	_____ days
Employer provided	yes ___ no ___	yes ___ no ___

Generally, you should have long-term disability insurance that provides a benefit of approximately 60 percent of your gross (pre-tax) income. Since disability benefits payments are tax free if you pay the premium, they should replace your current after-tax earnings. One exception to this guideline would be a person who is just getting started in a field (starting up a small business or someone beginning work at an entry level in professional service field) and reasonably expects his income to be significantly higher in future years. You can obtain a policy that enables you to buy a higher level of benefits ("future increase option") in the future without a health exam, or you can simply shop for a larger policy down the road. Other exceptions to the guideline are a person who has significant assets and is close to being financially independent or a person who earns a high income and spends far less than that. In both such cases, you may wish to buy only enough coverage to replace a more modest portion of current income.

State disability insurance programs and the Social Security disability insurance program do not provide adequate disability coverage. State programs typically only pay benefits for up to a maximum of one year, which isn't going to cut it if you truly suffer a long-term disability that can last years. While one year of coverage is better than none, the premiums for such short-term coverage often are higher per dollar of benefit than through the best private insurer programs.

Although the Social Security program pays long-term benefits, you will receive payments only if you are not able to perform any substantial, gainful activity for more than a year or if your disability will result in death. In fact, most applicants for Social Security disability benefits coverage are turned down. Furthermore, Social Security disability payments are only intended to provide for basic subsistence living expenses.

Worker's compensation, if you have coverage through your employer, will not pay benefits at all if you get injured or become sick away from your job. Such narrow coverage that only pays benefits under a limited set of circumstances is not the comprehensive insurance you need.

I recommend that your disability policy contain the following benefits:

➤ **Definition of Disability.** Guarantees you benefits if you cannot perform your regular occupation. If you work as a teacher, for example, your disability policy wouldn't require you to take a job as a cashier.

➤ **Noncancelable and Guaranteed Renewable.** Guarantees that your policy cannot be canceled because of poor health conditions. If you purchase a policy that requires periodic physical exams, you could lose your coverage when you are most likely to need it.

➤ **Insurer's Financial Health.** The insurance company should have strong financial health with the leading credit rating agencies (A.M. Best, Duff & Phelps, Moody's, Standard & Poor's, and Weiss Research).

➤ **Benefit Period.** You need a policy that would pay you benefits until an age at which you would become financially self-sufficient. For most people, that would require obtaining a policy that pays benefits to age 65 or 67 (when Social Security retirement benefits begin). If you are close to being financially independent and expect to accomplish that or retire before your mid-60s, also know that many companies offer policies that pay benefits for five years.

➤ **Waiting Period.** This is the "deductible" on disability insurance, which is the time between your disability and when you begin collecting benefits. As with other types of insurance, I recommend that you take the highest deductible (i.e., longest waiting period) that your financial circumstances allow. The minimum waiting period on most policies allowed is 30 days and the maximum can be up to 1 to 2 years. I generally recommend a waiting period of at least 90 or 180 days.

> **Residual Benefits.** I recommend this option, which pays you a partial benefit if you have a disability that prevents you from working full-time.

> **Cost-of-Living Adjustments.** This feature automatically increases your benefit payment once you are disabled by a set percentage or in step with inflation.

To get disability insurance proposals, start with considering if there are any professional associations for your occupation or profession. If that's not an option, interview some good agents in your area who specialize in disability insurance. See Chapter 19, "Hiring Financial Help," for more about hiring help.

Life Insurance

If, after having reviewed Chapter 15, you've determined you need some life insurance because you have financial dependents and you're not yet financially independent, remember that your goal here is adequate income protection in the event of the death of an income provider. Life insurance should not be viewed as an investment vehicle!

Use this worksheet to determine how much term life insurance to purchase:

1. Your annual after-tax employment income $ _____
   (Look at last year's tax return or Form W-2.)

2. To replace your income for this many years: Multiply by: _____

5 years	× 5
10 years	× 9
15 years	× 12
20 years	× 15
25 years	× 17
30 years	× 19

3. Multiply line 1 by line 2 _____

This analysis assumes that your beneficiaries invest the life insurance proceeds and earn a modest rate of return—7 percent, while inflation runs at about 3 percent per year.

If you were to only earn 5 percent (the current money fund rate) with an inflation rate of 3 percent, you need to increase the amount of life insurance needed in the preceding calculations by 15 percent.

If you can earn 9 percent versus an inflation rate of 3 percent, then you can decrease by 15 percent the amount of life insurance you buy based upon the preceding calculations.

If you bought a term life policy many years ago or you didn't really shop around, get quotes now. You may be able to save a lot on the cost of your coverage by switching carriers.

A good place to obtain term life insurance proposals is a quotation service such as ReliaQuote (www.realiaquote.com; 888-847-8683).

Will, Trusts, and Estate Planning

Although some of us don't like to admit or think about it, we are all mortal. Because of the way our legal and tax systems work, it's beneficial when people die to have legal documents in place specifying what should be done with assets and other important details.

A will is the most basic of such documents, and for most people, particularly those who are younger or don't have great assets, the only critical one. Through a will, you can direct to whom your assets will go upon your death, as well as who will serve as guardian for your minor children. In the absence of a will, state law dictates these important issues. Thus, your friends, less closely related relatives, and charities will likely receive nothing. Also, make sure that your named beneficiaries on IRA accounts, for example, reflect your current wishes. Many people mistakenly believe that a will overrides their beneficiary statement or insurance.

Without a will, your heirs are powerless, and the state will appoint an administrator to supervise the distribution of your assets at a fee of around 5 percent of your estate. A bond must also be posted at a cost of hundreds of dollars.

In the event that both you and your spouse die without a will, the state (courts and social service agencies) will decide who will raise your children. Even if you cannot decide at this time who would raise your children, you should at least appoint a trusted guardian who could decide for you.

If you previously completed a will, how many years ago was it prepared, and have any significant changes happened in your life since then (e.g., move, birth of child, passing of a named beneficiary, etc.)?

Along with your will, prepare a living will (called a health care proxy in some states) and medical power of attorney. These documents help your doctor and family members make important decisions regarding your health care should you be unable to make them yourself.

Even if you have a will, and supporting medical and legal documents, that might not be enough. If you hold significant assets outside tax-sheltered retirement accounts, in most states, those assets must be "probated"—which is the court-administered process for implementing your will. Establishing and placing your assets in a living trust can eliminate much of the hassle and cost of probate. Attorney probate fees can run quite high in some states—up to 5 percent of the value of the probated assets.

Finally, if your net worth (assets minus liabilities) exceeds $2,000,000 upon your death, significant estate taxes will be levied by the federal and perhaps your state's government. (This amount increases to $3,500,000 in 2009.) Estate planning can help to minimize the portion of your estate subject to taxation.

One simple but powerful estate planning strategy is to give money to your desired heirs to reduce your taxable estate. If you're in the fortunate position of having great wealth, you may give up to $12,000 each to as many recipients as desired.

A relatively simple strategy for a married couple to use to double the amount that they can pass on free of federal estate tax (currently $2,000,000) is to establish a bypass trust. The software recommended later in this section can assist you with that.

Remember that wills, living trusts, and estate planning are nothing more than a form of insurance. It takes time and money to do these things, and the benefits may be a long time off.

The simplest and lowest cost way to prepare a will and living trust is to use one of the high-quality, user-friendly software packages developed by attorneys. You do not need an attorney to prepare a legal will and living trust. Most attorneys, in fact, have their administrative staff prepare wills using a software package! What makes a will valid is that it is witnessed by three people.

Computer-generated wills have not caused any unusual problems. Hiring an attorney becomes more valuable when the value of your estate exceeds $2,000,000, the level at which estate taxes begin.

WillMaker (Nolo Press) is an excellent program for preparing wills as well as other standard legal documents (e.g., health care directives, durable powers of attorney for finances). I do not recommend "fill in the blank" will kits, which are prone to errors and challenge, which you may have seen for $10 or less at the local drug or stationary supply store.

If doing it all yourself seems overwhelming, by all means hire an attorney. Be sure to retain the services of one who specializes in wills, trusts, and related issues. Also, don't be shy about questioning costs and doing some comparison shopping. See Chapter 19 for advice on hiring professionals.

Auto Insurance

Locate a copy of your most recent auto insurance statement. Often called a "declaration," this statement should detail your coverage types and amounts, and premiums (cost).

Let's go through each of the elements of your policy:

➤ **Liability.** Auto accidents can harm other people and damage property, and for accidents in which you're at fault, you can be sued. The liability portion of your policy covers for these claims and comes in varying amounts—e.g., $15K, $30K, $50K, $100K, 300K, and so on. This coverage amount is per accident. I recommend that you have liability coverage of at least two times the value of your assets. If you have significant assets, you can more cost effectively pick up additional liability protection after $300K or $500K of liability coverage on your auto policy through an umbrella or excess liability policy, as discussed later in this chapter.

➤ **Medical payments.** This optional rider generally provides $5K or $10K in medical benefits to you or other passengers in your car for medical expenses not covered by their health insurance policy. I consider this coverage non-essential because it is capped at a relatively small amount, and if someone lacks health insurance, $5K or $10K in benefits won't cover much. If you're at fault and you're sued, your liability coverage will protect you.

➤ **Uninsured motorist.** This coverage allows you (and your vehicles' passengers) to be compensated for pain and suffering, lost wages, and out-of-pocket medical expenses when you're in an accident with an uninsured or underinsured motorist. Think of this coverage as buying liability coverage for the other guy (or gal) if he doesn't have sufficient coverage. Once you have adequate health and disability insurance that would take care of lost wages and medical expenses in an accident, being able to collect for pain and suffering isn't really necessary.

➤ **Collision.** This provides reimbursement for damage done to your car in an accident. To reduce your premiums, choose as high a deductible (e.g., $500 or $1,000) as you are comfortable with.

➤ **Other than collision.** Sometimes known as comprehensive coverage, this provides insurance for damage done to your car for things other than accidents. For example, if you're driving down the road and a rock skips off the road and cracks your windshield, this coverage will pay for damage, after your deductible. As with collision coverage, to reduce your premiums, choose as high a deductible (e.g., $500 or $1,000) as you are comfortable with.

➤ **Other riders.** Other typical add-ons that insurers and agents may put on your policy include towing, rental car reimbursement, etc. As I recommended in Chapter 15, skip these because they ultimately cover small potential dollar items and aren't worth insuring for. Spend your insurance money on protecting against the big potential losses.

Good companies to get an auto insurance policy quotation from include Amica (www.amica.com; 800-242-6422), Geico (www.geico.com; 800-841-3000), Liberty Mutual (www.libertymutual.com), and State Farm (www.statefarm.com). USAA (www.usaa.com; 800-531-8000) is an attractive source for auto insurance, but membership is limited to officers and enlisted personnel, National Guard, Selected Reserve officers and enlisted personnel, officer candidates in commissioning programs, recently retired or separated military personnel, and children of USAA members.

Home Insurance

Let's walk through the elements of a homeowners' insurance policy—get out yours if you own a home. (If you're renting, you may wish to obtain a renter's policy for two major reasons. First is to protect your personal property. Second is for some liability protection.) Here are the major elements on a homeowners' policy:

➤ **Dwelling.** Your home insurer should determine approximately how much it would cost (based on size and cost per square foot) to rebuild your home should it be a total loss. Make sure that your policy comes with "guaranteed replacement cost" coverage. This makes the insurer pay for the full cost to rebuild your home should it cost more than the dwelling coverage portion of your policy. Please note, though, that different insurers define their guarantees differently. Most place some sort of a cap on the coverage—for example at 20 or 30 percent above the dwelling coverage.

➤ **Other structures.** This would cover separate structures such as a shed or freestanding garage.

➤ **Personal property.** This portion of the policy covers the contents of your home—furniture, clothing, personal possessions, etc. The coverage amount is typically derived as a portion (e.g., three-quarters) of the dwelling portion of your policy. A good policy will cover the full cost to replace damaged items—be sure this is what you're paying for or inquire about the cost of a rider to provide this benefit.

➤ **Loss of use.** This again is standard coverage and often a portion (e.g., 20 percent) of the dwelling coverage. If you can't reasonably live in your home after it is damaged, this part of your policy will pay for you to rent and enjoy a similar standard of living.

➤ **Personal liability.** If someone sues you for an accident relating to your home, this portion of the policy kicks in. As with your auto insurance, you should have enough liability to protect at least twice your assets. For coverage greater than $500,000, you would typically get excess liability coverage in a separate policy (see the next section).

➤ **Medical payments to others.** This is standard on most policies and provides limited coverage for out-of-pocket costs for accidents on your property.

Be sure to get catastrophic coverage as needed in your area—see the section in Chapter 16, "Managing Risks Involves More Than Buying Insurance," for details on flood, earthquake, and other such risks and how to reduce your risks of suffering a catastrophe.

Use the recommended list of insurers in the auto insurance section for homeowner's insurance.

Excess Liability Insurance

If you have assets that total into the hundreds of thousands or millions of dollars, given your current assets and future earnings, which could be garnished in a lawsuit settlement, you have a lot to lose. Excess liability insurance, which is sold in increments of a million dollars, can offer protection against a large lawsuit.

Many people are surprised at the relatively low cost. The first additional million might cost $200, and up to $5 million should cost about $700.

You generally obtain this insurance through your current home and auto insurers. Be sure to shop around, as prices vary, sometimes significantly.

18

Information and Edutainment Resources

"Advertising is legalized lying."
—H.G. Wells

Growing up, I remember learning about the stock market during the early 1970s from my father. We'd talk on the phone to my dad's stockbroker and would on occasion visit him in his office. Friday night, we'd watch Louis Rukeyser's program, *Wall Street Week*, on PBS, one of only several major networks. We'd have to wait for the next morning's *Wall Street Journal* to see how our stocks did the prior day. Cable television, the Internet, and personal finance publications were almost non-existent. Since that time, the number of published, online, and media resources devoted to personal finance, and related advertising, has skyrocketed. This chapter will help you sift through and make sense of the morass.

Understanding the Role of Advertising

Most of the free and low-cost personal finance resources are paired with lots of advertising. It's no great surprise that companies with something to sell like to reach those seeking to invest, wanting to buy a home or refinance a mortgage, searching for insurance, and so on.

Advertising creates conflicts of interest. Consider a free web site that derives all of its revenue from advertising. If the site covers, say, investments or insurance, how likely is it to criticize products or tactics used by the sites' advertisers? The Internet has further exacerbated and accelerated the trend begun in the media of the blurring distinction between advertising and news.

Just ask the famous television news anchor Jane Pauley. In October 2006, her lawyers filed a lawsuit against *The New York Times*, one of the nation's oldest and largest circulation newspapers. Pauley was outraged when her smiling full-page photo graced the cover of an advertising supplement a year earlier. She maintains that she was never told that she would be featured in an advertising supplement. Pauley was interviewed regarding mental health issues by someone she thought was a *New York Times* reporter but was instead an employee of DeWitt Publishing, which produces advertising supplements for publications. (Pauley had previously gone public about her personal struggles with bipolar disorder.)

Not surprisingly, drug companies, which pour billions annually into advertising, were heavy advertisers in the supplement featuring Pauley. She clearly didn't need the money and didn't seek this kind of publicity. (And, her husband—*Doonesbury* cartoonist Garry Trudeau—never seems to be short of fodder for his comic strip.) So, how could an intelligent media veteran like Pauley have been deceived?

Although *The New York Times* denied these charges, the lawsuit sheds light on this and the business pressures that are causing advertising to have more and more influence on the news. "*NYT*'s practice of intentionally blurring the distinction between advertisements and news was criticized by the 'public editor' of *The New York Times* in a November 2005 article." The piece, written by editor Byron Calame, was entitled, "Cracks in the Wall Between Advertising and News." Here's the core of Calame's comments about his own paper:

> "The search for revenue, not surprisingly, means the advertising staff of *The Times* is scrambling ever harder to come up with attractive new options for advertisers. Sometimes that can lead to pressures to let advertisers tie their pitches more closely to the credibility of the news columns. And that can blur the distinction between advertising and articles—risking erosion of the readers' right to assume that the news columns are pure journalism, both in print and online."

Remember—this is what an editor of the paper was allowed to publicly write about in the *Times*. Imagine what you would hear privately (and what I have observed in my two decades' worth of interaction with many people in the news media and having been involved with numerous publications). That's why the phrase "pure journalism" is somewhat laughable. As one of my students from my teaching days for the University of California system so astutely observed, the sections of *The New York Times* are like a shopping guide. Sections such as "Fashion & Style," "Home & Garden," and "Automobiles" were not created and expanded over the years for the sake of "pure journalism!" Can you imagine the serious writers at the *Times* sitting around in a conference room high above the street in their mid-town Manhattan office building saying that what the paper really needs in order to maintain its editorial significance in the world are more articles about the latest ladies' handbags and gardening tools! The existence and creation of these newer sections of the paper came about and were motivated by a desire to capture more advertising dollars.

How (Some) Papers Choose What Content to Publish

I've been interviewed by hundreds of print and online publications, and radio and television programs. I've encountered many caring, dedicated editors and producers who do their best. But, I've also come across those who make me want to run from them as fast as possible or beat my head against the wall.

In the worst cases, editors have refused to cover certain topics or censored portions of stories because they feared offending particular advertisers. And, while I've had plenty of positive experiences with public television and public radio, I've learned that those entities share many of the same problems as their commercial peers. They may pander to advertisers or not care enough about the quality of the content they provide to their viewers, listeners, and readers.

Editors and producers with the best of intentions may end up doing a poor job. The major reason for this is a lack of personal finance expertise combined with stubbornness and unwillingness to gain such expertise or consult those who have it. Consider the following exchange that I had with one newspaper editor over the content of his newspaper section devoted to personal money issues. One day when I was speaking with that section's editor, he began complaining about his paper, his boss, his lousy computers, etc. I was sympathetic, as newspapers across the country face competitive pressures from the many news and information sources including the Internet. I had some ideas for how he could improve his section without spending more money by changing some of the content. So, I offered to review (without charge or strings attached) a week's worth of the daily money sections and provide some written ideas. There was nothing in it for me except to satisfy my curiosity as to what would happen to my ideas. He mailed me the sections and said he looked forward to my feedback.

Among the main suggestions that I made were the following:

> ➤ There was no information provided for mutual fund prices and returns. The only financial data in the section were the daily "Most Active" stock listings for the

NYSE, AMEX, and NASDAQ and stock prices for companies in the small state where the paper was located. This list changes every day, and the acronyms are unintelligible to most people. Interestingly, many of the most actively traded shares' acronyms make no sense because they are for exchange traded funds (ETFs). How many of the following listings make sense: SemiHTr, EvgrnE nya, iShSP100 cbo. Few people (except those who work in the investment field or write about it) know what these are, and even fewer own them, especially among the typical readers of a daily newspaper. The local company stock prices made up about just a few percent of all listed stocks on the exchanges. I recommended replacing the most active quotes with a daily report of widely held and leading mutual funds (which far more of the paper's readers owned) and stocks that would include at least some of the local companies. Overall, this would have taken less space and been more useful to the readers.

➤ Each day there was a column that took up nearly ¼ of a page that reported on what the stock market did on the prior trading day and included various quotes from numerous market followers and economists on why the market did what it did. Recent articles were entitled "Stocks Stumble on Weak Data," "Dow Drops on Interest Rate Fears," and "Stocks Dip as Oil Rises Amid Threats." This column rehashed day-old news and repeated what people heard the night before on the evening news on television, on radio, or online.

My other ideas for what could replace the preceding largely revolved around news and information that people could use and couldn't get anywhere else. I provided several examples of items that would fit that bill.

In the lengthy response that I got back from the editor, each and every one of my ideas was rejected. I was essentially told that, "…the vagaries of newspapers are difficult for outsiders to understand." I never take any of this kind of feedback personally, but such a comment is telling and silly. The editor also justified keeping all of the stock listings the way they were because some readers had called and complained in the past when they didn't run. One of the lessons you learn providing advice and in consulting is that you can't help people who don't really want to be helped. Change is difficult, and many people resist it. This is another reason to be thoughtful about where you get your money information and advice.

Question What You Read and Hear

The news media is dependent upon advertisers but suffers from an even larger potential problem. Too many reporters, journalists, etc. lack sufficient expertise (and time) to do a thorough and informed job when they cover personal money topics. And, these folks are under tremendous pressure to meet short-term deadlines and to entertain and bring in viewers. All of this can lead to significant errors and inaccuracies in stories or segments. These errors are often introduced from sources that the news media utilizes but don't sufficiently check out. Here are two examples that I came across in just one week.

A multi-billion dollar investment firm sent out a stock market commentary in September 2006, just after the five-year anniversary of the September 11 terrorist attacks. In it the firm said:

> "What has been most surprising in the past five years is how strong corporate earnings have been relative to a decent economy and how little that strength has helped propel U.S. equities. For the past three years, in fact, earnings for the S&P 500 have registered double-digit growth (with that growth—contrary to most market expectations—accelerating in 2006), while the major indices have been flat."

I did a double take when I read the last sentence, "For the past three years...the major indices have been flat." I couldn't believe that was even close to being true. The stock market took a major drubbing in the early 2000s but had a huge rebound beginning in early 2003.

Before leaping to any conclusions as to the accuracy or lack thereof in this commentary, I wanted to get the facts about the stock market's performance over the three-year period through the issuance of this commentary in September of 2006. Here's what I found for the cumulative three-year returns for the major stock market indexes:

| Total U.S. Stock Market Index | 44.6% (13 percent per year annualized) |
| Total International Stock Index | 86.5% (23 percent per year annualized) |

So, you can clearly see that this firm's statement that stock prices had been flat the prior three years was incredibly wrong and off base. Since the stock market averages returns of about 10 percent per year, stocks worldwide produced returns well above average, especially overseas.

I couldn't believe such a large investment firm could be so clueless. The only possible agenda that I could see was that if their investment portfolios hadn't been faring well, they were trying to make it sound like the overall stock market had been treading water and going nowhere so their clients wouldn't feel like they were missing out on a party. When I examined the company's mutual funds' investment performance on Morningstar, I found that its domestic stocks funds, which carried a relatively steep average expense ratio in excess of 1.5 percent annually, had underwhelming and mediocre risk adjusted returns (rating 3.0 on a scale of 1 being worst to 5 being best). The firm did not offer diversified foreign funds, which meant that its clients missed out on the strong performance overseas.

Wanting to understand why the firm would publish such an erroneous report, I called it. I tried several times, in fact, and no one called back. I made one last attempt to call and finally got called back—more than one month after I originally contacted the company. The principal who called me fumbled quite a bit when I asked him to explain the sentence that said that stock prices had been flat over the three years prior to the commentary in question. He first said that he was not able to publish as many commentaries as his firm would like because of all of his responsibilities. He then said that what the firm was really trying to say was that since January 2004 (which was less than three years from the report's publication), the market hadn't gone anywhere. Lopping off the last quarter of 2003 did erase a strong up period for most stock markets worldwide, but the major indices had still increased significantly using January 1, 2004 as the starting point. (Remember that these returns are over just two and three-quarter years.)

| Total U.S. Stock Market Index | 28.7% (10 percent per year annualized) |
| Total International Stock Index | 59.0% (18 percent per year annualized) |

So, even despite this manager's attempt to spin out an explanation, he was still way off base. Even allowing him to say that he really meant performance since the beginning of 2004, stocks during the ensuing period did as well or better than they have historically.

Here's another example—this time from a press release—with problematic assertions and data. A firm that provides information to consumers seeking to get out of consumer debt made the following statement in a release it sent out in the fall of 2006:

> "The number of homeowners spending at least 30% of their gross income on housing grew from 27% in 2000 to 35% in 2005. For renters, it increased from 37% in 2000 to 46% in 2005. At the same time, wages and income have remained the same."

I underlined the last sentence, which is asserting that during the five-year period from 2000 through 2005, people's wages and income did not grow at all. I was sent this press release via e-mail, so I highlighted the paragraph and sentence in particular and sent it back to the firm's president, asking what data supported this statement.

Here's the response that I got back:

> "Thanks for your note (pasted below) the other day. I thought I'd send you a previous press release we did, which stated (in the third paragraph) that the median family income is now $43,200, which represents only a 1.6% increase in the past five years. I hope that answers your question that you posted below. If you have any other questions, we would certainly like to answer them."

> "…The median income is now $43,200, a small 1.6% increase from 2001."

I went to the Federal Reserve report cited as the source for this data in the press release. Here's my response back after I examined the data in that report:

> "Well, it states that over the period 2001–04, the median value of real (inflation-adjusted) income rose 1.6 percent. So, it's not over five years and it went up even after adjusting for inflation. Your original statement which I questioned would appear in error."

Disappointingly, I got no further response. No correction was sent, and this erroneous information appeared and was repeated in many publications and news reports.

Everyone makes mistakes. But it's troubling when inaccurate releases are sent to the news media or information is conveyed to the public, and those who are responsible make no effort to correct clear errors. It's disturbing how many news' media outlets will run with something given to them without verifying its accuracy.

By all means, be a consumer of financial news. But, be a skeptical consumer. Don't blindly accept news as factually correct and unbiased. Learn what sources to trust and which to sidestep.

Books

Personal finance books, when done well and by an author with expertise and objectivity in the subject area, offer a crash course at a reasonable price. The best books provide enormous value. You can spend hundreds or thousands of dollars attending some "financial seminars" and learn a fraction of what you can from the best books. Even worse are the many examples I've learned about over the years where high-priced seminars, CDs, audiotapes, and so on end up by being nothing more than infomercials and don't teach you anything useful.

The challenge is to find the best books, and it isn't easy for most people. For starters, if you're not an expert in the field, it's difficult and challenging to evaluate the competence and professional track record of various authors. Nobel Prize winner Niels Bohr eloquently stated, "An expert is a man who has made all the mistakes which can be made in a very narrow field." After a lifetime of money mistakes, you'll be an expert or more of an expert, but you don't get do-overs!

Publishers make your job of book and author evaluation even more challenging because most of them exercise woefully far too little due diligence when deciding who and what to publish. The single most important factor for most publishers isn't the quality of the writing or legitimacy of the advice or author's credentials and professional background. What matters most is simply how well the publisher thinks that the book will sell.

In the financial world, one of the keys to a book selling well is the author's having a "platform" to promote his book. Those who are already doing lots of media interviews and conducting seminars around the country are attractive to publishers. Hype sells. Cutesy stories sell. And by the time that the truth comes out—if ever—millions of copies may have already sold and nothing will probably happen. Here are some examples to illustrate these points from what I call the Personal Finance Book Hall of Shame:

➤ **Beardstown Ladies.** This Midwest investment club wrote a best-selling book, on the cover of which was prominently displayed their claimed 23+ percent annual returns picking stocks, which placed these amateurs among the legions of the best of the best professional investment managers of all time. (In large type on the book's cover it said, "How We Beat the Stock Market—and You Can, Too 23.4% ANNUAL RETURN." I was highly suspicious given the extraordinary returns the group boasted of and the fact that when I interviewed the club's leaders, they were unable to provide any proof. It ultimately came out that the club really only earned about 9 percent per year—a far cry from the claimed 23+ percent—and well *below* the market averages. In a rare outcome, the book's publisher was successfully sued in a class action lawsuit.

➤ **Wade Cook.** What more of a red flag does one need about Wade Cook's approach and advice than to see claims on his books such as "Double your money every 2½ to 4½ months with rolling stocks" or "Get 14% to 34% monthly returns—consistently." Given that stocks have returned an average *annual* return of just about 10 percent, clearly Cook is promising pie-in-the-sky, too-good-to-be-true returns. For complete details about Cook's history, visit www.johntreed.com, click on the link to "Real Estate Investment," then click on "Real estate guru ratings" and then the link for "Wade Cook."

➤ **Day trading books.** In the late 1990s, when stock markets around the world were reaching a frothy boil and technology stocks seemed to be soaring to the moon, a blizzard of day trading books were published by many business book publishers. If you don't know what day trading is, that's fine—ignorance on this topic is not only blissful but also more profitable. Day trading is gambling on very short-term moves in stock prices. It literally means buying a stock early in the trading day in the hopes and expectation of selling it later that same day at a profit. The short-term movements of stock prices are not predictable, and day trading is a dangerous, gambling type approach to playing the stock market. Day trading increases one's transaction costs, and when you do have profitable trades, their taxes as well (short-term profits are taxed at high ordinary income tax rates which for most people are more than double the rate applied to profits realized after holding for more than one year). If day trading stocks wasn't risky enough, books appeared that advocated day trading even more dangerous financial instruments such as futures and options. One electronic day trading book proclaims it as "...Wall Street's Hottest Phenomenon" while another trumpets, "...Catch the Wave." Well, those who grabbed their surfboards quickly got wiped out.

➤ **Suze Orman.** She began her career as a secretary at a brokerage firm, and by the late 1990s, Orman was seemingly everywhere dispensing financial advice. *Forbes'* columnist William Barrett did a review of Orman's background compared with her claims and found some major misrepresentations. (To find his well-documented article, simply type "Suze Orman Forbes" into Google's search engine.) Financial writer Charles Jaffee has done a number of articles detailing the inadequacy of much of Orman's financial advice. He also said, "...I couldn't help but do a double take during one of her recent shows on CNBC. In talking about debt, Orman said: 'One of the books I wrote, I did a whole section on good debt and bad debt. In fact, I was the one who created that terminology, good debt/bad debt, in the United States back in 1999.' A quick check of a not-too-complete database found hundreds of stories written throughout the 1990s using the terms good debt and bad debt and describing them roughly in the fashion Suze claims to have originated." I know I was using the term back in 1990 and used it extensively in my best-selling book, *Personal Finance For Dummies*, which I wrote in 1993 and is now in its 5th edition. A final and important point relates to Orman's financial ties with companies that she recommends. A number of readers expressed concern to me that Orman appears in commercials and advertising for a specific long-term care insurance and credit reports (among others) and asked if I thought this was a conflict of interest. It clearly is— how can she objectively review and recommend products and services in the financial services industry if she's receiving fees from those same companies?

Who's Your Rich Dad?

As a final example, I put forth the *Rich Dad, Poor Dad* series of books, by Robert Kiyosaki. With regards to mutual funds and 401(k)s, in addition to his saying that they are "...way too risky," Kiyosaki also says, "...those vehicles are only good for about 20 percent of the population, people making $100,000 or more." I couldn't disagree more. In fact, my experience is that mutual funds are tailor made for non-wealthy people who don't have the assets to properly create a diversified portfolio themselves.

Jonathan Clements, who covers investing and personal finance for *The Wall Street Journal* and who reviewed Kiyosaki's latest book, *Why We Want You to Be Rich: Two Men—One Message*, co-written with Donald Trump, agrees. "His scorn for mutual funds is also a little puzzling. He argues that funds don't have to accurately disclose expenses, that a bank wouldn't lend money to buy funds because they're too risky...and that you can't do a tax-deferred 1031 exchange from one fund to another, like you can with real estate."

Clements succinctly and accurately refutes all of these erroneous assertions by Kiyosaki and Trump. "In truth, funds are far clearer about their expenses than other investments, you can borrow against funds held in a brokerage-firm margin account and investors make tax-deferred exchanges all the time, by trading within their retirement accounts," says Clements.

Kiyosaki also says that he doesn't like mutual funds because "...mutual funds have got no insurance from a stock market crash. To me, that's sad, and I am concerned." The best way to reduce the risk of investing in stocks is to be diversified not only in a variety of stocks but also in other investments that don't move in tandem with the stock market.

Kiyosaki absurdly claims that he invests with the benefit of insurance when investing in real estate with which, "...my banker requires me to have insurance from catastrophic losses." This is an unfair comparison since such an insurance policy would cover losses from, say, a fire but not a decline in market value of the real estate due to overall market conditions.

I recently read an online article by Kiyosaki, entitled "Why mutual funds are lousy long-term investments." He says that mutual fund companies keep 80 percent of the return while the investor, who puts up all of the capital and takes all of the risk, only gets 20 percent of the return.

I wondered what planet he is living on that he asserts that mutual funds keep 80 percent of investors' returns? For sure, there are a variety of funds with differing fees. With stock funds, for example, the lowest cost funds measure their expenses in tenths of one percent, whereas the most costly funds charge well in excess of one percent.

The typical stock fund charges about one percent per year and returns on average about 10 percent per year. Thus, fees take about 10 percent of the return, not 80 percent! If you buy a low-cost stock index fund and pay just 0.2 percent per year in fees, that would represent only 2 percent of your total returns—again a far cry from 80 percent.

Also, in the article, Kiyosaki says, "The problem with funds is fees. The longer you invest in a mutual fund, the more you pay in fees. I've pointed out before that when I buy a piece of real estate or a stock, I pay the sales commission once, but when I purchase a mutual fund, I pay a sales commission for as long as I own the fund."

Having read a good deal of his writings over time, I know that Kiyosaki is incredibly biased against mutual funds and in favor of real estate investing.

Of course, since a mutual fund is performing an ongoing service (monitoring and making changes to the portfolio) for you in managing your money, you pay for that service in the form of an annual management fee. (It's not a commission.) When you purchase a piece of real estate, you pay lots of closing costs. It's not true that there are no ongoing costs to managing real estate. For example, if you choose to hire a management company, it would typically take about 6 percent of the rental income per year as a fee. If you choose to manage the property yourself, you will spend plenty of hours on the necessary tasks. (It's also worth noting that Kiyosaki was gushing about real estate investing as that market was peaking in recent years, and he was down on the stock market, which has had an incredible run the last several years.)

If you buy an individual stock, you pay a commission, but it's not fair to say that there's nothing after that. Stocks require some monitoring, and you will need to subscribe to various publications and journals to do a good job of that.

Real estate expert John T. Reed has a highly detailed review of Kiyosaki at www.johntreed.com. Click on the "real estate investment" section and then click on "real estate guru ratings."

One final and interested tidbit about Kiyosaki's book, *Rich Dad's Prophecy: Why the Biggest Stock Market Crash in History Is Still Coming... and How You Can Prepare Yourself and Profit from It!*. The book was published in October 2002. This was great timing on Kiyosaki's part, as the book was published at the stock market lows (see the following graph). In this work, he said don't buy stocks, and the rest of his books glorified real estate investing, which peaked in the mid 2000s.

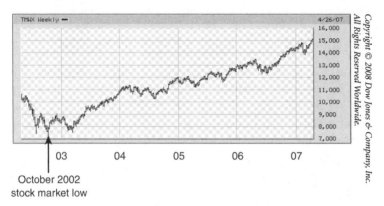

October 2002
stock market low

Figure 18.1   *Dow Jones-Wilshire 5000 U.S. Composite Index*

Financial Books and Authors Worth Reading

In a typical year, I see dozens of new financial books. My office has in excess of 1,000 titles—I should open a library! There are two shelves closest to my desk, which are reserved for the very best books. The rest get put on the other shelves. Here are books that make the shelves closest to my desk and that I recommend for your consideration:

> John Bogle—Vanguard's founder and now retirement chairman and author of *Bogle on Mutual Funds*.
>
> Jonathan Clements—*Wall Street Journal* reporter and book author.
>
> James C. Collins—*Built to Last* and *Good to Great*.
>
> Charles Ellis—*Winning the Loser's Game*.
>
> Burton Malkiel—*A Random Walk Down Wall Street*.
>
> Nolo Press—Book publisher of legal education and self-help books.

Jeremy Siegel—*Stocks for the Long Run.*

Eric Tyson—Various *...For Dummies* books on *Personal Finance, Investing, Real Estate,* and *Mutual Funds.*

Liz Weston—Columnist and book author of *Your Credit Score* and *Deal with Your Debt.*

19

Hiring Financial Help

"Finding the occasional straw of truth awash in an ocean of confusion and bamboozle requires intelligence, vigilance, dedication and courage. But, if we don't practice these tough habits of thought, we cannot hope to solve the truly serious problems that face us—and we risk becoming a nation of suckers, up for grabs by the next charlatan who comes along."
—Carl Sagan in "The Fine Art of Baloney Detection"

Making the best personal financial decisions requires knowledge, research, and good judgment. Don't expect perfection—you can do just about everything right, but things may not work the way you hoped for reasons beyond your control. That doesn't mean, however, that you should not bother working to maximize your ability and chances of making the best decisions given a reasonable input of time and energy on your part.

I was pleasantly surprised when I read Steven Scott's book, *The Richest Man Who Ever Lived: King Solomon's Secrets to Success, Wealth, and Happiness*. Books with a title such as this give me cause to pause. It sounded too good to be true. But, the book had a lot of practical and powerful information.

In discussing how to make wise decisions, Scott cites the timeless wisdom from Solomon's book of *Proverbs*. Throughout the *Proverbs*, Scott says, Solomon highlights the value of seeking outside counsel. "Where no counsel is, the people fall. But in a multitude of counselors, there is safety."

Solomon also discussed the value in finding wise counsel and sidestepping the rest: "He that walks with wise men shall become wise. But a companion of fools shall be destroyed."

Because I write financial advice books and columns, some people erroneously think that I'm a so-called "do it yourself" advocate. I am not. People who read my books and columns are seeking wisdom and information, and I do my best to meet their needs and expectations. Obviously, through reading this book, you've demonstrated a healthy and substantial interest in making the most of your money and financial decisions.

At critical junctures, hiring competent and ethical help pays off. Too often, though, people fail to hire the right expert and fail to do enough homework before making the hiring decision. This chapter covers who, when, and how to hire the best financial help.

The Keys to Finding the Best Advisors

In my early twenties, I had a spare couple of thousand dollars to invest. Precious metals were getting a lot of coverage in the press as interest rates and inflation were rising fast. On the basis of some official-looking ads placed in *The Wall Street Journal*, I contacted a company called the International Gold Bullion Exchange (IGBE). To make a long story short, the company was a scam—I was lucky that I only lost about $2,000 (although if I had simply invested that money into a diversified stock fund, it would be worth more than $25,000 today).

I had learned a powerful lesson at a relatively young age. I had not done my homework about the company that I chose to do business with and had blindly gone down that path without any outside perspectives, counsel, or second opinions. Even if I was sure that I wanted to invest some money in gold, I had not adequately researched my investment options in that arena. I had not learned about different companies providing products and services in that field and had done insufficient comparison shopping. I was young, naïve, and impatient. I assumed that since IGBE was a regular advertiser in respected business publications, it was a legitimate firm.

I should have sought out objective information and advice *before* I decided to send money to this fraudulent company. If I had done enough basic reading, for example, I would have learned that the field of commodities and precious metals had more than its fair share of problematic companies over the years. If I had called around to different companies to learn about the industry and various players, I would have heard stories about serious problems at IGBE.

Over the years, I've not only learned from my personal experiences, but I've also heard what thousands of others have done wrong and right. Here are the main insights I've come to believe about making the best decisions with outside help and assistance:

➤ **Educate yourself first.** No matter the subject area—investing in mutual funds, buying a home, securing life insurance—you've got to learn the basics and lingo. Otherwise, you're not going to be able to know who is bamboozling you and what the deal is with what you're considering. How can you possibly evaluate the competence of someone you're considering hiring if you yourself are ignorant in the area in question? Getting a crash course through a good book on the topic can be a cost-effective and excellent way to start. The biggest challenges with selecting books are finding those written by authors who have sufficient expertise and high ethical standards. After reading this book, you should be well on your way to being able to screen the best from the rest. Also, in Chapter 18, "Information and Edutainment Resources," I provided a short list of books that you should find helpful on various financial topics.

➤ **Clearly identify in what area(s) you think you need help.** Are you having trouble living within your means? Perhaps you have lots of financial quandaries and don't know where to begin and how to prioritize. Or maybe you're one of those rare, fortunate few who have the "problem" of rapidly accumulating piles of cash that you don't know how to invest. This chapter should help you to fine-tune the kind of specialist you may want to hire.

➤ **Search hard for the best information and people you can find.** If you simply hire the first person you come across or are referred to, you're going to make plenty of mistakes. The same holds true for selecting financial advice publications. You've got to scrutinize, ask probing questions, check references, and prove to yourself that someone is worth listening to or hiring.

The Good That Good Brokers Do

I get many letters and e-mails from people writing in to tell me about the problems and situations where they have been unhappy with salespeople. I have long spoken out and highlighted the conflicts of interest that exist among various players in the financial services' industry. Brokers who work on commission certainly head the list of those who may not have your best interests in mind when they recommend particular strategies or products.

I have highlighted the inevitable conflicts of interest that come into play when you are seeking advice from someone who has a vested financial interest in a transaction you may make. Obviously, if you go to your local Honda dealer, he's not going to sing the praises of buying a Chevy (if he doesn't sell them), and he is even more unlikely to suggest going without a car and living someplace where you can access good public transportation.

Good brokers can do well by their clients. Brokers, who get paid on commission, work in various facets of the financial services industry. Real estate agents work with home buyers and house sellers; insurance agents deal in life, disability, home, auto and other insurance lines; securities brokers deal with investments; and so on.

Good financial salespeople can add value. Here are the attributes of the best financial brokers I've interacted with over the years:

> **They're upfront about being brokers and don't hide behind obfuscating titles.** Good agents and brokers call themselves what they are. A real estate agent isn't a housing consultant and an insurance agent isn't a risk reduction counselor.

> **They think first about recommending what's best for their client and not what's best for maximizing their own short-term commissions.** Years ago, I remember working with an excellent real estate agent who advised me not to buy at a particular time. It was the right advice for many reasons at that time and enabled me to buy after the real estate market softened and I was better positioned to purchase. Guess who my got my future business (and referrals) when I was ready to buy?

> **They know what their expertise is and when to seek outside experts.** A good insurance agent, who specializes in, say, health and disability policies, won't try to dabble in investments or selling real estate.

> **They welcome educated customers, shopping around, and second opinions.** A good agent isn't threatened by questions, outside research, and your obtaining other opinions. Note: In the case of real estate agents, I advocate working with just one agent at a time in a given geographic area.

Financial Advisors and Planners

Open up your local yellow page directory, and you can quickly see how many people call themselves financial planners, financial advisors, financial services providers, and so on. And for good reason—after all, tens of millions of people have the challenge of living within their means, planning for major expenditures such as buying a car, a home, for retirement, higher education expenses, starting a small business, securing proper insurance coverage, etc. Financial consultants and planners purport to be able to help with this far-ranging list of money challenges. And, the best ones out there are able to tackle at least some of these topics competently and ethically.

Your challenge if you desire to hire a financial planner is to

➤ **Define in what areas you need help.** Are you having budgeting problems and trouble with consumer debt and being able to save money? Have you got the problem of cash languishing in low-interest accounts and you want to know how to best invest this money for your financial future? Or, is your problem that you and your spouse argue about money and can't agree on common goals? The first step toward finding the right help and beginning to correct a problem is to clearly define and acknowledge the problem. For example, saying, "I don't know how much I should be saving toward retirement and in what accounts and investments," states a specific problem. So does the question, "How do I prioritize among competing financial savings goals of saving for retirement, a home purchase, and my kids' college education?"

➤ **Identify potential experts for providing that type of help.** If you seek help with budgets, spending, and dealing with debt, you're obviously looking for a different type of advisor than is someone seeking an investment manager to direct a six-figure nest egg. Although you may find a firm that does both of these things well, that's unlikely given the different skill sets required. Ask people and professionals you respect for their recommendations. There's nothing wrong with calling people from a phone directory listing so long as you ask plenty of tough questions and really do your homework before you commit to hiring someone.

➤ **Interview and screen potential candidates.** Once you've developed a short list of potential planners, interview them. It's amazing how uncomfortable it makes most people feel to ask tough questions, but you've got to do it! There's so much at stake for you! Here are the key questions you should ask:

➤ What is your approach to working with clients?

➤ What are your areas of expertise?

➤ What educational and professional training prepared you to be a financial advisor?

➤ How are you compensated—hourly, asset management fees, and/or commissions?

Presuming you are satisfied with the answers you get to the preceding questions, I would then advocate your asking:

➤ Can I have a copy of your Form ADV? (Obtain both Parts I and II.) This is a form investment advisors file with the Securities and Exchange Commission that provides details on a firm's approach, key personnel, fees, etc.

➤ Do you retain professional liability insurance?

➤ Can you provide references of people with whom you've worked?

➤ **Select the "best" advisor.** While I endorse collecting information, facts, and references for the potential candidates, in the end, you've got to make a decision. That often comes down to personal comfort and instincts. Be careful, however, not to simply select someone with the best bedside manner, the most polished, the most credentialed, or who has the most famous or highest net worth clients. The folks who select on these superficial criteria after not asking sufficient questions end up getting burned the worst by lousy planners. Focus on evaluating the candidates on the issues important to you. By all means, consider your personal comfort with the advisor; just don't allow that to overwhelm everything else.

Budget Counselors

The vast majority of organizations offering budget or credit counseling services are beholden to the credit card and other consumer debt purveyors. Their goal is typically to place you on what's called a debt management plan if you come to them with a lot of debt and seek advice for how to deal with it.

Here are excerpts from a pitch from a credit counseling agency (interspersed are my comments on the pitch). Here are three common supposed reasons to go to them for help with your debts:

> *"Help you pay less. The credit counseling agencies...negotiate with your creditors for better repayment terms, including lower interest rates and waived late fees."*

The fact of the matter is that you can do anything an agency does on your behalf. You can negotiate better payment terms. Here's a simple test to show you how easy this can be done. Suppose that you have credit card debt on which you're currently getting whacked with 18 percent (or worse) interest charges. There are many credit cards to which you can transfer your debt balances, with far-lower interest rates. Once you've identified such a card, when you call your current credit card company to report that you're transferring your balance onto a low rate card (and wish to cancel your current card), you will almost be guaranteed to get an offer for as good a rate from your current company!

> *"Help to pay off your debt faster. By creating a realistic and manageable payment plan, you'll be able to pay off your debt in as few as 3 to 5 years (as compared to potentially 20 to 30 years on your own)."*

What these agencies fail to disclose here—and it's a huge omission—is that participating in their debt management plans can greatly tarnish your credit report.

> *"Help make it easier to pay every month. By consolidating all your credit card and other unsecured debt payments into one, you won't have to juggle multiple payments."*

Well, you won't have to juggle because you are expected to make the one monthly consolidated payment. The only thing that's "easier" about that is that you're supposed to just write one check. Coming up with the money to make that monthly payment (whether it's one or many) is the hard part for people in trouble with consumer debt.

If you've had problems with living within your means, managing your debt, and sticking to a regular savings and investing plan, please thoroughly read Chapter 7, "Valuing Saving and Spending." The key to getting out of debt is to reverse the process (spending exceeding earnings) that got you into debt. You may well have to make some significant changes and sacrifices in the ways in which you spend money.

To find the few counselors/advisors who will help with spending and debt issues, you might actually start your search by using the advice I provide in the financial planner section earlier in this chapter and seeking planners in your area that do this kind of work or asking them for referrals to budget counselors they know and like. You could also try using your local yellow pages or going online and looking up Credit and Debt Counseling or Budget Counseling.

Investment Managers

If your savings and investment balances total well into the six-figures, you may be considering hiring an investment manager (by this I mean someone who manages money for a living, not a financial planner). I'm not referring to a financial advisor who recommends investments but rather a firm that actually manages the money by selecting stocks, bonds, etc.

Let me say upfront that most people who seek to hire an investment manager probably should not. The first reason is that most people lack sufficient assets to justify doing so. Suppose you have $250,000. That's a lot of money to most people, but to a money manager who has hundreds of millions or more likely billions of dollars under management, it's pocket change. Even if you could meet a manager's investment minimums, the percentage management fee you would pay would be relatively quite high. And, if you meet the minimum, then you're stuck turning over all of your assets to a single manager—not a good idea for diversification purposes. Most investment managers have investment minimums of several million dollars or more.

Another reason you probably shouldn't hire an investment manager is a lack of expertise on your part to evaluate that person. Even if you are one of those rare people who have plenty of millions to invest, how much do you know about evaluating an investment manager? The common answer I hear when I pose this question and people answer honestly is probably little to nothing unless you happen to be in the profession. Consider that investment firms such as Fidelity, T. Rowe Price, and Vanguard have entire departments devoted to the evaluation of investment managers, both before their hiring and to monitor their efforts after.

How One Large Firm Evaluates Money Managers

I got an inside look at selecting and monitoring money managers when I interviewed Joe Brennan, who is a principal at mutual fund behemoth Vanguard. Brennan heads up the company's Portfolio Review group. Many of Vanguard's stock funds are managed by outside money management firms—that is, firms that Vanguard contracts with to manage a particular mutual fund. For example, Vanguard's Wellesley Income fund is managed by the Wellington Management Company, a Boston, Massachusetts-based firm in business since 1928 and that has managed the Wellesley Income Fund since 1970. Wellington Management Company manages more than $500 billion. It has ten offices located around the world. If you wanted to invest in a privately managed account with Wellington, you could not. The company deals only with institutions.

Brennan's Portfolio Review group at Vanguard employs 30 full-time people. Vanguard uses 27 external money management firms, which manage more than $300 billion. "It's a continuous search process. We select and monitor portfolio managers and funds," says Brennan (who is not related to current Vanguard Chairman John Brennan).

Wellington is not unusual among money managers in not dealing with individuals. Often, this is a function of not wanting to deal with "small" accounts and not wanting the time and labor-intensive task of dealing with individuals. "Some of Vanguard's outside managers take individual accounts—the minimum may be $10 million plus. Most just serve the institutional marketplace," says Brennan.

Clearly with 30 full-time people, Vanguard devotes substantial resources to the task of selecting and monitoring investment managers. "The challenge for individuals is to have the resources and time to interview, and the expertise to evaluate. That's our full-time job. We have trained investment professionals—people who have done this for a living. We also have the analytic tools to evaluate managers. And, we visit firms and they visit us," says Brennan.

> Vanguard actually has three levels of review that provide
> checks and balances on the important task of selecting and
> tracking money managers the firm hires. The three groups
> include 1) The Portfolio Review group; 2) an internal com-
> mittee of senior management of Vanguard; and 3)
> Vanguard's Board of Directors. Among other things,
> Vanguard ensures that the firms they hire are in compliance
> with the myriad regulatory issues that apply to money man-
> agement firms.

Some money managers will offer individuals so-called separate accounts and pitch them as customized money management. However, the reality is that there will be hundreds of accounts with the same holdings and approach, and you pay a relatively high fee for such accounts.

"Wrap accounts" (managed investment accounts) are another product you will hear about and are sold by brokers as the way to get access to the best private money managers. The reality is that wrap accounts are quite costly, and some of the best managers won't manage wrap account money because it is more operationally intensive.

So, the bottom line on money management firms is that the bigger and more successful firms cannot be accessed by individuals but can be through the nation's leading mutual fund companies. And, because of the purchasing power of fund companies, you get access to the leading money managers for a lower cost than a wealthy individual could going to such firms directly.

Real Estate Agents

One type of sales agent you will surely encounter is one who works with consumers on residential real estate transactions. Real estate agents can add value to a housing transaction if they are knowledgeable and patient with their customers. That said, real estate agents can also lead to problems if they cause a consumer to make a decision without performing sufficient due diligence and thought. In the final analysis, it's up to each person to be sure she has done her homework, gained sufficient knowledge, and satisfied her concerns.

Real estate agents are salespeople who are compensated on commission. Blindly relying on such an individual in an advisory capacity with such significant money at stake is a recipe for potential disaster.

With the rapid escalation of housing prices during much of the 1990s and early 2000s, agents sharing a 5 to 6 percent commission amounted to larger and larger numbers. Always keep in mind that commissions are negotiable and a cost borne by both sellers and buyers. Even though sellers "pay" the commission from the proceeds of their house sale, the cost of commission is included in the total price paid for the home by the buyer. If you can negotiate a lower commission, the price of the home could be lowered, too.

While larger and more expensive homes typically take longer to sell, it doesn't, for example, take four times as long to sell a home worth $600,000 compared to one worth $150,000. The national median (meaning half the homes sell for more, half sell for less) home price is about $230,000. Especially if your home is in one of the higher-priced markets in the following table, you can and should negotiate for a lower commission rate when selling your home.

Median Home Prices	$Thousands
San Francisco-Oakland-Fremont, CA	751.9
San Jose-Sunnyvale-Santa Clara, CA	748.2
Anaheim-Santa Ana, CA (Orange Co.)	726.2
Honolulu, HI	640.0
San Diego-Carlsbad-San Marcos, CA	613.1
Los Angeles-Long Beach-Santa Ana, CA	576.3
New York-Wayne-White Plains, NY-NJ	549.2
Bridgeport-Stamford-Norwalk, CT	495.5
NY: Nassau-Suffolk, NY	478.0
New York-Northern New Jersey-Long Island, NY-NJ-PA	473.7
NY: Newark-Union, NJ-PA	443.8
Washington-Arlington-Alexandria, DC-VA-MD-WV	443.4
Boston-Cambridge-Quincy, MA-NH**	421.2

Median Home Prices	$Thousands
Barnstable Town, MA	406.3
Riverside-San Bernardino-Ontario, CA	395.7
NY: Edison, NJ	393.6
Sacramento-Arden-Arcade-Roseville, CA	380.6
Miami-Fort Lauderdale-Miami Beach, FL	376.2
Boulder, CO	373.2
Reno-Sparks, NV	353.4
Sarasota-Bradenton-Venice, FL	350.9
Las Vegas-Paradise, NV	319.1
New Haven-Milford, CT	292.6
Providence-New Bedford-Fall River, RI-MA	291.1
Trenton-Ewing, NJ	290.4
Worcester, MA	285.7
Baltimore-Towson, MD	285.1
Portland-Vancouver-Beaverton, OR-WA	283.4
Chicago-Naperville-Joliet, IL	278.5
Norwich-New London, CT	274.0
Phoenix-Mesa-Scottsdale, AZ	272.2
Orlando, FL	271.7
Cape Coral-Fort Myers, FL	271.6
Atlantic City, NJ	257.3
Hartford-West Hartford-East Hartford, CT	256.6
Denver-Aurora, CO	255.2
Kingston, NY	248.6

Median Home Prices	$Thousands
Tucson, AZ	247.3
Allentown-Bethlehem-Easton, PA-NJ	243.4
Portland-South Portland-Biddeford, ME	242.7
Virginia Beach-Norfolk-Newport News, VA-NC	237.3
Philadelphia-Camden-Wilmington, PA-NJ-DE-MD	235.1
Minneapolis-St. Paul-Bloomington, MN-WI	233.0
Tampa-St. Petersburg-Clearwater, FL	231.6
Hagerstown-Martinsburg, MD-WV	229.4
Milwaukee-Waukesha-West Allis, WI	227.7
Eugene-Springfield, OR	227.6
OVERALL U.S.A.	**227.5**

Source: National Association of Realtors

When listing a house to sell, be aware that when you sign a listing agreement with your agent, a determination is made as to what portion of the total commission will be advertised, typically in the multiple listing service (MLS), as the commission payable to an agent representing a buyer. For example, suppose you agree to pay the listing agency a total commission of 5 percent of the sale's price of your house, but only 2 percent of the sale's price goes to the agent representing a buyer. If other similarly priced houses for sale are listed in the MLS advertising greater commissions—say of 2.5 or 3 percent—some agents may not be enthusiastic to show their buyers your house if they only get 2 percent. This may not sound like a big difference, but it is—consider that on a $300,000 sales price, a 2 percent commission comes to $6,000, but a 3 percent commission yields a $9,000 commission. To reduce your commission as a seller, have your listing agent reduce her take but don't reduce below the norm the portion of the commission (which is advertised in the Multiple Listing Service) paid to the agent who brings you a buyer.

When seeking the services of an agent, be sure to consider the following:

➤ **Experience and expertise.** How long has the agent been working with home buyers and house sellers, and what success has she had? Be sure to ask the agent for an activity list of all her transactions over the past year.

➤ **Negotiation and interpersonal skills.** An agent interacts with many people in a transaction. Does the agent know how to get along with others while advocating for your best interests?

➤ **Ethics.** Can you trust the agent? Does she perform work that she promises to and within the timeframe that she says?

Please refer to *Home Buying For Dummies* and *House Selling For Dummies*, both of which I've co-written with residential real estate expert Ray Brown, for lots of specifics regarding how to win the real estate game.

Tax Preparers and Advisors

Some aspects of the U.S. tax laws are complicated. Why else would there be so many accountants and tax advice guides!

Hiring a competent tax advisor makes sense if you're dealing with something for the first time or are dealing with a multi-part problem that is complicated. Or, perhaps you just want a second opinion.

Ideally, you should hire a tax advisor who

➤ Has experience dealing with the sorts of issues you're struggling with.

➤ Is focused on taxes and works at it full-time and/or has many years of experience.

➤ Suits your comfort level about being aggressive or conservative in pursuing deductions and other areas. Ask about his history with tax audits and the results.

➤ Provides solid references.

➤ Carries errors and omission (liability) insurance.

Several different types of tax practitioners are eager to earn your business. Preparers, enrolled agents (EAs), and Certified Public Accountants (CPAs) do the bulk of tax return preparation for individuals in the United States. EAs and CPAs may represent you before the IRS should your tax return be audited or otherwise questioned. Tax preparation and advisory fees vary from $50 up to several hundred dollars per hour.

Tax attorneys deal with more unusual tax problems with the IRS and business deals. They do not typically handle routine tax preparation.

Regardless of whom you choose to work with, organize your records as best you can before you sit down with your tax advisor. Remember, advisors charge for their time. Don't hire a tax preparer to organize a shoebox full of receipts.

In addition to tax advisors, also consider tax preparation software and tax guides to help you navigate through the annual tax headache. Chapter 9, "Your Spending Plan," has advice for strategies to reduce your taxes.

Insurance Agents

As I discuss in Chapters 15 through 17, many folks make mistakes buying insurance, in part due to the influence of commission-compensated insurance brokers. That's why, in addition to finding ethical and competent insurance agents, you should be aware and make use of insurance that can be bought directly without brokers and utilize shopping services to help you ensure that you get value for your money.

When you do deal with insurance agents, be sure you work with those who specialize in the line of insurance you seek. For example, don't buy disability insurance from an agent for whom it's a sideline.

Attorneys

The primary reason you would seek the counsel of an attorney for financial purposes is to do estate planning, divorce, or bankruptcy (and possibly in some states for a real estate transaction). Hire an attorney with lots of experience in the specific area (e.g., estate planning, real estate) you need help with.

Check references for competency and ethics, and be sure to comparison shop to get value for your money. Ask an attorney for a budget for a project. Because an attorney bills for his time and can profit more from conflict and dragging things out, beware of open-ended arrangements. Express your concern about managing costs, and don't hesitate to question how much something is going to cost or has been charged.

Legal book publisher Nolo Press has an excellent web site (www.nolo.com) with all sorts of background information about a multitude of important legal topics. Click on the link for the "Lawyer Directory" (http://lawyers.nolo.com) that can assist you with learning more about the best ways to hire an attorney. It also includes a lawyer directory if you'd like help with finding attorneys with specific expertise. This directory is being rolled out state-by-state and is still under development.

Index